Originality & Imagination

Originality &
Imagination

THOMAS McFARLAND

The Johns Hopkins University Press
BALTIMORE & LONDON

The Johns Hopkins University Press, Baltimore, Maryland 21218
The Johns Hopkins Press Ltd., London

Earlier versions of chapters 1 and 2 appeared in *New
Literary History* 5 (Spring 1974), 447–76, and *New Literary
History* 13 (1981–82), 421–82, respectively. Chapter 3 was
published, in abridged form, in *The Wordsworth Circle* 13
(1982), 59–68. Chapter 4 is a revised version of an essay
that originally appeared in *New Perspectives on Coleridge
and Wordsworth*, edited by Geoffrey H. Hartman (New
York and London, 1972), pp. 195–246.

*The paper in this book is acid-free and meets the guidelines for
permanence and durability of the Committee on Production Guidelines
for Book Longevity of the Council on Library Resources.*

Library of Congress Cataloging in Publication Data
McFarland, Thomas, 1926–
Originality and imagination.

Bibliography: p.
Includes index.
1. Imagination—Addresses, essays, lectures.
2. Originality—Addresses, essays, lectures.
3. Aesthetics—Addresses, essays, lectures.
I. Title.
BH301.I53M38   1985   700'.19   84–47949
ISBN 0–8018–2517–2 (alk. paper)

For my brother
JOHN SYLVESTER MCFARLAND

Contents

Preface

*K*ant said, near the end of the *Critique of Pure Reason*, that human reason in its transcendental employment is directed toward three topics: the freedom of the will, the immortality of the soul, and the existence of God. It takes only a little reflection to realize that all three are a single collocation, and that if one exists, all must exist. "If God exists, the soul exists," said Victor Hugo in *Le Tas de Pierres*. But the converse is also true: if any one does not exist, then the others do not exist either. "I cannot conceive a supreme moral Intelligence," wrote Coleridge, "unless I believe in my own immortality." Actually, the phrase "immortality of the soul" is a pleonasm, for if consciousness is merely an effect of bodily processes, then neither "soul" nor "immortality" exists; and on the other hand, if any such entity as soul exists as distinct from bodily states, then by definition it would be exempt from the vicissitudes of those states.

The stakes are great, and the news is not good. When Plato said in his *Laws* that soul is the oldest of all things and rules over bodies, he planted the banner of the most hopeful possibility. Hume, however, cast his lot with an opposite conception. Personal identity, he said, is merely "a bundle or collection of different perceptions," and we "feign" the "notion of a *soul*, and *self*" in order to connect this collection together.

It is significant that Hume wrote more than two thousand years later than Plato did, for the historical progress of human conceiving has led inexorably away from the assurance of soul toward the hegemony of material processes. The theologian today who actually believes in God is a rara avis indeed; and as early as the seventeenth century, Bossuet, one of those who did believe, or at least seriously wanted to believe, was, in Paul Hazard's description, already at bay.

The news, in truth, has never really been good. St. Paul himself had to hedge the immortality of the soul, and the consequent validity of Christian faith, in a thicket of "ifs". "If there be no resurrection of the dead, then is Christ not risen: And if Christ be not risen, then is our preaching vain, and your faith is also vain." Even in the time of the crusades, when the sea of faith was at the full, Christian guarantees were not accepted unequivocally. On one occasion reported by Joinville in the thirteenth century, a bishop addressed King Louis. " 'Your Majesty,' he said, 'the Lords Spiritual of the realm here present, have directed me to tell you that the cause of Christianity, which it is your duty to guard and defend, is being ruined in your hands.' On hearing these words the king crossed himself and said: 'Pray tell me how that may be.' 'Your Majesty,' said the bishop, 'it is because at the present time excommunications are so lightly regarded that people think nothing of dying without seeking absolution, and refuse to make their peace with the Church.' " Indeed, Nietzsche claims that even Plato did not really believe in soul. "Plato: a great Cagliostro. . . . Is Plato's integrity beyond question? . . . we know at least that he wanted it to be *taught* as absolute truth what he himself did not regard as even conditionally true: namely, the separate existence and separate immortality of 'souls.' "

By the seventeenth century, the word *soul* was no longer effective in philosophical argument. Although philosophers of the seventeenth and eighteenth centuries frequently invoke the word, their use is equivocal; more and more, *soul* is displaced, in formal argumentation, by special technical language. Descartes wrote an offhand treatise on "the passions of the soul," but when he needed a true diamond bearing to take the weight of skepticism and serve as fulcrum for his entire position, he resorted to the *"cogito."* Likewise Kant, writing in the late Enlightenment, was forced to conduct his own defense of soul in what he called a "unique technical language" ("ganz eigener technischer Ausdrücke"); instead of "soul," he fortified himself with the armor plate of "transcendental unity of apperception." And it was not only Hume, but John Locke and Joseph Butler as well, who substituted the phrase *personal identity* in serious discussion of soul.

Discredited as a possible focus of cognitive discussion, soul was even then in retreat toward the status of mere trope. In our time, it exists only metaphorically, like Gaston Bachelard's "fire," and fits literary contexts only, not scientific ones. The tradition of Freud speaks of psychoanalysis, not of soul analysis; and the Freudian psyche is not in any sense (pace Bruno Bettelheim) the Platonic or Christian soul. The assaults of thinkers like Ernst Mach and Gilbert Ryle have tended to undermine even the concept of the unified ego; and the linguistic theories of Chomsky, which posit the potential of language as given intact in the subject, hastily disclaim this seeming evidence of *a priori* human domain as simply an effect of evolutionary channelings.

Yet two bastions of *a priori* human domain, the ideas of "originality" on the one hand, and of "imagination" on the other, have proved curiously resistant to this historical process of deterioration. Indeed, as "soul" became weaker, they became stronger. Earlier historians of "imagination" have been puzzled because that term and its aura did not rise to prominence until the eighteenth century and did not achieve full honorific status until the Romantic era. Thus, though one of them, Murray Bundy, understood that "Aristotle's *De Anima*," the chief ancient locus for a philosophical treatment of imagination, "may become more significant for literary criticism than the *Poetics*," he attributed the relative lack of "a theory of the poetic mind" in ancient thought to a diversion of attention. "It was obvious, almost from the outset, that classical antiquity did not evolve such a view because it did not habitually think of poetry as the product of certain conditions and habits of mind. Its outstanding critical term was *mimesis*, imitation: the Greeks were primarily concerned with the relation of poetry to external reality, not to the nature of the mind of the artist." Yet a larger truth of the situation, I suggest, is that the relative diminuendo of imagination's importance for ancient thought, the absence of escalation in its significance, the deficiency of emotional aura surrounding it, had less to do with theories of the poetic mind than with the fact that the existential urgencies contiguous to the term were still at that juncture validly maintained by the concept of soul.

A more recent commentator than Bundy, James Engell, finds that "the concept of the imagination is the quintessence of Romanticism." He asserts that "the creative imagination became the way to unify man's psyche and, by extension, to reunify man with nature, to return by the paths of self-consciousness to a state of higher nature, a state of the sublime where senses, mind, and spirit elevate the world around them even as they elevate themselves." Engell urges again that the imagination is "protean." "It deals with the very source of genius and creation and touches the nerve center of human achievement. It brings with it self-confidence and self-reliance. A premium on the imagination encourages the genius and the poet in their faith that what they say is more than decorative, that their creations can awaken the soul and reach truth." Still another commentator, Mary Warnock, says of Wordsworth that "the whole purpose" of one of his long passages is "to suggest that, quite soberly considered, there is something in the connexion he makes between the imaginative ability to perceive and recreate the 'forms of the ancient hills' and 'salvation from the universe of death.' If imagination will save us, it is the very same imagination which enables us to grasp the forms in the first place and then to visit and revisit them in our mind's eye thereafter."

The import of such and similar understandings converges to a single burning focus: the historical rise of imagination's importance witnessed a transfer of mental energy from the weakening concept of soul to an alternative vehicle. Imagination, and its twin Romantic ideal, originality, were then, and still are, transformations of the human intensity earlier conveyed by soul. Blake, who habitually used Christian tropes, though he was not a Christian, asserted comprehensively that "the imagination is not a state; it is the Human Existence itself." Sartre, who did not use Christian tropes and was a declared atheist, said with equal insistence that "the imagination" is "the necessary condition for the freedom of empirical man in the midst of the world."

The foregoing quotations all serve to illustrate the status and function of the imagination, but it would be easy to enlist parallel quotations that do the same for originality. The linkage of the two conceptions is not adventitious. Neither was greatly treasured in antiquity; each began to accelerate in urgency during the eighteenth century; both burst into full flower in the Romantic period. "Originality is the fundamental law of modern poetry," wrote Schelling near the advent of the nineteenth century, "but this was not so in antiquity."

Both conceptions continue to be mysteriously valued in our own day. Indeed, originality and imagination seem to have been intuitively linked together almost from the time they began their rise. Addison, in his series of papers in 1712 on "the pleasures of the imagination," lays stress on "novelty," on "everything that is new or uncommon," and then insists that novelty "raises a pleasure in the imagination, because it fills the soul with an agreeable surprise, gratifies its curiosity, and gives it an idea of which it was not before possessed." In 1728 Zachary Mayne said that "*Imagination*, when under the Conduct and Direction of *Reason*, is the Instrument of that noble Faculty of the Mind, called *Invention*." Joseph Warton writes in 1746 that "the chief faculties of a poet" are "invention and imagination." In 1767 William Duff observed that "Original Genius is distinguished from every other degree of this quality, by a more vivid and a more comprehensive Imagination"; "as Invention is the peculiar and distinguishing province of every species of Genius, Imagination claims an undivided empire over this province." In 1777 Tetens, in speaking of the imagination, says that "von ihr kommt alles Originelle"—"everything original comes from it." By 1783 James Beattie could say almost as a matter of course that "Invention is by all philosophers considered, as an operation" of "Imagination." "By Imagination, we *invent;* that is, produce arrangements of ideas and objects, that were never so arranged before." By the time of high Romanticism, Coleridge, in his *Biographia Literaria* in 1817, links originality and imagination to convey his deepest praise of Wordsworth. "Last, and pre-eminently, I challenge for this poet the gift of IMAGINATION in the highest and strictest sense of the word. . . . In imaginative power, he stands nearest of all modern writers to Shakespeare and Milton; and yet in a kind perfectly unborrowed and his own." In Wordsworth's poetry, he says again, it is "impossible to deny the presence of original genius."

And yet both imagination and originality were then and still are mysterious. What Herder said in the late 1780s still pertains to the real situation. "Of all the powers of the human mind the imagination has been least explored, probably because it is the most difficult to explore . . . —it seems to be not only the basic and connecting link of all the finer mental powers, but in truth the knot that ties body and mind together."

The present volume takes license from Herder's declaration of work still to do, although it makes no attempt to roam in fields better left to the hopes of the physiologist, the psychologist of perception, and the theorist of computer possibilities. It attempts rather a survey of cultural topography, those areas of paradox and poetico-philosophical function out of which arise the twin peaks of originality and imagination. It circles these masses, sights them from varying perspectives, ascends or tries to ascend them by likely-looking paths. The range from which they rise is that of *a priori* human domain, and it is one that has been located and trodden by many others, coming from different directions, laden in different ways, faced with different contours of ascent. All report the same range; no two record exactly the same forms.

A word may be in order about the structure of this volume. My various books have found their origins and evolved their shapes each in a different way; none has developed itself like any other. This one, however, is so idiosyncratic in its coming to be that perhaps it will be of interest to take note of its special process.

The germ of the book was a preoccupation with peripheral but unresolved problems incidental to a comprehensive and long-standing study of Coleridge. There seemed a patent contradiction between Coleridge's intellectual indebtedness—dramatically highlighted by the problem of his plagiarisms—and the widespread Romantic emphasis on originality. The situation was compounded by the mutual indebtedness of Coleridge and Wordsworth, a special example of which was the two friends' extraordinary emphasis on the powers and efficacies of the imagination.

It was this latter emphasis that I addressed, almost by chance, in a statement that has evolved into the fourth chapter of the present book. I was asked to deliver a paper to the English Institute for a session on Coleridge and Wordsworth, and I took the opportunity to precipitate some of the unresolved data in my mind by investigating Coleridge's obligations to Tetens in the formulation of the doctrine of secondary imagination. At that time, however, I had no intention of writing a book on these questions and was content to let the statement stand alone. A year or so later I was asked to contribute a paper to a special issue of *New Literary History*, which was to be devoted to the topic of originality. With that as stimulus, I composed "The Originality Paradox," which now, in somewhat revised form, constitutes the first chapter of this book.

For a while I was content to allow the two statements, the one published in a volume of English Institute essays, and the other in an issue of *New Literary History* (which curiously enough changed its focus so that mine, I believe, was the only contribution that in fact addressed the original plan), to stand as separate articles.

But the topics refused to lie still in my thoughts. As more and more historical data accreted in my mind, gradually the two subjects seemed more and more to impinge on and even merge into one another. I found myself drawn by a need to supply a formal bridge between them. I began to conceive of the two essays not as separate statements but as foundation statements for a book that would attempt to involve the entire spectrum of their mutual implications. Such a book I envisioned as combining practical examination of poetic texts with theoretical discussion of abstract ideas.

Because of other commitments, however, I could anticipate no substantial periods of time in which the volume could be composed, and I feared it might be delayed indefinitely and possibly never written at all. Then a possibility occurred to me. I might be able to continue the book in the same way that the foundation chapters had come into existence: I could wait until someone asked me to deliver a paper, and then, if there were sufficient leeway in the terms of the invitation, use that occasion to work up another chapter of my larger endeavor, crafting it more finely with each subsequent delivery. People did ask; the book did progress. When it was somewhat more than half completed I had the rare good fortune to be allowed an idyllic year in California with no routine duties, and during that time I substantially finished the volume as it now appears.

So I wish to thank Harold Bloom for inviting me to deliver the English Institute lecture that became "The Origin and Significance of Coleridge's Theory of Secondary Imagination," and Ralph Cohen for asking me to compose the essay that became "The Originality Paradox." I wish also to thank Jonathan Culler for generously answering some queries about Derrida, and Wesley Trimpi for long and useful conversations about Coleridge's doctrine of imagination. Paul Alpers provided me friendly criticism of my views on the relation of pastoral to Coleridge's poetry. My friends David Bromwich, Albert Cook, Samuel R. Levin, and A. Walton Litz read the volume before it was printed, and I am exceedingly grateful for their discerning advice.

The matter having been broached at all, it is perhaps desirable to say something of the specific etiology of the other chapters. The second chapter, which is here called "Field, Constellation, and Aesthetic Object," was composed for a conference on Anglo-German literary relations held at the University of Houston in 1981, was again delivered, with refinements, as a lecture at the Claremont complex, this time under the auspices of the Francis Bacon Foundation and the Claremont Graduate School, and eventually came to rest in one form in an issue of *New Literary History*, and in another in a volume called *English and German Romanticism: Cross-Currents and Controversies*, edited by James Pipkin and published at Heidelberg by Carl Winters Universitaetsbuchhandlung. The third chapter, which is here called "The Best Philosopher," was originally delivered as a lecture at the University of Michigan in Ann Arbor, delivered again in England at the Wordsworth Summer Conference at Dove Cottage in the Lake District, still again at the University of California at Berkeley, and once more at the University of Washington in Seattle. A truncated version, without the theoretical matrices, was published in *The Wordsworth Circle*.

The fifth chapter, which is called "The Poetic Working of Secondary Imagination," and the sixth, which is called "The Higher Function of Imagination," and which together complete my original plan for the book, were not written as lectures; indeed, the sixth is much too long to have been delivered under such conditions. The fifth, however, which was composed with no specific occasion in mind other than its necessary role in the book, was subsequently delivered at Queen's University, Kingston, Ontario, as the first George Whalley Memorial Lecture.

Lastly, I wish to express my gratitude to the Center for Advanced Study in the Behavioral Sciences, Stanford, California, and to the National Endowment for the Humanities for fellowships that made available the unencumbered year in California during which I was able to complete the book.

I regret that I was unable to profit from Roland Mortier's *L'Originalité. Une nouvelle catégorie esthétique au siècle des lumières*, which did not appear until after this volume was written.

The index for this volume was compiled by Thomas A. Reed.

Key to Brief
Titles Cited

Brief titles that appear in the notes refer either to full citations occurring shortly before or to the editions listed below.

Addison
> Joseph Addison, Sir Richard Steele, et al., *The Spectator*, ed. Gregory Smith. Everyman's Library, 4 vols. (London: J. M. Dent; New York: E. P. Dutton, 1961–63).

Agassi
> Joseph Agassi, *Faraday as a Natural Philosopher* (Chicago: University of Chicago Press, 1971).

Alpers
> Paul Alpers, "What Is Pastoral?" *Critical Inquiry* 8 (Spring 1982), 437–60.

Ameriks
> Karl Ameriks, *Kant's Theory of Mind: An Analysis of the Paralogisms of Pure Reason* (Oxford: Clarendon Press, 1982).

Amiel
> *The Private Journal of Henri Frédéric Amiel*, trans. Van Wyck and Charles Van Wyck Brooks (New York: Macmillan Co., 1935).

Anxiety
> Harold Bloom, *The Anxiety of Influence: A Theory of Poetry* (New York: Oxford University Press, 1973).

Arnold, *Culture*
> Matthew Arnold, *Culture and Anarchy*, ed. R. H. Super (Ann Arbor: University of Michigan Press, 1965). Volume 5 in *The Complete Prose Works of Matthew Arnold*.

Arnold, *Essays*
> Matthew Arnold, *Essays in Criticism, Second Series* (London: Macmillan & Co., 1905).

Baader
> *Franz von Baaders sämmtliche Werke*, ed. Franz Hoffmann et al., 16 vols. (Leipzig: H. Bethmann, 1850–60).

Babbitt
  Irving Babbitt, *Rousseau and Romanticism* (New York: Meridian
  Books, 1955 [1919]).

Baker
  James Volant Baker, *The Sacred River: Coleridge's Theory of the
  Imagination* (Baton Rouge: Louisiana State University Press, 1957).

Bate, *Burden*
  Walter Jackson Bate, *The Burden of the Past and the English Poet*
  (Cambridge, Mass.: Harvard University Press, 1970).

Bate, *Classic to Romantic*
  Walter Jackson Bate, *From Classic to Romantic: Premises of Taste in
  Eighteenth-Century England* (New York: Harper Torchbooks, 1961
  [1946]).

Bate, *Coleridge*
  Walter Jackson Bate, *Coleridge* (New York: Macmillan Co., 1968).

Beattie
  James Beattie, *Dissertations Moral and Critical* (London: Printed for
  W. Strahan; and T. Cadell, in the Strand; and W. Creech at
  Edinburgh, 1783).

Beck
  Lewis White Beck, *Early German Philosophy: Kant and His Predecessors*
  (Cambridge, Mass.: Harvard University Press, 1969).

Beer
  John Beer, *Coleridge the Visionary* (London: Chatto & Windus, 1959).

Bettelheim
  Bruno Bettelheim, *Freud and Man's Soul* (New York: Alfred A.
  Knopf, 1983).

Biographia
  Samuel Taylor Coleridge, *Biographia Literaria, or, Biographical Sketches
  of my Literary Life and Opinions*, ed. James Engell and W. Jackson
  Bate, 2 vols. (London: Routledge & Kegan Paul; Princeton, N.J.:
  Princeton University Press, 1983). Volume 7 in *The Collected Works of
  Samuel Taylor Coleridge*, ed. Kathleen Coburn, Bollingen Series 75.

Blake
  The Poetry and Prose of William Blake, ed. David V. Erdman,
  commentary by Harold Bloom, third printing, with revisions
  (Garden City, N.Y.: Doubleday & Co., 1968).

Bradley
  A. C. Bradley, *Oxford Lectures on Poetry* (London: Macmillan & Co.,
  1934 [1909]).

Brandes
 Georg Brandes, *Wolfgang Goethe,* trans. Allen W. Porterfield, 2 vols.
 in 1 (New York: Crown Publishers, 1936).

Brinkley
 Coleridge on the Seventeenth Century, ed. Roberta F. Brinkley (New
 York: Greenwood Press, 1968).

Burke
 Edmund Burke, *A Philosophical Enquiry into the Origin of our Ideas of
 the Sublime and Beautiful,* ed. J. T. Boulton (London: Routledge &
 Kegan Paul, 1967 [1958]).

Caird
 Edward Caird, *The Critical Philosophy of Immanuel Kant,* 2 vols.
 (Glasgow: James Maclehose & Sons, 1889).

Carlyle
 The Works of Thomas Carlyle in Thirty Volumes, centenary ed., [ed. H.
 D. Traill], 30 vols. (London: Chapman & Hall [1896–99]).

Carlyon
 Clement Carlyon, *Early Years and Late Reflections,* 4 vols. (London:
 Whittaker & Co., 1836–58).

Cassirer, *Enlightenment*
 Ernst Cassirer, *The Philosophy of the Enlightenment,* trans. Fritz A. C.
 Koelln and James P. Pettegrove (Boston: Beacon Press, 1955).

Cassirer, *Kant*
 H. W. Cassirer, *Kant's First Critique: An Appraisal of the Permanent
 Significance of Kant's Critique of Pure Reason* (London: George Allen &
 Unwin; New York: Humanities Press, 1968 [1954]).

Cassirer, *Leibniz*
 Ernst Cassirer, *Leibniz's System in seinen wissenschaftlichen Grundlagen*
 (Hildesheim: Georg Olms Verlagsbuchhandlung, 1962 [1902]).

Chronology
 Mark L. Reed, *Wordsworth: The Chronology of the Middle Years, 1800–
 1815* (Cambridge, Mass.: Harvard University Press, 1975).

Cobban
 Alfred Cobban, *Edmund Burke and the Revolt Against the Eighteenth
 Century,* 2d ed. (London: George Allen & Unwin, 1960).

Coburn
 Kathleen Coburn, *Inquiring Spirit: A New Presentation of Coleridge
 from His Published and Unpublished Prose Writings* (New York:
 Pantheon Books, 1951).

Coleridge, *Poems*
> *The Complete Poetical Works of Samuel Taylor Coleridge,* ed. Ernest Hartley Coleridge, 2 vols. (Oxford: Clarendon Press, 1912).

Collected Letters
> *Collected Letters of Samuel Taylor Coleridge,* ed. Earl Leslie Griggs, 6 vols. (Oxford: Clarendon Press, 1956–71).

Collingwood
> R. G. Collingwood, *The Principles of Art* (Oxford: Clarendon Press, 1947).

Couturat
> *Opuscules et fragments inédits de Leibniz,* ed. Louis Couturat (Hildesheim: Georg Olms Verlagsbuchhandlung, 1961 [1903]).

Crick
> Francis Crick, *Of Molecules and Men* (Seattle: University of Washington Press, 1966).

Darwin
> Erasmus Darwin, *The Botanic Garden: A Poem in Two Parts,* 2 vols. (London: Printed for J. Johnson, St. Paul's Church-Yard, 1791).

Dennis
> *The Critical Works of John Dennis,* ed. Edward Niles Hooker, 2 vols. (Baltimore: The Johns Hopkins Press, 1939–43).

De Quincey
> *The Collected Writings of Thomas De Quincey,* ed. David Masson, 14 vols. (Edinburgh: Adam & Charles Black, 1899–90).

Derrida
> Jacques Derrida, "Limited Inc.," in *Glyph 2: Johns Hopkins Textual Studies* (Baltimore: The Johns Hopkins University Press, 1977).

De Vleeschauwer, *Déduction transcendentale*
> H. J. De Vleeschauwer, *La Déduction transcendentale dans l'oeuvre de Kant,* 3 vols. (Antwerp: De Sikkel; Paris: Édouard Champion; The Hague: Martinus Nijhoff, 1934–37).

De Vleeschauwer, *Kantian Thought*
> Herman-J. De Vleeschauwer, *The Development of Kantian Thought: The History of a Doctrine,* trans. A.R.C. Duncan (London: Thomas Nelson & Sons, 1962).

Diary
> *Diary, Reminiscences, and Correspondence of Henry Crabb Robinson,* ed. Thomas Sadler, 3 vols. (London: Macmillan & Co., 1869).

Du Bos
> Abbé Jean Baptiste Du Bos, *Critical Reflections on Poetry, Painting and Music,* trans. Thomas Nugent, 3 vols. (London: Printed for J. Nourse, 1748).

Duff

William Duff, *An Essay on Original Genius and its Various Modes of Exertion in Philosophy and the Fine Arts, Particularly in Poetry* (London: Edward & Charles Dilly, 1767).

Durham

Critical Essays of the Eighteenth Century, 1700–1725, ed. W. H. Durham (New Haven, Conn.: Yale University Press, 1915).

Durkheim

Emile Durkheim, *Suicide: A Study in Sociology,* trans. John A. Spaulding and George Simpson (New York: Free Press, 1966).

Eliot

T. S. Eliot, *Selected Essays,* new ed. (New York: Harcourt, Brace & Co., 1950).

Elledge

Eighteenth-Century Critical Essays, ed. Scott Elledge, 2 vols. (Ithaca, N.Y.: Cornell University Press, 1961).

Ellmann

Richard Ellmann, *Yeats: The Man and the Masks* (New York: W. W. Norton & Co., 1978 [1948]).

Emerson

The Complete Works of Ralph Waldo Emerson, ed. E. W. Emerson, centenary ed., 12 vols. (Boston: Houghton Mifflin & Co., 1903–12).

Emerson, *Lectures*

The Early Lectures of Ralph Waldo Emerson, vol. 1, ed. Stephen E. Whicher and Robert E. Spiller (Cambridge, Mass.: Harvard University Press, 1966).

Engell

James Engell, *The Creative Imagination: Enlightenment to Romanticism* (Cambridge, Mass.: Harvard University Press, 1981).

Erdmann

Johann Edward Erdmann, *A History of Philosophy,* vol. 2, trans. Williston S. Hough (London: George Allen & Unwin; New York: Macmillan Co., 1915).

Erkenntnisproblem

Ernst Cassirer, *Das Erkenntnisproblem in der Philosophie und Wissenschaft der neueren Zeit,* 3 vols. (Berlin: Verlag von Bruno Cassirer, 1906–20).

Everest

Kelvin Everest, *Coleridge's Secret Ministry: The Context of the Conversation Poems 1795–1798* (New York: Barnes & Noble, 1979).

Ewing
A. C. Ewing, *A Short Commentary on Kant's Critique of Pure Reason* (Chicago: University of Chicago Press, 1959 [1938]).

Farmer
An Essay on the Learning of Shakespeare, Addressed to Joseph Cradock, Esq., by Richard Farmer, M.A., 2d ed. with large additions (Cambridge: Printed by J. Archdeacon, Printer to the University; for W. Thurlbourn & J. Woodyer, in Cambridge, 1767).

Ferrier
[J. F. Ferrier], "The Plagiarisms of S. T. Coleridge," *Blackwood's Edinburgh Magazine* 47 (1840), 287–99.

Fichte
Johann Gottlieb Fichte, Ausgewählte Werke in Sechs Bänden, ed. Fritz Medicus, 6 vols. (Darmstadt: Wissenschaftliche Buchgesellschaft, 1962 [1910–12]).

Ficino
Theologia Platonica de immortalitate animorum duo de viginti libris, Marsilio Ficino Florentino, Philosopho sacerdote ac Medico, Graecè Latineque doctissimo, authore comprehensa . . . (Parisiis, 1559); facsimile edition (Hildesheim: Georg Olms Verlag, 1975).

Fischer
Ludwig Fischer, *The Structure of Thought: A Survey of Natural Philosophy*, trans. W. H. Johnston (London: George Allen & Unwin, 1931).

Fleming
Donald Fleming, Introduction to Jacques Loeb, *The Mechanistic Conception of Life* (Cambridge, Mass.: Harvard University Press, Belknap Press, 1964).

Foakes
Coleridge on Shakespeare: The Text of the Lectures of 1811–1812, ed. R. A. Foakes (London: Routledge & Kegan Paul, 1971).

Foucault
Michel Foucault, *Les mots et les choses; une archéologie des sciences humaines* (Paris: Gallimard, 1966).

Frankenstein
Mary Shelley, *Frankenstein: or, The Modern Prometheus* (Boston: Sever, Francis & Co., 1869).

Freud
The Standard Edition of the Complete Psychological Works of Sigmund Freud, trans. and ed. James Strachey, Anna Freud et al., 24 vols. (London: Hogarth Press and the Institute of Psycho-Analysis, 1966–74).

Friend
Samuel Taylor Coleridge, *The Friend,* ed. Barbara E. Rooke, 2 vols. (London: Routledge & Kegan Paul; Princeton, N.J.: Princeton University Press, 1969). Volume 4 in *The Collected Works of Samuel Taylor Coleridge,* ed. Kathleen Coburn, Bollingen Series 75.

Fruman
Norman Fruman, *Coleridge, the Damaged Archangel* (New York: George Braziller, 1971).

Frye, *Anatomy*
Northrop Frye, *Anatomy of Criticism* (Princeton, N.J.: Princeton University Press, 1957).

Frye, *Symmetry*
Northrop Frye, *Fearful Symmetry: A Study of William Blake* (Princeton, N.J.: Princeton University Press, 1969 [1947]).

Garin
Eugenio Garin, *Italian Humanism: Philosophy and Civic Life in the Renaissance,* trans. Peter Munz (Oxford: Basil Blackwell, 1965).

Gay
Peter Gay, *The Enlightenment: An Interpretation,* 2 vols. (New York: Alfred A. Knopf, 1967–69).

Gedenkausgabe
Johann Wolfgang Goethe, *Gedenkausgabe der Werke, Briefe und Gespräche,* ed. Ernst Beutler, 27 vols. (Zurich: Artemis Verlag, 1948–71).

Gérard, *Discordant Harp*
Albert S. Gérard, *English Romantic Poetry: Ethos, Structure, and Symbol in Coleridge, Wordsworth, Shelley, and Keats* (Berkeley and Los Angeles: University of California Press, 1968), chap. 2, "The Discordant Harp: The Structure of Coleridge's Conversation Poems."

Gerard, *Essay*
Alexander Gerard, *An Essay on Genius* (London: W. Strahan; T. Cadell in the Strand; and W. Creech at Edinburgh, 1774).

Germany
Crabb Robinson in Germany, 1800–1805: Extracts from his Correspondence, ed. Edith J. Morley (London: Oxford University Press, 1929).

Goethes Gespräche
Goethes Gespräche, ed. Wolfgang Herwig, 4 vols. (Zurich und Stuttgart: Artemis Verlag, 1965–72).

Hallie
Philip P. Hallie, *The Scar of Montaigne: An Essay in Personal Philosophy* (Middletown, Conn.: Wesleyan University Press, 1966).

Hamann
  Johann Georg Hamanns Briefwechsel, ed. Walther Ziesemer and Arthur Henkel, 7 vols. (Wiesbaden: Insel-Verlag, 1955–79).

Hartley
  David Hartley, *Observations on Man, His Frame, His Duty, and His Expectations*, 2 vols. (London: S. Richardson for J. Leake and William Frederick, 1749).

Hartman
  Geoffrey Hartman, *Wordsworth's Poetry, 1787–1814* (New Haven, Conn.: Yale University Press, 1964).

Havelock
  Eric Havelock, *Preface to Plato* (Cambridge, Mass.: Harvard University Press, 1963).

Haven
  Richard Haven, *Patterns of Consciousness: An Essay on Coleridge* (Amherst: University of Massachusetts Press, 1969).

Haydon
  The Diary of Benjamin Robert Haydon, ed. Willard Bissell Pope, 5 vols. (Cambridge, Mass.: Harvard University Press, 1960–63).

Hazlitt
  The Complete Works of William Hazlitt, ed. P. P. Howe, after the edition of A. R. Waller and Arnold Glover, 21 vols. (London: J. M. Dent & Sons, 1930–34).

Hegel
  G.W.F. Hegel: Werke in zwanzig Bänden, Theorie-Werkausgabe, ed. Eva Moldenhauer and Karl Markus Michel, 21 vols. (Frankfurt am Main: Suhrkamp Verlag, 1967–71).

Heidegger
  Martin Heidegger, *Poetry, Language, Thought*, trans. Albert Hofstadter (New York: Harper & Row, 1971).

Heine
  Heinrich Heine: Historisch-kritische Gesamtausgabe der Werke, Düsseldorfer Ausgabe, ed. Manfred Windfuhr, 15 vols. (Hamburg: Hoffman und Campe, 1973–).

Herder, *Ideen*
  Johann Gottfried Herder, *Ideen zur Philosophie der Geschichte der Menschheit*, 2 vols. (Berlin: Aufbau-Verlag, 1965).

Herders Werke
  Herders sämmtliche Werke, ed. Bernhard Suphan, 33 vols. (Berlin: Weidmann, 1877–1913).

Hofstadter
>Douglas R. Hofstadter, review of *Alan Turing: The Enigma, New York Times Book Review*, 13 November 1983.

Hollander
>John Hollander, "Originality," *Raritan: A Quarterly Review* 2 (Spring, 1983), 24–44.

House
>Humphry House, *Coleridge: The Clark Lectures 1951–52* (London: Rupert Hart-Davis, 1962).

Hulme
>T. E. Hulme, *Speculations: Essays on Humanism and the Philosophy of Art*, ed. Herbert Read (London: Routledge & Kegan Paul, 1949 [1924]).

Hume
>David Hume, *A Treatise of Human Nature*, ed. L. A. Selby-Bigge, 2d ed., rev. by P. H. Nidditch (Oxford: Clarendon Press, 1978).

Irving
>Washington Irving, *The Sketch Book of Geoffrey Crayon, Gent.*, 3d ed., 2 vols. (London: John Murray, 1820).

Jackson
>J. R. de J. Jackson, *Method and Imagination in Coleridge's Criticism* (Cambridge, Mass.: Harvard University Press, 1969).

Jacobi
>*Friedrich Heinrich Jacobis Werke*, ed. Friedrich Roth and Friedrich Köppen, 7 vols. in 6 (Leipzig: Gerhard Fleischer, 1812–25).

Jaeger, *Early Christianity*
>Werner Jaeger, *Early Christianity and Greek Paideia* (Cambridge, Mass.: Harvard University Press, Belknap Press, 1961).

Jaeger, *Paideia*
>Werner Jaeger, *Paideia: The Ideals of Greek Culture*, trans. Gilbert Highet, 3 vols. (New York: Oxford University Press, 1960).

James, *Scepticism*
>D. G. James, *Scepticism and Poetry: An Essay on the Poetic Imagination* (London: George Allen & Unwin, 1960 [1937]).

James, *Principles*
>William James, *The Principles of Psychology*, 2 vols. (New York: Henry Holt & Co., 1890).

Janke
>Wolfgang Janke, *Fichte: Sein und Reflexion—Grundlagen der kritischen Vernunft* (Berlin: Walter de Gruyter & Co., 1970).

Jaspers
Karl Jaspers, *Nietzsche: An Introduction to the Understanding of His Philosophical Activity,* trans. Charles F. Wallraff and Frederick J. Schmitz (Tucson: University of Arizona Press, 1965).

Jean Paul
Jean Pauls sämtliche Werke, historical-critical ed., ed. Eduard Berend, 19 vols. (Weimar: Hermann Böhlaus Nachfolger, 1927–44).

Johnson
Samuel Johnson, *The Lives of the English Poets,* ed. George Birkbeck Hill, 3 vols. (Oxford: Clarendon Press, 1905).

Jones
Ernest Jones, *The Life and Work of Sigmund Freud,* 3 vols. (New York: Basic Books, 1953–57).

Jonson
Ben Jonson, ed. C. H. Herford and Percy Simpson, 11 vols. (Oxford: Clarendon Press, 1925–52).

Kabbalah
Harold Bloom, *Kabbalah and Criticism* (New York: Seabury Press, 1975).

Kant
Kants gesammelte Schriften, ed. by the Royal Prussian Academy of Sciences, 31 vols. (Berlin: Druck und Verlag von Georg Reimer; continued to the present by Walter de Gruyter & Co., 1902–).

Keats, *Letters*
The Letters of John Keats, 1814–1821, ed. Hyder Edward Rollins, 2 vols. (Cambridge, Mass.: Harvard University Press, 1958).

Keats, *Poems*
The Poems of John Keats, ed. Jack Stillinger (Cambridge, Mass.: Harvard University Press, Belknap Press, 1978).

Kemp Smith
Norman Kemp Smith, *A Commentary to Kant's* Critique of Pure Reason, 2d ed. (New York: Humanities Press, 1950).

Kierkegaard
Søren Kierkegaard, *The Concept of Dread,* trans. Walter Lowrie (Princeton, N.J.: Princeton University Press, 1957).

Knight
G. Wilson Knight, *The Starlit Dome* (London: Methuen, 1941).

Koyré
Alexandre Koyré, "Les Philosophes et la machine," *Critique* 4 (1948), 324–33, 610–29.

Laing
R. D. Laing, *The Politics of Experience* (New York: Pantheon Books, 1967).

Lamb
The Letters of Charles and Mary Anne Lamb, ed. Edwin Marrs, Jr., 5 vols. (Ithaca, N.Y.: Cornell University Press, 1975–).

La Mettrie
La Mettrie's L'Homme Machine: A Study in the Origins of an Idea, critical ed. with an introductory monograph and notes by Aram Vartanian (Princeton, N.J.: Princeton University Press, 1960).

Lawall
Gilbert Lawall, *Theocritus' Coan Pastorals: A Poetry Book* (Cambridge, Mass.: Harvard University Press, 1967).

Lay Sermons
Samuel Taylor Coleridge, *Lay Sermons*, ed. R. J. White (London: Routledge & Kegan Paul; Princeton, N.J.: Princeton University Press, 1972). Volume 6 in *The Collected Works of Samuel Taylor Coleridge*, ed. Kathleen Coburn, Bollingen Series 75.

Leavis, *Pursuit*
F. R. Leavis, *The Common Pursuit* (London: Chatto & Windus, 1972 [1952]).

Leavis, *Revaluation*
F. R. Leavis, *Revaluation: Tradition & Development in English Poetry* (London: Chatto & Windus, 1969 [1936]).

Leibniz
Die philosophischen Schriften von Gottfried Wilhelm Leibniz, ed. C. J. Gerhardt, 7 vols. (Hildesheim: Georg Olms Verlagsbuchhandlung, 1960; facsimile reprint of the 1875–90 edition).

Levin, *Memories*
Harry Levin, *Memories of the Moderns* (London: Faber & Faber, 1981).

Levin, *Perspectives*
Walter Jackson Bate, "Coleridge on the Functions of Art," in *Perspectives of Criticism*, ed. Harry Levin (Cambridge, Mass.: Harvard University Press, 1950).

Levy
Paul Levy, *Moore: G. E. Moore and the Cambridge Apostles* (New York: Holt, Rinehart & Winston, 1979).

Lichtenbergs Aphorismen
Georg Christoph Lichtenbergs Aphorismen, ed. Albert Leitzmann, 5 vols. (Berlin: B. Behrs Verlag, 1902–8).

Lichtenberg's Visits
    Lichtenberg's Visits to England, trans. Margaret L. More and W. H.
    Quarrell (Oxford: Clarendon Press, 1938).

Lindsay
    A. D. Lindsay, Preface to Elie Halévy, *The Growth of Philosophic
    Radicalism,* trans. Mary Morris (New York: Macmillan Co., 1926).

Locke
    John Locke, *An Essay Concerning Human Understanding,* ed. Peter H.
    Nidditch (Oxford: Clarendon Press, 1975).

Loeb
    Jacques Loeb, *The Mechanistic Conception of Life,* ed. Donald Fleming
    (Cambridge, Mass.: Harvard University Press, Belknap Press, 1964).

Lowes
    John Livingston Lowes, *The Road to Xanadu: A Study in the Ways of
    the Imagination* (Boston: Houghton Mifflin Co., 1927).

McFarland, *Coleridge*
    Thomas McFarland, *Coleridge and the Pantheist Tradition* (Oxford:
    Clarendon Press, 1969).

McFarland, *Romanticism*
    Thomas McFarland, *Romanticism and the Forms of Ruin: Wordsworth,
    Coleridge and Modalities of Fragmentation* (Princeton, N.J.: Princeton
    University Press, 1981).

Man in the Modern Age
    Karl Jaspers, *Man in the Modern Age,* trans. E. and C. Paul (New
    York: Doubleday Anchor Books, 1957).

Mannheim
    From Karl Mannheim, ed. Kurt H. Wolff (New York: Oxford
    University Press, 1971).

Marks
    Emerson R. Marks, *Coleridge on the Language of Verse* (Princeton,
    N.J.: Princeton University Press, 1981).

Mathematische Schriften
    Leibnizens mathematische Schriften, ed. C. I. Gerhardt, 7 vols. (Halle:
    H. W. Schmidt, 1849–63).

Mayne
    [Zachary Mayne], *Two Dissertations Concerning Sense, and the
    Imagination. With an Essay on Consciousness* (London: Printed for J.
    Tonson in the Strand, 1728).

Mayo
    Robert Mayo, "The Contemporaneity of the *Lyrical Ballads,*" *PMLA*
    69 (1954), 486–522.

Middle Years, I

The Letters of William and Dorothy Wordsworth, II, The Middle Years, Part I, 1806–1811, ed. Ernest de Selincourt, revised by Mary Moorman (Oxford: Clarendon Press, 1969).

Middle Years, II

The Letters of William and Dorothy Wordsworth, III, The Middle Years, Part II, 1812–1820, 2d ed., ed. Ernest de Selincourt, revised by Mary Moorman and Alan G. Hill (Oxford: Clarendon Press, 1970).

Mill

Collected Works of John Stuart Mill, ed. J. M. Robson et al., 25 vols. (Toronto: University of Toronto Press, 1963–).

Miscellaneous Criticism

Coleridge's Miscellaneous Criticism, ed. T. M. Raysor (London: Constable, 1936).

Misreading

Harold Bloom, A Map of Misreading (New York: Oxford University Press, 1975).

Newman

John Henry Cardinal Newman, The Idea of a University, Defined and Illustrated, new ed., ed. Charles Frederick Harrold (New York: Longmans, Green & Co., 1947).

Newton

Eric Newton, The Romantic Rebellion (New York: Schocken Books, 1964).

Nietzsche

Friedrich Nietzsche: Werke in drei Bänden, ed. Karl Schlechta, 3 vols. (Munich: Carl Hanser Verlag, 1954–56).

Nietzsches Briefwechsel

Friedrich Nietzsches Briefwechsel mit Franz Overbeck, ed. Richard Oehler and C. A. Bernoulli (Leipzig: Insel-Verlag, 1916).

Notebooks

The Notebooks of Samuel Taylor Coleridge, ed. Kathleen Coburn, 3 vols. (London: Routledge & Kegan Paul, 1957–).

Ortega, *Dehumanization*

José Ortega y Gasset, The Dehumanization of Art and Other Essays on Art, Culture, and Literature, trans. Helene Weyl et al. (Princeton, N.J.: Princeton University Press, 1968).

Ortega, *Velazquez*

José Ortega y Gasset, Velazquez, Goya and the Dehumanization of Art, trans. Alexis Brown (New York: W. W. Norton & Co., 1972).

Paley
> Morton D. Paley, *Energy and the Imagination: A Study of the Development of Blake's Thought* (Oxford: Clarendon Press, 1970).

Pater
> Walter Pater, *Appreciations, With an Essay on Style* (London: Macmillan & Co., 1924 [1889]).

Paton
> H. J. Paton, *Kant's Metaphysic of Experience: A Commentary on the First Half of the* Kritik der reinen Vernunft, 2 vols. (London: George Allen & Unwin; New York: Humanities Press, 1965 [1936]).

Philosophical Lectures
> The Philosophical Lectures of Samuel Taylor Coleridge, Hitherto Unpublished, ed. Kathleen Coburn (London: Pilot Press, 1949).

Poggioli
> Renato Poggioli, *The Theory of the Avant-Garde*, trans. Gerald Fitzgerald (Cambridge, Mass.: Harvard University Press, 1968).

Pope
> The Twickenham Edition of the Poems of Alexander Pope, ed. John Butt et al., 11 vols. in 12 (London: Methuen & Co.; New Haven: Yale University Press, 1939–69).

Praz
> Mario Praz, *The Romantic Agony*, trans. Angus Davidson (New York: Meridian Books, 1956 [1933]).

Prelude
> Wordsworth, *The Prelude: A Parallel Text*, ed. J. C. Maxwell (Harmondsworth, Middlesex: Penguin Books, 1971).

Proclus
> Proclus, *A Commentary on the First Book of Euclid's Elements*, trans., with introduction and notes, by Glenn R. Morrow (Princeton, N.J.: Princeton University Press, 1970).

Prose
> The Prose Works of William Wordsworth, ed. W.J.B. Owen and Jane Worthington Smyser, 3 vols. (Oxford: Clarendon Press, 1974).

Quint
> David Quint, *Origin and Originality in Renaissance Literature: Versions of the Source* (New Haven, Conn.: Yale University Press, 1983).

Radley
> Virginia L. Radley, *Samuel Taylor Coleridge* (New York: Twayne Publishers, 1966).

Randall
> John Herman Randall, *The Career of Philosophy*, volume 2, *From the*

German Enlightenment to the Age of Darwin (New York: Columbia University Press, 1965).

Ransom
John Crowe Ransom, *The World's Body* (New York: Charles Scribner's Sons, 1938).

Raysor
Samuel Taylor Coleridge, *Shakespearean Criticism*, 2d ed., ed. Thomas Middleton Raysor. Everyman's Library, 2 vols. (London: J. M. Dent; New York: E. P. Dutton, 1960).

Renan
Ernest Renan, *Nouvelles études d'histoire religieuse* (Paris: Calmann Lévy, 1884).

Richards
I. A. Richards, *Coleridge on Imagination,* 3d ed. (London: Routledge & Kegan Paul, 1962).

Robinson
Henry Crabb Robinson on Books and their Writers, ed. Edith J. Morley, 3 vols. (New York: AMS Press, 1967).

Said
Edward Said, *Beginnings: Intention and Method* (New York: Basic Books, 1975; Baltimore: The Johns Hopkins University Press, 1978).

Saintsbury
Loci Critici: Passages Illustrative of Critical Theory and Practice from Aristotle Downwards, ed. George Saintsbury (Boston: Ginn & Co., 1903).

Sartre, *Critique*
Jean-Paul Sartre, *Critique de la raison dialectique* (Paris: Gallimard, 1960).

Sartre, *Imagination*
Jean-Paul Sartre, *The Psychology of Imagination* (New York: Citadel Press, 1963).

Schelling
Friedrich Wilhelm Joseph von Schellings sämmtliche Werke, ed. K.F.A. Schelling (Stuttgart: J. G. Cotta'scher Verlag, 1856–61). The edition is in two *Abtheilungen,* the first consisting of volumes numbered 1–10, the second of volumes numbered 1–4. To avoid cumbersome identifications of *Abtheilungen,* references to the first are cited as volumes I–X, to the second as volumes XI–XIV.

Schiller
Schillers sämtliche Werke, secular ed., ed. Eduard von der Hellen, in association with Richard Fester et al., 16 vols. (Stuttgart: J. G. Cotta'sche Buchhandlung Nachfolger [1904–05]).

Schneider
Elisabeth Schneider, *Coleridge, Opium and* Kubla Khan (Chicago: University of Chicago Press, 1953).

Schofield
Robert E. Schofield, *Mechanism and Materialism: British Natural Philosophy in An Age of Reason* (Princeton, N.J.: Princeton University Press, 1970).

Schopenhauer
Arthur Schopenhauer, *Sämtliche Werke,* ed. Arthur Hübscher, 3d ed., 7 vols. (Wiesbaden: F. A. Brockhaus, 1972).

Schrickx
W. Schrickx, "Coleridge and Friedrich Heinrich Jacobi," *Revue belge de philologie et d'histoire* 36 (1958), 812–50.

Segal
Charles Segal, *Poetry and Myth in Ancient Pastoral: Essays on Theocritus and Virgil* (Princeton, N.J.: Princeton University Press, 1981).

Sharpe
William Sharpe, *A Dissertation Upon Genius* (London: C. Bathurst, 1755).

Shawcross
Biographia Literaria, by S. T. Coleridge, edited with his Aesthetical Essays by J. Shawcross, 2 vols. (London: Oxford University Press, 1907).

Shelley
The Complete Works of Percy Bysshe Shelley, ed. Roger Ingpen and Walter E. Peck, 10 vols. (New York: Gordian Press, 1965).

Shelley, *Letters*
The Letters of Percy Bysshe Shelley, ed. Frederick L. Jones, 2 vols. (Oxford: Clarendon Press, 1964).

Sidney
The Prose Works of Sir Philip Sidney, ed. Albert Feuillerat, 4 vols. (Cambridge: Cambridge University Press, 1968–70).

Simmel
Georg Simmel on Individuality and Social Forms, ed. Donald N. Levine (Chicago: University of Chicago Press, 1971).

Snell
Bruno Snell, *The Discovery of the Mind: The Greek Origins of European Thought,* trans. Thomas G. Rosenmeyer (New York: Harper Torchbooks, 1960).

Sperry
> Stuart M. Sperry, *Keats the Poet* (Princeton, N.J.: Princeton University Press, 1973).

Spingarn
> J. E. Spingarn, *A History of Literary Criticism in the Renaissance*, 2d ed. (New York: Columbia University Press, 1954 [1908]).

Spinoza
> *Spinoza Opera*, commissioned by the Heidelberg Academy of Sciences, ed. Carl Gebhardt, 4 vols. (Heidelberg: Carl Winters Universitaetsbuchhandlung, 1972).

Spranger
> Eduard Spranger, *Wilhelm von Humboldt und die Humanitätsidee* (Berlin: Reuther und Reichard, 1909).

Stahl
> E. L. Stahl, "S. T. Coleridges Theorie der Dichtung im Hinblick auf Goethe," in *Weltliteratur: Festgabe für Fritz Strich zum 70. Geburtstag,* ed. Walter Muschg and Emil Staiger (Bern: Francke Verlag, 1952).

Sterling
> John Sterling, *Essays and Tales,* ed. J. C. Hare, 2 vols. (London: John W. Parker, 1848).

Stirner
> Max Stirner, *The Ego and His Own,* ed. John Carroll (New York: Harper & Row, 1971).

Strich
> Fritz Strich, *Goethe und die Weltliteratur,* 2d ed. enl. (Bern: Francke Verlag, 1957), pt. 2, sec. 1, "Die befreiende Macht der englischen Literatur."

Suther
> Marshall Suther, *Visions of Xanadu* (New York: Columbia University Press, 1965).

Table Talk
> *The Table Talk and Omniana of Samuel Taylor Coleridge,* ed. T. Ashe (London: George Bell & Sons, 1888).

Tetens
> Johann Nicolas Tetens, *Philosophische Versuche über die menschliche Natur und ihre Entwickelung,* 2 vols. (Leipzig: M. G. Weidmanns Erben und Reich, 1777).

Theocritus
> *The Greek Bucolic Poets,* ed. and trans. J. M. Edmonds, Loeb Classical Library (Cambridge, Mass.: Harvard University Press, 1960).

Tocqueville
> Alexis de Tocqueville, *Democracy in America*, Henry Reeves text, rev. Francis Bowen, ed. Phillips Bradley, 2 vols. (New York: Vintage Books, 1954).

Traherne
> Thomas Traherne, *Centuries, Poems, and Thanksgivings*, ed. H. M. Margoliouth, 2 vols. (Oxford: Clarendon Press, 1958).

Trilling
> Lionel Trilling, *The Liberal Imagination: Essays on Literature and Society* (Garden City, N.Y.: Doubleday Anchor Books, 1954).

Tuveson
> Ernest Lee Tuveson, *The Imagination as a Means of Grace: Locke and the Aesthetics of Romanticism* (Berkeley and Los Angeles: University of California Press, 1960).

Uebele
> Wilhelm Uebele, *Johann Nicolaus Tetens nach seiner Gesamtentwicklung betrachtet, mit besonderer Berücksichtigung des Verhältnisses zu Kant* (Berlin: Reuther & Reichard, 1911).

Vaihinger
> Hans Vaihinger, *Die transcendentale Deduktion der Kategorien* (Halle: Max Niemeyer, 1902).

Valéry
> *The Collected Works of Paul Valéry*, ed. Jackson Mathews, et al. 15 vols. (Princeton, N.J.: Princeton University Press, 1956–75).

Vaughan
> *The Complete Poetry of Henry Vaughan*, ed. French Fogle, Stuart Editions (New York: New York University Press, 1965).

Vendler
> Helen Vendler, *On Extended Wings: Wallace Stevens' Longer Poems* (Cambridge, Mass.: Harvard University Press, 1969).

Visionary Company
> Harold Bloom, *The Visionary Company: A Reading of English Romantic Poetry*, rev. & enl. ed. (Ithaca, N.Y.: Cornell University Press, 1971).

Walzel
> Oskar Walzel, *Deutsche Romantik*, vol. 1, *Welt- und Kunstanschauung*, 5th ed. (Leipzig: Verlag und Druck von B. G. Teubner, 1923).

Walzer
> Richard Walzer, "Al-Fārābi's Theory of Prophecy and Divination," *Journal of Hellenic Studies* 77 (1957), 142–48.

Watson
> George Watson, *Coleridge the Poet* (London: Routledge & Kegan Paul, 1966).

Weinberg
> Steven Weinberg, *The First Three Minutes: A Modern View of the Origin of the Universe* (New York: Basic Books, 1977).

Weldon
> T. D. Weldon, *Kant's* Critique of Pure Reason, 2d ed. (Oxford: Clarendon Press, 1958).

Wellek
> René Wellek, *A History of Modern Criticism: 1750–1950*, 4 vols. to date (New Haven, Conn.: Yale University Press, 1955–).

Wetzels
> Walter D. Wetzels, *Johann Wilhelm Ritter: Physik im Wirkungsfeld der deutschen Romantik* (Berlin: Walter de Gruyter & Co., 1973).

Whalley
> George Whalley, "Coleridge Unlabyrinthed," *University of Toronto Quarterly* 32 (1963), 324–45.

Wheeler
> K. M. Wheeler, *The Creative Mind in Coleridge's Poetry* (Cambridge, Mass.: Harvard University Press, 1981).

White
> H. O. White, *Plagiarism and Imitation During the English Renaissance: A Study in Critical Distinctions* (Cambridge, Mass.: Harvard University Press, 1935).

Whitehead
> Alfred North Whitehead, *Science and the Modern World*, Lowell Lectures, 1925 (New York: Macmillan Co., 1925).

Williams
> Raymond Williams, *The Country and the City* (New York: Oxford University Press, 1973).

Wilson
> Arthur M. Wilson, *Diderot* (New York: Oxford University Press, 1972).

Winters
> Yvor Winters, *Forms of Discovery: Critical & Historical Essays on the Forms of the Short Poem in English* ([Denver]: Allan Swallow, 1967).

Wolfson
> Harry Austryn Wolfson, *The Philosophy of Spinoza: Unfolding the Latent Processes of His Reasoning*, 2 vols. (Cambridge, Mass.: Harvard University Press, 1948).

Woodring
   Carl Woodring, *Politics in English Romantic Poetry* (Cambridge,
   Mass.: Harvard University Press, 1970).

Woolf
   Virginia Woolf, "The Leaning Tower," *Collected Essays*, vol. 2
   (London: Hogarth Press, 1966).

Wordsworth, *Poems*
   The Poetical Works of William Wordsworth, ed. Ernest de Selincourt
   and Helen Darbishire, 5 vols. (Oxford: Clarendon Press, 1940–49).

Wordsworth, *William Wordsworth*
   Jonathan Wordsworth, *William Wordsworth: The Borders of Vision*
   (Oxford: Clarendon Press, 1982).

Yarlott
   Geoffrey Yarlott, *Coleridge and the Abyssinian Maid* (London:
   Methuen & Co., 1967).

Yeats
   Harold Bloom, *Yeats* (New York: Oxford University Press, 1970).

Young
   [Edward Young], *Conjectures on Original Composition*, in a letter to
   the author of *Sir Charles Grandison* (London: A. Millar and R. and J.
   Dodsley, 1759).

Originality & Imagination

• 1 •

The Originality Paradox

W̶e cannot think of man except by invoking simultaneously the opposed categories of individual and society. The "pivotal point," insists Simmel, of the "concept of individuality" is that "when man is freed from everything that is not wholly himself, what remains as the actual substance of his being is man in general, mankind, which lives in him and in everyone else." It is only by this truth that there can exist the conception of a "lonely crowd," for the paradox of that title reflects the paradox of human consciousness. Neither individuality nor communality can be felt without the other, although each strains against its complement. The paradox reflects no adventitious alignment of possibilities, but rather an irreducible truth of what it is to be human. "The fact is," points out Kierkegaard, "that at every moment the individual is himself and the race."[1]

Any attempt to resolve the paradox is unsuccessful. Romanticism's very emphasis on the isolated ego ("From my youth upwards," intones Manfred, "My spirit walked not with the souls of men . . . / My joy was in the Wilderness,—to breathe / The difficult air of the iced mountain's top") is an attitude that leads to nothingness.

> MANFRED (*alone*): We are the fools of time and terror: Days
> Steal on us and steal from us; yet we live,
> Loathing our life, and dreading still to die.

Zarathustra too inhabits the peaks of isolation; but Nietzsche's own lot was despair and collapse. Indeed, Durkheim, in his classic treatise, identifies one genesis of suicide as precisely the isolation of the individual from the group: "we may call egoistic the special type of suicide springing from excessive individualism"; for such

---

[1]*Simmel*, p. 220; Kierkegaard, p. 26.

suicide is an awareness of the "complete emptiness of an egoistic life."[2] On the other hand, too much communality leads just as inexorably to nothingness. "Love," urges Wordsworth, does not "easily thrive / In cities, where the human heart is sick."[3]

The intensification of the paradox arising from an alteration of relationship between the individual ego and its conditions of communality—an alteration that becomes clearly visible with the Romantic era—is a counterpart, both logically and historically, of a problem with regard to individual talent and the existence of intellectual tradition. Romantic egotism, which was a response to the palpable diminution of the meaningful self,[4] is paralleled by the cultural rise of an emphasis on originality. The intensification of the individual/group polarity marks out, as it were, an abscissa; and that of the individual/tradition problem an ordinate.

The latter complication I call the *originality paradox*. Although

[2]*Manfred*, II, 144–45, 156–57, 258–60; Durkheim, pp. 209, 325.

[3]*Prelude*, 1805–1806 version, XII, 201–2 (p. 498). Elsewhere Wordsworth finds the "mighty City" a "blank confusion" that causes men to be "melted and reduced / To one identity" (VII, 695–703 [p. 292]). What Wordsworth felt at the beginning of the nineteenth century, as both technology and population stirred into ominous increase (his lines were written contemporaneously with the proleptic unease of Malthus's *Essay on the Principle of Population as it Affects the Future Improvement of Society*), was darkened, as both conditions advanced, into Joseph Conrad's nightmare: "The vision of an enormous town presented itself, of a monstrous town more populous than some continents and in its man-made might as if indifferent to heaven's frowns and smiles; a cruel devourer of the world's light. There was . . . darkness enough to bury five millions of lives" (Author's Note to *The Secret Agent*). The problem is historically cumulative. Aristotle, who said that "a great city is not to be confounded with a populous one," felt that the number of five thousand citizens proposed by Plato in the *Laws* (with supernumeraries, perhaps not much more than a hundred thousand people) was excessive (*Politics*, 1326a25, 1265a5–20). By Conrad's time, five million was the number, and the increase was accompanied by desolation. At this writing the population of Mexico City is said to be eighteen million humans. Even by the mid-nineteenth century James Thomson's *City of Dreadful Night* had as inhabitants "the saddest and weariest men on earth," subject to "infections of incurable despair," while in the twentieth century T. S. Eliot thinks despondently "of all the hands / That are raising dingy shades / In a thousand furnished rooms." H. G. Wells writes of a "limitless crowd of dingy people" that shows "no gleam of hope or anything" (all three passages quoted in Williams). And our own experience of megalopolis is even more light-devouring. It is in our time, indeed, that it has become necessary to distinguish between "group"—people for whom interrelationship exists—and "collective"—the anonymous crowd or "pluralité de solitudes," characterized by "interchangeabilité" (Sartre, *Critique*, pp. 306–14).

[4]Cf. Eric Newton: "I am inclined to think that the advent of romantic movements is a by-product of the decay of humanism. . . .This consciousness . . . always results in Man being displaced from his central position as the measure of all things and being involved once more in a struggle . . . which always belittles him" (Newton, p. 62). Cf. Carl Woodring's statement that Romanticism is "egoistic *revolt* in headlong *flight*" (Woodring, p. 25). The so-called *mal du siècle* of Chateaubriand's René is the true reality underlying that era's egotistic vaunts. "A mysterious apathy

both complications, of course, occur in chronological sequences, the problem of individual and group is always perceived as a lateral relationship, occupying a common temporal plane. The problem of individual and tradition, conversely, always is perceived as a vertical effect in time. To be sure, the relationships of a cultural figure to his contemporaries form a part of this problem; yet even those relationships are perceived in terms of temporal precedences, however minute their intervals may be. The complication is thus properly schematized as an ordinate, and its cultural spatiality is created by its opposed relationship to the abscissa, that is, to individuality in tension with communality.

Although the examples that follow in this chapter are devoted preferentially to the illustration of the originality paradox, rather than to the illustration of the tension between the individual and society, we shall not entirely lose sight of the latter. The largest purpose of its invocation, however, has already been served: that is, to dramatize, by its immediacy in our common experience, the unavoidability and importance of the matters under discussion. We are aware in countless daily ways of the impact of increasing population on our personal situations; only in our special role as intellectuals, however, do we apprehend the corresponding complications of too heavy a cultural past. So it is for these latter complications that the other awarenesses are invoked as prolegomena.

The elements of both tensions are constant in human experience even if their psychic spatiality is expanded in Romanticism. Romantic, or Byronic, egotism, it is necessary to insist, was not invested by the Romantics. Childe Harold is no more egotistic than Almanzor; nor Almanzor than Tamburlaine.[5] The same, mutatis

---

gradually took hold of my body. My aversion for life, which I had felt as a child, was returning with renewed intensity. Soon my heart supplied no more nourishment for my thought, and I was aware of my existence only in a deep sense of weariness." For further statement on the sense of melancholy and self-diminishment characteristic of Romanticism, see Babbitt, p. 237; Praz, p. 31. The surface of Romanticism was, in Watts-Dunton's phrase, "the renascence of wonder"; but the deeper reality, to use Hegel's rubric as developed by Judith Shklar, was "the unhappy consciousness."

[5]See, e.g., Eugene M. Waith, *The Herculean Hero: In Marlowe, Chapman, Shakespeare and Dryden* (New York: Columbia University Press, 1967). The failure adequately to realize this truth seems to me to constitute a limitation on the discussion in Peter L. Thorslev, *The Byronic Hero: Types and Prototypes* (Minneapolis: University of Minnesota Press, 1962). Simmel says: "The conscious emphasis on individuality as a matter of principle certainly does seem to have been the original accomplishment of the Renaissance. This took place in such a way that the will to power, to distinction, and to becoming honored and famous was diffused among men to a degree never before known" (*Simmel*, p. 217). The egotistic emphasis in the Renaissance, even in

mutandis, holds true for the conception of originality. It is not the case, as one sometimes hears, that earlier writers were not concerned with originality; they were concerned, but not so deeply and not so insistently as were the Romantics.[6] It is merely a note of special intensity that is sounded, not one without any cultural precedent whatever, when Coleridge, in summing up Wordsworth's achievement, speaks as follows: "But in imaginative power, he stands nearest of all modern writers to Shakespear and Milton; and yet in a kind perfectly unborrowed and his own."[7] But a special note it is. As legatees of the Romantic, we are so inured to the high value placed on originality that we perhaps are not cognizant of how beside the point Coleridge's concluding words might have sounded in earlier praise of artistic achievement. For example, the following commendation of Webster's *Duchess of Malfi* by John Ford looks to the conception of the "masterpiece," and not at all to the conception of originality; the work of art rivals those of the past rather than separates itself from them:

> Crown him a poet, whom nor Rome, nor Greece,
> Transcend in all theirs, for a masterpiece:
> In which, whiles words and matter change, and men
> Act one another, he, from whose clear pen
> They all took life, to memory hath lent
> A lasting fame, to raise his monument.[8]

We are reared, as it were, on Emerson's advice to "insist on yourself; never imitate";[9] and we recollect only by an act of historical

---

a special instance such as Cesare Borgia, can hardly match, however, the extreme theoretical apotheosis of egotism as reflected in Max Stirner's Romantic treatise, *Der Einzige und sein Eigenthum* (1845). It is significant that Stirner's celebration of egotism ("I am *owner* of my might, and I am so when I know myself as *unique*") involves a total rejection of society, e.g.: "The egoist has broken the ties of the family and found in the State a lord to shelter him. . . .But where has he run now? Straight into a new *society*, in which his egoism is awaited by the same snares and nets that it has just escaped. . . .The State always has the sole purpose to limit, tame, subordinate, the individual" (Stirner, pp. 261, 147, 150).

[6]See, e.g., White, pp. 15–16, 118–19. Castelvetro, in particular, called strongly for originality (pp. 26–27). But the matter, in keeping with the paradox that invests originality, is ambiguous. On the one hand, "year by year, man by man, grew the steadily increasing demand for liberty, for originality," and on the other, "Englishmen from 1500 to 1625" were "without any feeling analogous to the modern attitude toward plagiarism" (pp. 201–2). As early as 1711, however, Addison, in a signal adumbration of Romantic emphasis (see below, nn. 11, 12), was saying that "an Imitation of the best Authors is not to compare with a good Original" (Addison, I, 484).

[7]*Biographia*, II, 151.

[8]John Webster, *The Duchess of Malfi*, ed. John Russell Brown, The Revels Plays (Cambridge, Mass.: Harvard University Press, 1964), p. 5.

[9]*Emerson*, II, 83.

imagination that the rise of this opinion replaced the ascendancy, which lasted for many centuries, of the doctrine of imitation.[10] Until a change was gradually effected in the eighteenth century, the dominant view was that summed up in the capsuled wisdom of Pope's "Essay on Criticism."

> Learn hence for ancient rules a just esteem;
> To copy nature is to copy them.

> True Wit is Nature to advantage dress'd,
> What oft was thought, but ne'er so well express'd.

The event and date that most unmistakably signalize the shift in emphasis was the publication of Edward Young's *Conjectures on Original Composition* in 1759. "*Imitators*," writes Young, "only give us a sort of Duplicates of what we had, possibly much better, before; increasing the mere Drug of books, while all that makes them valuable, *Knowledge* and *Genius*, are at a stand. The pen of an *Original* Writer, like *Armida*'s wand, out of a barren waste calls a blooming spring: Out of that blooming spring an *Imitator* is a transplanter of Laurels, which sometimes die on removal, always languish in a foreign soil."[11] In such a statement, the function of originality is clearly revealed to be parallel to that of individuality; originality is invoked to avoid "Duplicates of what we had." It is, furthermore, closely bound up with the conception of "Genius," which is itself an analogue of the unduplicatibility, always hoped for even if only precariously real, of the individual. "The mind of a man of Genius is a fertile and pleasant field, pleasant as *Elysium*, and fertile as *Tempe*; it enjoys a perpetual Spring. Of that Spring, *Originals* are the fairest Flowers: *Imitations* are of quicker growth, but fainter bloom."[12] Originality, for Young, is not an isolated conception, but one that occupies a place in the relationship of individual to tradition. Originality is seen in fact as a variant of imitation:

[10]See, e.g., John D. Boyd, *The Function of Mimesis and Its Decline* (Cambridge, Mass.: Harvard University Press, 1968).

[11]Young, p. 10. It is necessary to realize that Young's essay did not create an abrupt and idiosyncratic break with the mimetic tradition, but signalized instead a gradual change in emphasis shared by the age as a whole. In the 1740s, for instance, William Melmoth, as Walter Jackson Bate points out, "shared a growing interest of his day in 'original genius'" and "thought that original 'invention is depressed and genius enslaved' by imitation of the ancients" (Bate, *Classic to Romantic*, p. 52).

[12]Young, p. 9. Cf. Emerson: "To all that can be said of the preponderance of the Past, the single word Genius is a sufficient reply. . . .The profound apprehension of the Present is Genius, which makes the Past forgotten. Genius believes its faintest presentiment against the testimony of all history . . .And what is Originality? It is being, being one's self, and reporting accurately what we see and are" (*Emerson*, VIII, 201).

> Must we then, you say, not imitate antient Authors? Imitate them,
> by all means; but imitate aright. He that imitates the divine *Iliad*,
> does not imitate *Homer*; but he who takes the same method, which
> *Homer* took, for arriving at a capacity of accomplishing a work so
> great. Tread in his steps to the sole Fountain of Immortality; drink
> where he drank, at the true *Helicon*, that is, at the breast of Nature:
> Imitate; but imitate not the *Composition*, but the *Man*. For may not
> this Paradox pass into a Maxim? *viz.* "The less we copy the
> renowned Antients, we shall resemble them the more."(pp. 20–21)

That the conception of "Originals" existed in polar tension to
the conception of tradition and thereby participated fully in the
originality paradox was central to Young's insistence. In 1728,
some thirty years before his *Conjectures* appeared, he formulated
the essentials of his entire subsequent contention.

> Above all, in this, as in every work of genius, somewhat of an
> original spirit should be at least attempted. . . .Originals only have
> true life, and differ as much from the best imitations as men from
> the most animated pictures of them. Nor is what I say at all
> inconsistent with a due deference for the great standards of antiq-
> uity; nay, that very deference is an argument for it, for doubtless
> their example is on my side in this matter. And we should rather
> imitate their example in the general motives and fundamental meth-
> ods of their working than in their works themselves. This is a
> distinction, I think, not hitherto made, and a distinction of
> consequence.[13]

The awareness of tradition is here, as later, hardly less evident
than the call for originality.

As time passed, however, and the industrial revolution, the
deluge of books, and the increase of population became more visible, the pressures grew heavier. There is a statement, usually attributed to Talleyrand, and whether apocryphal or not I do not
know, that runs something to the effect that only he who had
experienced the privileges possible before the French Revolution
could know the full sweetness of life. The sentiment, in whatever
form, has reappeared in instance after instance. Although it is
currently more usual to emphasize progressive and socially aware
currents in nineteenth-century thought, it would be equally possible to stress repeated expressions of apprehension about the rise of
democracy, which was the social and political analogue of the increasing weight of population and industrialization. Thus Tocqueville, who said that "it is evident to all alike that a great demo-

---

[13]"On Lyric Poetry," in Elledge, I, 414.

cratic revolution is going on among us," judged of one aspect of that revolution that "we have . . . abandoned whatever advantages the old state of things afforded, without receiving any compensation from our present condition. . . .The democracy of France, hampered in its course or abandoned to its lawless passions, has overthrown whatever crossed its path and has shaken all that it has not destroyed. . . . I can recall nothing in history more worthy of sorrow and pity than the scenes which are passing before our eyes." Tocqueville's was only one of many recognitions of an inexorable and uneasily attended process. Cavour, for a single other example, asks, "What means of defence have we against the inundation of the masses? Nothing stable, nothing effective, nothing durable. Is this a matter for congratulation or repining? I cannot say. Be it one or the other, it is, to my way of thinking, the inescapable future of mankind."[14]

Cavour's fear of "inundation" by masses of people was the abscissal counterpart of an intellectual fear of inundation by masses of books. Washington Irving, for instance, taking up this forbidding matter with the tongs of humor, draws a parallel between the checks upon natural growth and those upon publication. Without the principle of decay, nature would soon overwhelm all things with its luxuriance. In ancient times, writes Irving, there were difficulties of copying, preserving, and dispersing that restricted the accumulation and reproduction of manuscripts, and "to these circumstances it may, in some measure, be owing that we have not been inundated by the intellect of antiquity; that the fountains of thought have not been broken up, and modern genius drowned in the deluge."[15] But, he goes on, "the inventions of paper and the press have put an end to all these restraints." And then follows an apprehensive vision of intellectual overproduction.

> The stream of literature has swoln into a torrent—augmented into a
> river—expanded into a sea. A few centuries since, five or six
> hundred manuscripts constituted a great library; but what would you
> say to libraries, such as actually exist, containing three and four
> hundred thousand volumes; legions of authors at the same time
> busy; and the press going on with fearfully increasing activity, to
> double and quadruple the number? Unless some unforeseen mor-
> tality should break out among the progeny of the muse, now that
> she has become so prolific, I tremble for posterity. (p. 269)

[14]Tocqueville, I, 3, 11–12; Cavour, quoted in *Man in the Modern Age*, p. 13.
[15]Irving, I, 268.

Irving's prophetic vision has proved correct. His libraries of "three and four hundred thousand volumes" now usually number in the region of ten million volumes; Keyes Metcalf, the librarian of Harvard University, estimated some decades ago that an ideal collection should contain perhaps thirty million books.

Remarkably, however, and indicative of the paradoxicality of the matters treated in this chapter, the emphasis on being original has grown, rather than diminished, in the face of this flood. Originality, as we suggested, is an analogue of heroism and individuality; the "good book," in Milton's unforgettable words, "is the precious life-blood of a master spirit," and its reality is set against that of mass experience, of those "many" who live "a burden to the earth." And so it has remained. Armoring himself in the conception of originality, the aspiring creator has simply "denied," in the Freudian sense of defense mechanism, the cultural reality around him and thereby continued to produce. The innovations of the last hundred years or so, including many of those in Romanticism itself, culminating in Dadaism and Surrealism, are all attempts, by hyperemphasis on the conception of originality, to deny the relevance of the exponentially increasing deluge of culture.[16] A classic recognition of this truth is furnished by Ortega y Gasset's *Dehumanization of Art*. The whole point of modern trends, Ortega argues, is to free art from the weight of its tradition; the "enthusiasm for pure art" is "a mask which conceals surfeit with art and hatred of it."[17]

> When an art looks back on many centuries of continuous evolution without major hiatuses or historical catastrophes its products keep on accumulating, and the weight of tradition increasingly encumbers the inspiration of the hour.
>
> We can hardly put too much stress on the influence which at all

[16]Cf. Renato Poggioli: "Italian futurism is also called *antipassatismo*, the down-with-the-past movement. As the first name is highly suggestive of a tendency common to all avant-gardism, so the second emphasizes a posture that is certainly not exclusive with the avant-garde"; "Mayakovsky later gave extreme nihilistic expression to antitraditionalism and the cult of the *tabula rasa* when he said, 'I write *nihil* on anything that has been done before'"; "In a way both analogous and opposed to Rimbaud's negation, the nihilism of dada is not a specifically literary or aesthetic posture; it is radical and totalitarian, integral and metaphysical. It invests not only the movement's program of action but also its very raison d'être. 'Dada does not mean anything,' declared Tristan Tzara, and his negative statement ought to be extended to issues even more substantial than the mere name. 'There is a great destructive, negative task to be done: sweeping out, cleaning up'—so we read in yet another of the founder's manifestoes" (Poggioli, pp. 52, 62–63).

[17]Ortega, *Dehumanization*, p. 45.

times the past of art exerts on the future of art. In the mind of the artist a sort of chemical reaction is set going by the clash between his individual sensibility and already existing art. He does not find himself all alone with the world before him; in his relations with the world there always intervenes, like an interpreter, the artistic tradition. . . . That a work of a certain period may be modeled after works of another previous period has always been easily recognized. But to notice the negative influence of the past and to realize that a new style has not infrequently grown out of a conscious and relished antagonism to traditional styles seems to require somewhat of an effort.[18]

The "negative influence of the past" reveals itself, in other words, in the treasuring of "originality" and a concomitant denial of the tradition. Indeed, this movement became so pronounced, as Romanticism flowed into later forms—supposedly different from it but actually permutations of the Romantic awareness—that writers like Babbitt, Hulme, Lasserre, and T. S. Eliot generated a "classical" reaction to its tide. Eliot's powerful essay "Tradition and the Individual Talent" constitutes a rebuke to the insistence on originality at the expense of the past. Eliot attempts to restore the paradox, to see originality, as did Young, in polarity with tradition. His opening statement is, "In English writing we seldom speak of tradition." He remarks on

our tendency to insist, when we praise a poet, upon those aspects of his work in which he least resembles any one else. In these aspects or parts of his work we pretend to find what is individual, what is the peculiar essence of the man. We dwell with satisfaction upon the poet's difference from his predecessors, especially his immediate predecessors; we endeavour to find something that can be isolated in order to be enjoyed. Whereas if we approach a poet without this prejudice we shall often find that not only the best, but the most individual parts of his work may be those in which the dead poets, his ancestors, assert their immortality most vigorously.[19]

[18]Ibid., pp. 44, 43. It is significant, in view of our conception of the complementary axes of individual/tradition tension and individual/society tension, that Ortega's individual/tradition concern as exhibited in *The Dehumanization of Art* is the complement of an individual/society concern in *The Revolt of the Masses*, e.g.: "To-day we are witnessing the triumphs of a hyperdemocracy in which the mass acts directly, outside the law, imposing its aspirations. . . .The mass crushes beneath it everything that is different, everything that is excellent, individual, qualified and select. . . .Here we have the formidable fact of our times, described without any concealment of the brutality of its features" (New York: W. W. Norton & Co., 1957, pp. 17–18)

[19]Eliot, pp. 3–4.

Having thus declared himself for a redress of the balance between the individual talent and tradition, Eliot subtly illuminates the role of the latter.

> Yet if the only form of tradition, of handing down, consisted in following the ways of the immediate generation before us in a blind or timid adherence to its success, "tradition" should positively be discouraged. We have seen many such simple currents soon lost in the sand; and novelty is better than repetition. Tradition is a matter of much wider significance. It cannot be inherited, and if you want it you must obtain it by great labour. (p. 4)

By insisting that the difficulty of repossessing the tradition is one of the problems encountered by the individual talent, Eliot reasserts the dynamic interplay of the two realities.

> No poet, no artist of any art, has his complete meaning alone. His significance, his appreciation is the appreciation of his relation to the dead poets and artists. You cannot value him alone; you must set him, for contrast and comparison, among the dead. . . . The existing monuments form an ideal order among themselves, which is modified by the introduction of the new (the really new) work of art among them. . . . Whoever has approved this idea of order, of the form of European, of English literature will not find it preposterous that the past should be altered by the present as much as the present is directed by the past.[20]

Eliot, therefore, attempts to restore the paradox recognized by Young and seemingly dispersed by the progress of Romanticism. In an important regard, however, his perspective is different from that of Young. For the latter took as given the overwhelming existence of tradition and sought to extricate the conception of originality; Eliot takes as given the rampant stress on originality and seeks to restore the dignity of tradition.

It is interesting, however, and symptomatic of the real situation for which the originality cult constitutes a denial, that Eliot seems to find that any attempt to reduce even slightly the predominance of originality occludes the conception entirely. The banner waves over an empty fortress; the idea of individuality vanishes. "There is a great deal, in the writing of poetry, which must be conscious and deliberate. In fact, the bad poet is usually unconscious where he ought to be conscious, and conscious where he ought to be unconscious. Both errors tend to make him 'personal.' Poetry is not a turning loose of emotion, but an escape from emotion; it is

---

[20]Ibid., pp. 4–5. This insistence prefigures that *apophrades,* or return of the dead, which is one of Harold Bloom's "revisionary ratios" (see below, n. 25).

not the expression of personality, but an escape from personality" (p. 10). As personality is the experienced entity in which such abstractions as individuality and originality inhere, Eliot is here purchasing his insistence on tradition by sacrificing the paradox whose recognition he sought to renew. Yet the contention is central to his essay. "The emotion of art is impersonal" (p. 11); "the progress of an artist is a continual self-sacrifice, a continual extinction of personality" (p. 7).

The fragility of the complex of originality, individuality, and personality as revealed by Eliot's examination was a portent of the accelerating increase of the cultural past, which has, as it were, redoubled in the half century since he wrote. And his attempts at a classical revival were swept away in the new tide of Romanticism that followed World War II. The reassuring flame of originality once more burnt with a brightness even more feverish than that of the first Romantic epoch. But the phenomenon of hippiedom, which was neither more nor less than a claim to originality and its concomitants of individualism and personality, reached its apex, and what must be considered its moment of truth, in the pathos of Woodstock, where all the claims to uniqueness were assembled in grotesque and overwhelming duplication.

More sophisticated approaches to the abscissal and ordinal problems of individuality and its relationship to the race have tended, however, since the advent of the Second Romanticism, to introduce a new note. It is, if not precisely a note of despondency, at least a pessimistic overtone not found in Eliot's attitude. Thus Walter Jackson Bate, in the very title of his learned study *The Burden of the Past and the English Poet*, indicates an awareness of the increasingly heavy weight of tradition. And Harold Bloom, in his own rubric, *The Anxiety of Influence*, reveals even more unmistakably the sense of crisis.[21]

Although the word *anxiety* does not figure in Bate's title, its presence in his awareness of the situation is only slightly less emphatic than in the arguments of Bloom. Bate speaks of an "accumulating anxiety" during the last three centuries, "and the question it so directly presents to the poet or artist: *What is there left to do?* To say that this has always been a problem, and that the arts have still managed to survive, does not undercut the fact that it has

---

[21]In terms of the idea of "inundation" used by both Cavour and Irving, it is interesting to note that Bloom says that "the anxiety of influence is an anxiety in expectation of *being flooded*" (*Anxiety*, p. 57). And, again, "the precursors flood us, and our imaginations can die by drowning in them, but no imaginative life is possible if such inundation is wholly evaded" (p. 154).

become far more pressing in the modern world." Again, he speaks
of "the real problem—the essential anxiety," that of the artist's
"nakedness and embarrassment (with the inevitable temptations
to paralysis or routine imitation, to retrenchment or mere fitful
rebellion) before the amplitude of what two thousand years or
more of an art had already been able to achieve."[22] Bloom, for his
part, says that "the covert subject of most poetry for the last three
centuries has been the anxiety of influence, each poet's fear that no
proper work remains for him to perform.[23]

Bloom's book expresses very powerfully, not only in its title but
in its tone as well, the strains resulting from the exponential increase in culture. The style, by a kind of vatic intensity, seems
fitted to a sense of apocalypse. And his deliberately hyperbolical
statement, "the meaning of a poem can only be another poem" (p.
94), is by way of becoming a watchword in current literary study,
one roundly rejected by some and praised as brilliant by others.[24]
Whether we find the assertion one of thoroughgoing exaggeration
or of Delphic reverberation, however, it is assuredly one that indicates an almost despairing sense of the burden of the past.

Bloom's depression of cultural individuality, and his recognition
of the importance of the past, to some extent parallel the emphasis
of Eliot; the introduction of the element and tone of anxiety, however, constitutes a radical disjunction from Eliot's position. "We
need to stop thinking of any poet as an autonomous ego," says
Bloom, "however solipsistic the strongest of poets may be. Every
poet is a being caught up in a dialectical relationship . . . with
another poet or poets" (p. 91). For Bloom, the existence of the
individual poet is one of a struggle against beleaguering forces; the
strong poet must "wrestle" with his precursors; "self-appropria-
tion involves the immense anxieties of indebtedness, for what
strong maker desires the realization that he has failed to create
himself?" (p. 5). The poet must constantly struggle to "clear imaginative space" for himself. "Poetic history," says the author gloom-
ily, is "indistinguishable from poetic influence" (p. 5). Poetic production, indeed, is now conceived to be a process not of *creatio ex
nihilo*, but rather to be a series of deflections of the burden of the
past: every strong poet "misreads" his predecessors in order to
establish his own individuality. Every poem is thus a "misprision"
of an earlier one.

[22]Bate, *Burden*, pp. 3, 95.
[23]*Anxiety*, p. 148.
[24]I myself have been one of the praisers. See my review in *Commonweal* 99 (2
November 1973), 112–14.

If, as suggested earlier in this chapter, the treasuring of originality has in the last century or so become ever more similar to the defense mechanism of denial, Bloom elevates an expanded version of such awareness into the very principle of poetry itself. The varieties of "poetic misprision" (he enumerates six of them) are explicitly declared to be coordinate with Freudian defense mechanisms by which an ego maintains itself against alien realities.[25]

Freud supplies the paradigm for Bloom's insistence in other respects as well. The relation of the poet to his precursor is conceived by Bloom to be analogous to that of the growing son to his father, that is, an ambivalence of acceptance and rejection. Here, too, the foundation of the originality paradox in the unavoidable reciprocity of individual/group relationships is signalized: "intrapoetic relationships" are parallels of "family romance." Interestingly enough, and outside Bloom's arena of discussion, the augmentation of the anxiety of influence and of the burden of the past continues the parallel in changed conceptions of the relationship of the individual to his family situation. Where traditionally, and especially through the agency of Christianity, the family was associated with security, nurture, and love, now in our own time, with a historical progression roughly coeval with that of Romantic originality, the family has more and more come under attack as a burden on growth and a distorting element in human possibilities. We see this change most dramatically, perhaps, in the attitudes enunciated by R. D. Laing.[26]

---

[25]E.g., *Anxiety*, pp. 8, 13–15, 88–89.

[26]E.g.: "A family can act as gangsters, offering each other mutual protection against each other's violence. It is a reciprocal terrorism"; "from the moment of birth, when the Stone Age baby confronts the twentieth-century mother, the baby is subjected to these forces of violence, called love, as its mother and father . . . have been. These forces are mainly concerned with destroying most of its potentialities, and on the whole this enterprise is successful. By the time the new human being is fifteen or so, we are left with a being like ourselves, a half-crazed creature more or less adjusted to a mad world" (Laing, pp. 59, 36). Extreme though Laing's denunciation of the nuclear social unit is, it is not without prefiguration. As early as 1868, the changing conditions of communality elicited from Amiel an agonized realization. "Oh, the family! If the pious, traditional superstition with which we envelop this institution would let us tell the truth about the matter, what a reckoning it would have to settle! What numberless martyrdoms it has required, dissemblingly, inexorably! How many hearts have been stifled by it, lacerated and broken. . . .The family may be all that is best in this world, but too often it is all that is worst. . . . The truth is that the family relation exists only to put us to the proof and that it gives us infinitely more suffering than happiness" (*Amiel*, pp. 257–58). To understand how changed this awareness was from earlier views, we need only contrast Wordsworth's continual apotheosis of the family, as, for instance, in his letter to Fox, or in a poem like "The Old Cumberland Beggar". "The easy man / Who sits at his own door . . . they who live / Sheltered, and flourish in a little grove / Of their own kindred."

Although Bloom's work reflects a sense of crisis in the relations of the individual to the cultural past, it must be realized that this crisis consists of an intensification of elements permanently present, and not the historical appearance of new reality. To realize this is to grasp a major significance of the originality paradox. The paradox is in fact a paradox, and not a merely historical development, simply because it is always present and defies resolution.[27]

Indeed, even the most characteristic phenomena of Romanticism itself can be seen to participate in the paradox, the strong Romantic emphasis on originality notwithstanding. As a single instance, *Lyrical Ballads* and its date of 1798 have for untold numbers of literary historians, critics, and students been events of uncontested originality: they mark the advent of the Romantic movement in England. But in 1954 Robert Mayo, in a notable article, demonstrated that hardly an emphasis existed in the volume that was not repeatedly prefigured in popular literature of the preceding decade.

> Whatever aspect of the *Lyrical Ballads* we examine, whether it be the meters, the lyrical and narrative kinds, the subjects, attitudes, and themes of individual poems of groups of poems, we are struck by the great number of particulars in which the volume conforms to the tastes and interests of some segments of the literary world in 1798. This is not to deny that the merit of the work was phenomenal, that it was "original" in various respects (as reviewers said it was). . . . From one point of view the *Lyrical Ballads* stand at the beginning of a new orientation of literary, social, ethical, and religious values; and they are unquestionably a pivotal work in the transition from one century to the next. But from another point of view, equally valid, they come at the end of a long and complicated process of development, according to which a great deal in the volume must have seemed to many readers both right and inevitable. Wayward as the two poets were in some respects, in others they must have seemed to be moving briskly with various currents of the day.[28]

The paradox emerges to view not only here but whenever we look below the surface of cultural phenomena. Emerson seems, and certainly is, in one aspect of his commitment an unequivocal spokesman for originality and individuality: "A man is . . . a selecting principle, gathering his like to him wherever he goes. He takes only his own out of the multiplicity that sweeps and circles round him."[29] Less often recognized, however, is the fact that the

---

[27] As brief but choice illustration—we may even adopt it as a kind of microcosmic symbol of the paradox—consider a commentator's observation, "Milton's pledge to pursue 'Things unattempted yet in prose or rhyme' (1.16) is itself a quotation from the *Orlando furioso*" (Quint, p. 216).

[28] Mayo, p. 517.

[29] *Emerson*, II, 144.

author of *Self-Reliance* paradoxically conceded the full claims of tradition. "The truth is all works of literature are Janus faced and look to the future and to the past. Shakespear, Pope, and Dryden borrow from Chaucer and shine by his borrowed light. . . . There never was an original writer. Each is a link in an endless chain. To receive and to impart are the talents of the poet and he ought to possess both in equal degrees. . . . Every great man, as Homer, Milton, Bacon, and Aristotle, necessarily takes up into himself all the wisdom that is current in his time."[30]

Emerson does not here restrict the problem of originality and indebtedness merely to poetry, as most of our examples up to this point have done, but refers as well to science and philosophy. In doing so, he identifies the originality paradox as a truth of culture as such, and not merely a movement in the history of poetic literature. Leaving aside the formidable topic of the history of science,[31] we may briefly illustrate the paradox's larger cultural presence by reference to two kinds of complication occurring within the history of philosophy. The first is a contrast between the attitude of Leibniz and that of Nietzsche, and the second a paradox within Nietzsche's thought itself. As to the former complication, Leibniz's great editor, Johann Eduard Erdmann, writes: "Seldom, if ever, did such a well-read student come up to the University; and no great philosopher ever continued to be so eager for reading and so dependent upon it as did Leibnitz. . . . Even if he had not told us, we should have known that his best ideas came to him when he was reading. Any one who is fond of discovering plagiarisms would have an easy task with Leibnitz."[32] Such a realization could serve as another example for Emerson's dictum that "there never

---

[30]Emerson, *Lectures*, pp. 284–85. Cf. Goethe: "At bottom we are all collective beings, pretend as we will. For how little have we and are we that in the purest sense we can call our own. We must all receive and learn, both from those who came before us and from those who are with us. Even the greatest genius would not get far if he wanted to owe everything to his own inner self. This, however, many very good men do not understand, and with their dreams of originality they grope through a half-life in the dark. I have known artists who boast that they followed no master, rather that they were indebted to their own genius for everything. The fools!" (*Gedenkausgabe*, XXIV, 767).

[31]See, however, Thomas S. Kuhn, *The Structure of Scientific Revolutions* (Chicago: University of Chicago Press, 1962), for discussion of the tension between the individual scientific talent and the scientific community.

[32]Erdmann, p. 172. Cf. Emerson: "If we encountered a man of rare intellect, we should ask him what books he read. We expect a great man to be a good reader; or in proportion to the spontaneous power should be the assimilating power. . . .Our debt to tradition through reading and conversation is so massive, our protest or private addition so rare and insignificant,—and this commonly on the ground of other reading or hearing,—that, in a large sense, one would say there is no pure originality. All minds quote. Old and new make the warp and woof of every moment. There is no thread that is not a twist of these two strands" (*Emerson*, VIII, 178).

was an original writer." Its depression of the conception of originality in favor of that of an intellectual tradition assimilated
through reading, however, is paradoxically opposed by
Nietzsche's attack on that very commitment to reading.

> The scholar who actually does little else than wallow in a sea of
> books—the average philologist may handle two hundred a day—
> finally loses completely the ability to think for himself. He cannot
> think unless he has a book in his hands. When he thinks, he
> responds to a stimulus (a thought he has read)—and finally all he
> does is react. The scholar devotes all his energy to affirming or
> denying or criticizing matter that has already been thought out—he
> no longer thinks himself. . . . In him the instinct of self-defense has
> decayed, otherwise he would defend himself against books. The
> scholar is a decadent. With my own eyes I have seen gifted, richly
> endowed, free-spirited natures already "read to pieces" at thirty—
> nothing but matches that have to be struck before they can emit any
> sparks—or "thoughts." To read a book early in the morning, at
> daybreak, in the vigor and dawn of one's strength—that I call
> viciousness.[33]

This kind of attitude seems to justify Bloom's classification of
Nietzsche as one of "the great deniers" of influence.[34] But
Nietzsche, whose denunciation of antecedent thinkers and whose
sense of the anxiety of being a cultural "latecomer" provide Bloom
choice quotations, could not abrogate the paradox. Not only was
he himself a "bookman" of formidable cultural attainment,[35] but
also his emphatic claim to originality and intellectual self-reliance
existed side by side with an equally emphatic avowal of relationship to a precursor: "I am totally amazed, totally enchanted! I
have a precursor, and what a precursor! I hardly knew Spinoza:
that I should have turned to him just now was inspired by 'instinct.' Not only is his whole tendency like mine . . . but in five
main points of his doctrine I recognize myself."[36]

[33]*Nietzsche*, II, 1094.
[34]*Anxiety*, p. 50.
[35]Cf. Karl Jaspers: "As a result of Nietzsche's estrangement from the world . . . he
had to derive new experiences from a program of *reading* that covered a very
extensive range of topics. . . .Words and thoughts often pass directly from the
reading matter to Nietzsche. . . . That the term 'superman' is found in Goethe and
the term 'cultural philistine' . . . in Haym, is no more essential than his taking the
expressions 'perspectivism' and 'decadence' from Bourget. Such receptivity . . . is
indispensable to all creative work" (Jaspers, pp. 31–32).
[36]*Nietzsches Briefwechsel*, p. 149. But see further H. A. Wolfson: " 'How about
Spinoza?' challenged one of the listeners. 'Was he also a bookish philosopher?'
Without stopping to think, I took up the challenge. 'As for Spinoza,' I said, 'if we
could cut up all the philosophic literature available to him into slips of paper, toss
them up into the air, and let them fall back to the ground, then out of these
scattered slips of paper we could reconstruct his *Ethics*' " (Wolfson, I, 3).

If the originality paradox extends outward to intellectual man-
ifestations other than poetry, it also extends backward to literally
the earliest records of culture. The point should be documented,
because Bloom, in exempting Shakespeare from his considerations, says that he was one of "the giant age before the flood,
before the anxiety of influence became central to poetic consciousness."[37] But this is a view from the distorting perspective of
our own era; from a different vantage point there seems to have
been no time when at least the paradox, if not the anxiety, of
influence and originality did not exist.[38] Gilbert Lawall, for a single
instance, stresses that "Theocritus . . . is by no means a completely original poet; he owes much to earlier Sicilian traditions
represented by Stesichorus, Epicharmus, and Sophron, and he
owes something to Greek tragedy, New Comedy, Homer, the lyric
poets, and perhaps even Plato."[39] In keeping with the necessities
of the originality paradox, however, Lawall also notes that "Theocritus' manner of poetry has no model. He could refer to no poet,
past or present, when he came to explain his unique poetic personality" (p. 84). And both aspects of the paradox appear simultaneously in another kind of statement.

> Greek pastoral poetry as it takes shape in Theocritus' work is thus a
> composite or eclectic form. *Idyll* I is an excellent example. . . . The
> use of stanzas and refrains in Thyrsis' song derives from popular
> folk songs. The description of the cup is reminiscent of Homer's epic
> description of Achilles' shield. Some of the formulaic language of
> Thyrsis' song comes almost directly from Homeric hymns. The myth
> of Daphnis may be adapted from a lyric poem of the archaic poet
> Stesichorus. And, most importantly, Daphnis' character and predica-
> ment are patterned after the Euripidean Hippolytus. . . . Theocritus
> here seems to be trying to compress the whole history of archaic and
> classical Greek poetry into a single creation which, as a combination
> of all the earlier traditions and as a pastoral poem, is totally
> unprecedented. (p. 2)

[37]*Anxiety*, p. 11. Yet why then Greene's attack on the "vpstart Crow, beautified
with our feathers"?

[38]Thus Bate does not restrict himself to Bloom's perspective on this point; indeed,
to show that the past was always a burden, he summons a quotation from so remote
a culture as that of ancient Egypt (Bate, *Burden*, pp. 3–4). Cf. Emerson: "If we
confine ourselves to literature, 'tis easy to see that the debt is immense to past
thought. None escapes it. The originals are not original. There is imitation, model
and suggestion, to the very archangels, if we knew their history. The first book
tyrannizes over the second. Read Tasso, and you think of Virgil; read Virgil, and
you think of Homer; and Milton forces you to reflect how narrow are the limits of
human invention. The Paradise Lost had never existed but for these precursors; and
if we find in India or Arabia a book out of our horizon of thought and tradition, we
are soon taught by new researches in its native country to discover its foregoers"
(*Emerson*, VIII, 180).

[39]Lawall, pp. 83–84.

In addition to its currency in the actual structure of ancient literary practice, the originality paradox was recognized in ancient statements of theory. Quintilian, for instance, insists that there can be no doubt that a great part of art consists in imitation ("neque enim dubitari potest, quin artis pars magna contineatur imitatione"). He finds it "a universal rule of life that we should wish to copy what we approve in others," that we must "either be like or unlike those who have proved their excellence. It is rare for nature to produce such a resemblance, which is more often the result of imitation." But Quintilian honors the paradox. His strong theoretical justification of imitation, and thereby of tradition, is complemented by an emphasis no less strong on the necessity of originality: "Ante omnia igitur imitatio per se ipsa non sufficit"— "Above all, therefore, imitation does not of itself suffice." And he concludes that it is a disgrace to be content to owe everything we attain to imitation ("turpe etiam illud est, contentum esse id consequi, quod imiteris").[40]

The recognition of the originality paradox by classical antiquity, as well as our recognition of its presence in forms of culture other than the merely poetic, comes together on a common ground, and is unified in its meaning, in the historical nexus of Plato's rejection of the "imitative poets" as inhabitants of his ideal society.[41]

The rejection has perplexed critics down through the centuries, and it presents itself as paradoxical on its face. It here seems, as Sidney says, that Plato "will defile the fountaine out of which his flowing streames have proceeded," for "of all *Philosophers* hee is the most *Poeticall*"; "even *Plato*, who so ever well considereth, shall finde that in the body of his worke though the inside & strength were Philosophie, the skin as it were and beautie, depended most of Poetrie."[42] Furthermore, in attacking the poets, Plato paradoxically must reject Homer most of all, whose poetry, as the Platonic dialogues so amply attest, he knew and esteemed with all his heart.[43]

But in rejecting the poets, Plato was refusing an entire *paideia*.[44]

[40]*Institutio oratorio*, x.ii.1–7.

[41]*Republic*, 595A–608B. E.g., "Shall we, then, lay it down that all the poetic tribe, beginning with Homer, are imitators of images of excellence and of the other things that they 'create,' and do not lay hold on truth?" (600E).

[42]*Sidney*, III, 33, 5.

[43]E.g., " 'Do not you yourself feel [poetry's] magic and especially when Homer is her interpreter?' 'Greatly' " (*Republic*, 607D).

[44]Cf. Werner Jaeger: "Plato in his *Republic* . . . rejected Homer and Hesiod not as poetic fiction but as paideia, which for him meant the expression of truth" (Jaeger, *Early Christianity*, p. 48, see also pp. 91, 126, n.11, 127, n.6). See further, Jaeger, *Paideia*, II, 213–27.

It has always been understood that the earliest poets occupied a larger cultural role than do our own; they were, to quote one of many eighteenth-century recognitions of the fact, "the *Philosophers*, and *Divines* of those early times."[45] Or, as Eric Havelock has recently put it, the problem of Plato's attack on the poets "cannot be solved by pretending it does not exist, that is, by pretending that Plato cannot mean what he says. It is obvious that the poetry he is talking about is not the kind of thing we identify today as poetry."[46] In his discussion of the meaning of Plato's attack, Havelock elucidates certain matters that, in view of the arguments in the previous portion of this chapter, are seen to be the irreducible components of the originality paradox. Briefly, the contention is this. Poetry, and especially the Homeric epics, constituted, in the era before the invention of writing, the "tribal encyclopedia." Its primary purpose was not entertainment but the transmission and control of culture. A collage of quotations might be useful here.

> The history of Greek poetry is also the history of early Greek *paideia*. . . . the warp and woof of Homer is didactic . . . the tale is made subservient to the task of accommodating the weight of educational materials which lie within it. . . .
>
> It was of the essence of Homeric poetry that it represented in its epoch the sole vehicle of important and significant communication. It therefore was called upon to memorialise and preserve the social apparatus, the governing mechanism, and the education for leadership and social management. . . . This same verse was essential to the educational system on which the entire society depended for its continuity and coherence. All public business depended on it, all transactions which were guided by general norms. The poet was in the first instance society's scribe and scholar and jurist and only in a secondary sense its artist and showman. . . .
>
> In sum then, Plato's conception of poetry, if we apply it to that preliterate epoch in which the Greek institutions of the Classical age first crystallised in characteristic form, was basically correct. Poetry was not "literature" but a political and social necessity. It was not an art form, nor a creation of the private imagination, but an encyclopedia maintained by co-operative effort on the part of the "best Greek polities." (pp. 47, 61, 93–94, 125)

What is central to all these realizations is that "poetry" (or pre-Platonic *mousiké*) was a social, not an individual manifestation. As Havelock points out, the very achievement of oral memorization and reproduction involved a group psychology that necessarily

---

[45]Charles Gildon, in Durham, p. 64.
[46]Havelock, pp. 9–10.

repudiated the claims of the individual. Plato's attack on this tradition was accordingly a protest on behalf of the emerging sense of the individual in Greek consciousness. "At some time towards the end of the fifth century before Christ," summarizes Havelock,

> it became possible for a few Greeks to talk about their "souls" as though they had selves or personalities. . . . Scholarship has tended to connect this discovery with the life and teaching of Socrates and to identify it with a radical change which he introduced into the meaning of the Greek word *psyche*. In brief, instead of signifying . . . a thing devoid of sense and self-consciousness, it came to mean "the ghost that thinks," that is capable both of moral decision and of scientific cognition . . . an essence unique in the whole realm of nature. (p. 197)

It was in the service of this new conception of the individual that Plato launched his attack upon the poets. "We are now," concludes Havelock, "in a position more clearly to understand one reason for Plato's opposition to the poetic experience. It was his self-imposed task . . . to establish two main postulates: that of the personality which thinks and knows, and that of a body of knowledge which is thought about and known. To do this he had to destroy the immemorial habit of self-identification with the oral tradition. For this had merged the personality with the tradition, and made a self-conscious separation from it impossible."[47]

Plato's opposition, however, was not only allied with the emerging conception of individuality, but was itself a further definition of that individuality. "The 'personality,' as first invented by the Greeks and then presented to posterity for contemplation, could not be that nexus of motor responses, unconscious reflexes, and passions and emotions which had been mobilised for countless times in the service of the mnemonic process. . . . The *psyche* which slowly asserts itself in independence of the poetic performance and the poetised tradition had to be the reflective, thoughtful, critical psyche, or it could be nothing" (p. 200). In short, "the doctrine of the autonomous psyche is the counterpart of the rejection of oral culture."[48]

This is the heart of the matter. It is as though the relationship of a man to his society in preliterate poetry is rotated on its axis by the

---

[47]Ibid., p. 201. Cf. Plato's call for "a counter-charm to [poetry's] spell, to preserve us from slipping back into the childish loves of the multitudes" (*Republic*, 608A).

[48]Ibid. Cf. Plato: "Theft of property is uncivilized, open robbery is shameless. . . . Let no man, therefore, be deluded concerning this or persuaded either by poets or by any perverse myth-mongers into the belief that, when he thieves or forcibly robs, he is doing nothing shameful" (*Laws*, 941B).

Platonic/Homeric confrontation; and that it is there, in the Platonic nexus, that our culture creates, or at least recognizes for the first time, the psychic spatiality of abscissa and ordinate that we earlier described.[49] In this understanding, the attraction/rejection tension between Plato and Homer is the counterpart of the individual/ tradition tension that constitutes the originality paradox, and is in fact the archetypal exemplification of the depth, unavoidability, and constancy of that paradox.

Fully to validate such a judgment, however, it is necessary to modify Havelock's dictum that "Plato is talking about an over-all cultural condition which no longer exists." The configuration of elements has no doubt changed, but the elements themselves remain constants. We can see this in terms of the doctrine of "imitation" or mimesis. If we bear in mind that Young's eighteenth-century readjustment in favor of originality identified the other pole of the paradox as imitation, we are led to certain realizations; for the poet Plato attacked was the "imitator" (ὁ δὴ μιμητικὸς ποιητής). As the "master clue to Plato's choice of the word *mimesis* to describe the poetic experience," Havelock advances the fact that it "focuses initially not on the artist's creative act but on his power to make his audience identify almost pathologically and certainly sympathetically with the content of what he is saying" (p. 45). After an examination of the term in its Greek cultural context before Plato, he urges that "the translation 'imitation,' it can now be seen, does not adequately translate what [Plato] is talking about. Imitation in our language is governed by the presupposition that there is a separate existence of an original which is then copied. The essence of Plato's point, the raison d'être of his attack, is that in the poetic performance as practised hitherto in Greece there was no 'original' " (p. 159). And he concludes his discussion by noting that the term "*mimesis* is chosen by Plato as the one most adequate

[49]I am not wholly at ease with a certain trend in classical studies—what one might call a Whorfian naiveté—by which scholars of our own day, emboldened by the claims of anthropologists, actually ascribe ontological nonexistence to psychological functions unless they are linguistically manifested. Although Havelock is more guarded than Bruno Snell in discussing the rise of the conception of the individual, his discussion bears affinities to the latter's intriguing but, I suspect, overstated case (see "Homer's View of Man" and "The Rise of the Individual in the Early Greek Lyric," in Snell, pp. 1–22, 43–70). The fact that matters are not discussed surely cannot be shown to mean that they are therefore necessarily not present to individual awarenesses. For instance, although Young's *Conjectures on Original Composition* provides literary historians with a convenient watershed for talking about the rise of the conception of "originality" in contrast to the prevailing view of the eighteenth century, we must not forget that the eminently conservative and neo-classical Dr. Johnson told Boswell that "he was surprised to find Young receive as novelties what he thought very common maxims."

to describe both re-enactment and also identification, and as one most applicable to the common psychology shared both by artist and by audience" (p. 160). Precisely. It is this truth, though transmuted into eighteenth-century formulations, that we have identified as underlying Young's conception of "imitation." The imitation of a predecessor form is merely the surface manifestation; the kernel of the matter is the submission of the individual to the mind of the group.

We are therefore justified in elevating the struggle between the Platonic and the Homeric paideutic functions to the status of paradigm for the originality paradox. That paradox is a constant of all culture that is not preliterate (or at least of our own post-Hellenic Western culture); it cannot be resolved, although in differing historical epochs one aspect of it can be emphasized or partly repressed in favor of the other. It is not, moreover, merely a residual pattern in culture. Stemming as it does from the dynamic and necessary interaction of individual sense and group sense, it not only represents, but also generates, cultural realities. As a revealing example of such generation, as well as a witness to the impossibility of evading the paradox, we may in conclusion direct our attention to the phenomenon of plagiarism.

Plagiarism is a cultural occurrence about which there has been remarkably little theoretical discussion. The reason is not far to seek: the practice occupies a gray area, encroaching in many instances on clearly defined standards of propriety and ethics. Although plagiarism must surely be—one can hardly doubt the fact—a variant form of the phenomenon of imitation and influence, it brings the conception of individuality into conflict with itself and thereby tends to be rather uneasily dismissed from cultural consciousness. Plagiarism is the appropriating, in the name of an individual's needs, of the insignia of another individuality, and it is therefore censured in a way that imitation and influence are not; for the latter phenomena more unambiguously occupy the area of individual/group concerns. Still, in terms, say, of Bloom's listing of six varieties of "revisionary ratios," there seems to be no reason why plagiarism could not be added as an ugly duckling seventh.

The phenomenon does occur, and it cannot be totally ignored. The way it is dismissed from our cultural considerations, however, is by treating each instance, as it comes into our awareness, as a special case, and invoking ethical censures to isolate it still further. Perhaps the first understanding that needs to be achieved, therefore, is that the practice has always been more frequent than we allow ourselves to realize. I have elsewhere, in connection with studies of Coleridge, had occasion to point out the unusual degree of its incidence in certain major cultural figures: not only Coleridge, but Montaigne, John Webster, Plotinus, Ben Jonson, Dryden, Lessing.[50] Others could be added; for instance, Diderot. Indeed, the very greatest cultural figures, Shakespeare, and even Plato himself, are not entirely free from this ambivalent practice. I say "even" Plato himself, but probably an awareness of the originality paradox should change the "even" to "of course." Havelock, in the very act of emphasizing Plato's service to the idea of personal subjectivity and individuality, points out that he was "not an eccentric in the stream of history who produces to be sure a formidable body of doctrine but a doctrine of his own making. Rather he is one of those thinkers in whom the seminal forces of a whole epoch spring to life. He thinks the unconscious thoughts of his contemporaries" (p. 277). And Hegel insisted on this truth still more strongly.

It is in fact astonishing how many cultural figures have at some point incurred either outright charges of plagiarism or hints or suspicion of undue dependence. A strong case could be made for Wordsworth being as dependent on the words of others as is the neurotic plagiarist Coleridge, and in at least one instance Wordsworth was actually charged with plagiarism. Coleridge borrowed verbatim from Steffens, but he also charged Humphry Davy with plagiarizing from Steffens. Davy, for his part, accused Faraday of having plagiarized from Wollaston, and Davy's brother accused Faraday of having plagiarized from Davy (interestingly, a commentator who discusses these charges concludes that "there is not the slightest doubt that (a) Faraday was utterly honest and (b) that he was utterly wrong in stooping so low as to defend his honesty"). Again, James Ferrier bitterly charged Coleridge with plagiarism from Schelling and with great indignation set about showing that "one of the most distinguished English authors of the nineteenth century, at the mature age of forty-five, succeeded in founding by far the greater part of his metaphysical reputation—which was very considerable—upon *verbatim* plagiarisms from works written and published by a German youth, when little more than twenty years of age!" Yet, on the other hand, Karoline Herder confided to a correspondent that Schelling plagiarized from Johann Wilhelm Ritter (who himself suggested as much). "In addition he thinks

[50]See "The Problem of Coleridge's Plagiarisms," in McFarland, *Coleridge*, pp. 1–52, and passim; also Thomas McFarland, "Coleridge's Plagiarisms Once More: A Review Essay," *Yale Review* 62 (1974), 252–86.

nothing of literary theft, and gives out as his own invention what others have told and entrusted to him. This he has done to a certain Ritter in Jena, who is a great chemist and physicist—results that Ritter has discovered and trusted him with Schelling has presented as his own, but of course in a quite perverted way."[51]

In addition, there are countless places in other writers in which a kind of secondary plagiarism exists, that is, where wordings are changed but the indebtedness is almost too direct to be thought of as either influence or imitation, although here too the difficulty in precise demarcation of these realms is evident. For instance, a commentator notes of Sir Philip Sidney's influential treatise that "it can be said without exaggeration that there is not an essential principle in *The Defence of Poesy* which cannot be traced back to some Italian treatise on the poetic art." "His *Defence of Poesy* is a virtual epitome of the literary criticism of the Italian Renaissance."[52]

The indeterminacy of plagiarism's boundaries is a constant in cultural usage. As example, Erasmus Darwin, in an "Interlude" to his *Botanic Garden* in 1789, introduces a dialogue in which a speaker notes that "many passages, which have been stolen from antient Poets, have been translated into our language without loosing [*sic*] any thing of the beauty of the versification." His interlocutor responds, "I am glad to hear you acknowledge the thefts of the modern poets from the antient ones, whose works I suppose have been reckoned lawful plunder in all ages. But have not you borrowed epithets, phrases, and even half a line occasionally from modern poems?" The first speaker then says,

> It may be difficult to mark the exact boundary of what should be
> termed plagiarism: where the sentiment and expression are both
> borrowed without due acknowledgement, there can be no doubt;—
> single words on the contrary taken from other authors cannot
> convict a writer of Plagiarism, they are lawful game, wild by nature,
> the property of all who capture them;—and perhaps a few common
> flowers of speech may be gathered, as we pass our neighbour's
> inclosure, without stigmatising us with the title of thieves; but we
> must not therefore plunder his cultivated fruit.[53]

How close this equivocal prescription can become in actual practice to plundering "cultivated fruit" may be judged from comparing some of Darwin's lines with those of Milton. Darwin writes,

---

[51]Agassi, p. 118; Ferrier, p. 288; Wetzels, p. 24.
[52]Spingarn, pp. 257–58, 268. Paradoxically, Spingarn then urges that the treatise "can lay claim to distinct originality in its unity of feeling" (pp. 268–69).
[53]Darwin, II, 131–32.

So in Sicilia's ever-blooming shade
When playful PROSPERINE from CERES stray'd,
Led with unwary step her virgin trains
O'er Etna's steeps, and Enna's golden plains;
Pluck'd with fair hand the silver-blossom'd bower,
And purpled mead,—herself a fairer flower;
Sudden, unseen amid the twilight glade,
Rush'd gloomy DIS, and seized the trembling maid.—

The source is of course in the fourth book of *Paradise Lost*.

. . .Not that fair field
Of *Enna*, where *Proserpin* gath'ring flow'rs,
Herself a fairer Flow'r, by gloomy *Dis*
Was gather'd, which cost *Ceres* all that pain
To seek her through the world. . . .

There are also frequent incidents of verbatim plagiarism, although, again paradoxically, these same incidents, if the passages in question were simply enclosed in quotation marks, would immediately become culturally acceptable. As a case in point, I recently happened to notice in Georg Brandes's magisterial study of Goethe the following passage with respect to Goethe's interest in Spinoza:

Naturally Spinoza did not have the conception of life that he would have had had he known modern chemistry and physiology. For him the universe was merely a matter of extension and thought; he never rose to the living and fruitful infinite which history and natural science show us ruling in boundless space. Conceptions such as evolution and progress were foreign to him. The world, as he conceived it, seemed crystalized.[54]

The passage seemed vaguely familiar, and after a while I remembered why. Brandes was plagiarizing Renan.

L'univers pour Spinoza, comme pour Descartes, n'était qu'étendue et pensée; la chimie et la physiologie manquaient à cette grande école, trop exclusivement géometrique et mécanique. Étranger à l'idée de la vie et aux notions sur la constitution des corps que la chimie devait reveler . . . Spinoza n'arriva point à cet infini vivant et fécond que la science de la nature et de l'histoire nous montre présidant dans l'espace sans bornes à un développement toujours de plus en plus intense. . . . Spinoza ne vit pas clairement le progrès universel; le monde comme il le conçoit semble cristallisé.[55]

[54]Brandes, I, 435.
[55]Renan, pp. 508–9.

Brandes, however, though clearly "plagiarizing," does not follow his source any more closely than does the speech of Shakespeare's Volumnia (*Coriolanus*, V.iii.94–124) follow the wording in North's translation of Plutarch.[56] And yet one does not customarily regard Shakespeare's use of his sources as falling under the term *plagiarism*.[57]

If such comparative examples suggest an ambivalence in our willingness to invoke the accusation of plagiarism, so too do the relatively few theoretical treatments of the phenomenon also display ambivalence, an ambivalence that arises from the paradoxical nature of originality in its relation to tradition. Thus the Abbé Du Bos, in his *Réflexions critiques* of 1719, defines plagiarism as "giving for our own composition . . . verses which we have had neither trouble nor merit in transplanting from another man's performance"; but if "we happen to adopt the verses of a poet, who has wrote in a different language from our own, we are not then guilty of plagiarism. The verse becomes in some measure ours, because the new expression, with which we have clad another person's thought, is our property. There is some merit in committing such a theft, as it cannot be executed well without trouble." "Those," he continues, "who imagined they might lessen Boileau's reputation, by printing by way of comment, at the bottom of the text of his works, the verses of Horace and Juvenal which he inchased in his, were very much mistaken: The verses of the ancients, which this poet has so artfully turned into French, and so completely rendered an homogenous part of the work in which he ingrafts them, that the whole seems to be one connected thought of the same person, are as great an honour to Boileau, as those that flow quite new from his vein."[58]

Although such serious attempts to define the phenomenon of plagiarism and adjudicate its limits wear their ambivalence on their

[56]See Farmer, pp. 13–15.

[57]Indeed, Farmer's point in demonstrating Shakespeare's use of North's Plutarch is to free him from the charge of dependence on classical antiquity. "*Shakespeare* wanted not the Stilts of Languages to raise him above all other men. . . . The rage of *Parallelisms* is almost over, and in truth nothing can be more absurd. 'THIS was stolen from *one* Classick,—THAT from *another*';—and had I not stept in to his rescue, poor *Shakespeare* had been stript . . . naked of ornament. . . . I have removed a deal of *learned Rubbish,* and pointed out . . .*Shakespeare's* track in the ever-pleasing *Paths of Nature*" (Preface). Another eighteenth-century commentator goes further. "SHAKESPEAR is the only modern Author, . . . whom, in point of Originality, we can venture to compare with those eminent ancient Poets above-mentioned. In sublimity of Genius indeed, MILTON is inferior to neither of them; but it cannot be pretended that he was so complete an Original" (Duff, p. 287).

[58]Du Bos, II, 57–58.

sleeve, so to speak, there are certain historical cruxes where plagiarism is treated as being precisely congruent with the unavoidable realities, and even the desirabilities, of cultural creation. "Come then all ye youths," calls Vida in 1527,

> and, careless of censure, give yourselves up to STEAL and drive the spoil from every source! Unhappy is he . . . who, rashly trusting to his own strength and art, as though in need of no external help, in his audacity refuses to follow the trustworthy footsteps of the ancients, abstaining, alas! unwisely from plunder, and thinking to spare others. O vain superstition! . . . Not long do such men prosper—often they outlive their own works. . . . How [deeply] could they wish to have spared their idle labour and to have learnt other arts from their parents! Often I love to play on ancient phrase, and utter some far other thought in the same words. Nor will any wise man care to blame my self-confessing thefts—thefts open and to be praised and approved. . . . So far be it from me to wish to hide my stolen goods, and conceal my plunder, from any fear of the penalty of infamy![59]

The passage is unmistakable witness to the originality paradox. By its bold equation of plagiarism with wise submission to the tradition (he who trusts "to his own strength and art" is rash and "unhappy"), it pays homage to one side of the paradox; and by its awareness, even though ironically denied, of "censure" and "the penalty of infamy," it pays homage to the claims of individuality.

Nor is Vida's attitude, startling though it may sound, without cultural analogues. Thus Irving wonders "at the extreme fecundity of the press, and how it comes to pass that so many heads, on which nature seems to have inflicted the curse of barrenness, yet teem with voluminous productions." He finds the reason on a chance visit to "the reading room of the great British Library," which contains books "most of which are seldom read." "To these sequestered pools of obsolete literature," he continues, do "many modern authors repair, and draw buckets full of classic lore, or 'pure English, undefiled,' wherewith to swell their own scanty rills of thought." Maintaining this sardonic vein, he proceeds to reflect on the meaning of his new "secret". "After all, thought I, may not this pilfering disposition be implanted in authors for wise purposes; may it not be the way in which Providence has taken care that the seeds of knowledge and wisdom shall be preserved from age to age. . . . The beauties and fine thoughts of ancient and

---

[59]Saintsbury, pp. 85–86. See also *The De Arte Poetica of Marco Girolamo Vida*, trans. with commentary by Ralph G. Williams (New York: Columbia University Press, 1976), pp. xlii–xliv, 98–103.

obsolete writers, are caught up by these flights of predatory authors, and cast forth, again to flourish." And he concludes, tongue in cheek, but not wholly without seriousness: "Authors beget authors, and having produced a numerous progeny, in a good old age they sleep with their fathers, that is to say, with the authors who preceded them—and from whom they had stolen."[60]

This same unequivocal identification of plagiarism with not only the larger truths, but also the actual interests, of cultural endeavor is urged, although now quite without irony, by R. G. Collingwood. Significantly, the affirmation is made as part of an attack on "the individualistic theory of artistic creation." Collingwood believes that what the artist says should and must be "something that his audience says through his mouth; . . . There will thus be something more than mere communication from artist to audience, there will be collaboration between audience and artist." Thus Collingwood, like Eliot, seeks to depress "aesthetic individualism" in favor of a recognition of the group and its tradition. In doing so he accepts the cultural reality of plagiarism. Furthermore, even more radically than Vida, he regards the practice as healthier than the claim to originality. "We try to secure a livelihood for our artists . . . by copyright laws protecting them against plagiarism; but the reason why our artists are in such a poor way is because of that very individualism which these laws enforce. If an artist may say nothing except what he has invented by his own sole efforts, it stands to reason he will be poor in ideas. If he could take what he wants wherever he could find it . . . his larder would always be full."[61] And he unflinchingly accepts the full implications of his stand; in a memorable aphorism he says, "Let all such artists as understand one another, therefore, plagiarize each other's work like men."[62]

Collingwood's attack on the philosophy underlying the copyright law ("Let every artist make a vow, and here among artists I include all such as write or speak on scientific or learned subjects, never to prosecute or lend himself to a prosecution under the law of copyright" [p. 326]) is paralleled by Northrop Frye's animadversions against that same law. Rejecting "the low mimetic prejudices about creation that most of us are educated in," Frye maintains that "all art is equally conventionalized, but we do not ordinarily

[60]Irving, I, 147, 151, 153, 155.

[61]Collingwood, pp. 318, 312, 325.

[62]Ibid., p. 326. Cf. Goethe: "Does not everything that the past and the contemporary world have achieved belong by right to the poet? Why should he hesitate to pick flowers where he finds them?" (*Gedenkausgabe*, XXIII, 370).

notice this fact unless we are unaccustomed to the convention. In our day the conventional element in literature is elaborately disguised by a law of copyright pretending that every work of art is an invention distinctive enough to be patented." This state of things, he continues, makes it difficult "to appraise a literature which includes Chaucer, much of whose poetry is translated or paraphrased from others; Shakespeare, whose plays sometimes follow their sources almost verbatim; and Milton, who asked for nothing better than to steal as much as possible out of the Bible." Fittingly enough for our own concerns in this chapter, Frye concludes by invoking the tension of individual and society as elucidation for the tension of individual and tradition:

> The underestimating of convention appears to be a result of . . . the tendency, marked from Romantic times on, to think of the individual as ideally prior to his society. The view opposed to this, that the new baby is conditioned . . . to a society which already exists, has . . . the initial advantage of being closer to the facts it deals with. The literary consequence of the second view is that the new poem, like the new baby, is born into an already existing order of words, and is typical of the structure of poetry to which it is attached. The new baby is his own society appearing once again as a unit of individuality, and the new poem has a similar relation to its poetic society.[63]

All such unorthodoxies of attitude, manifesting themselves as they do near the intersection of our twin axes of concern, show that the practice of plagiarism is a variable ratio, not an inert quantity, in cultural matters. It is a practice that participates in and is witness to the paradox that surrounds the entire conception of originality. "People," said Goethe, in what must be the eternal limit on the claims for such a conception, "are always talking about originality; but what do they mean? As soon as we are born, the world begins to work upon us, and this goes on to the end. And, after all, what can we call our own except energy, strength, and will? If I could give an account of all that I owe to great predecessors and contemporaries, there would not be much left over."[64]

Goethe's general understanding is complemented by Coleridge's particular realization that "so countless have been the poetic metamorphoses of almost all possible thoughts and connections of thought, that it is scarcely practicable for a man to write in the

[63]Frye, *Anatomy*, pp. 96–97. Cf. Goethe: "There are no individuals. All individuals are also *genera:* that is to say, this individual or that, what you will, is representative of a whole species [*Gattung*]" (*Goethes Gespräche*, II, 166, no. 2336).
[64]*Gedenkausgabe*, XXIV, 158–59.

ornamented style on any subject without finding his poem, against his will and without his previous consciousness, a cento of lines that had pre-existed in other works; and this it is which makes poetry so very difficult, because so very easy in the present day. I myself have for many years past given it up in despair."[65]

And yet Coleridge's despair, no less than Goethe's energy, strength, and will, testifies to the claims of originality and individuality. Such claims, however attenuated they may be by those of tradition and society, can never be entirely stilled. And both the need for originality and its conditions of attenuation, revealing themselves now as the counsel to "insist on yourself; never imitate," and now as the insight that "there never was an original writer," constitute together that inescapable cultural dilemma— presumed only at peril to their work, whether by artists, theorists, critics, or historians, to be either resolved or resolvable—that we have called the originality paradox.[66]

---

[65]*Collected Letters*, III, 469–70.
[66]Cf. Emerson: "Our knowledge is the amassed thought and experience of innumerable minds: our language, our science, our religion, our opinions, our fancies we inherited. Our country, customs, laws, our ambitions, and our notions of fit and fair,—all these we never made, we found them ready-made; we but quote them. . . .But there remains the indefeasible persistency of the individual to be himself. . . . Every mind is different; and the more it is unfolded, the more pronounced is that difference" (*Emerson*, VIII, 200–201).

• 2 •

Field, Constellation,
and Aesthetic Object

*T*he conception of originality is constantly and unavoidably involved in paradox. That involvement is essential, not accidental. It stems from the larger paradox of human existence, whereby we always hear and necessarily respond to the ineradicably conflicting claims of our social natures on the one hand and our individual natures on the other.

The claims are rarely in equipoise. At times the social voice will historically become more insistent, as for instance in Marxist ideology, and at other times the call of the individual, as in Rousseau's *Confessions*, will seem of overwhelming importance. When one or the other gains the ascendance that defines a historical epoch, then cultural conceptions will veer toward the more clamorous summons and attempt to mute the voice of the conflicting reality. But the veering is necessarily temporary, and indeed its attendant conceivings will be necessarily characterized by half-truth, distortion, and illusion; and this effect will obtain no matter how absolute the good faith of those who formulate the conceivings.

The correction, itself also involved in illusion, is historical. The systolic contraction will inevitably give way to a diastolic relaxation that reintroduces the muted voice, but then a new contraction will take place in favor of the truth newly heard. Such relaxation, followed by a new contraction, has recently occurred in our cultural conceptions.

The decade of the 1970s witnessed a revolution in our perception of the interrelation of literary events, and by extension the interrelation of cultural events in general. Before then the New Critical emphasis on the work of art as isolated object, inspected purely in its interior coherence somewhat as a fine blue-white diamond is reverently laid for viewing on a black velvet cloth, had tended to evict the older historical studies whereby *race, milieu,* and

31

moment, or at all events biographical considerations and sources
and influences, were the keys to elucidation. "The first law to be
prescribed to criticism," said the New Critical standard-bearer,
John Crowe Ransom, was "that it shall be objective, shall cite the
nature of the object rather than its effect upon the subject."[1] Historical studies continued to be produced, of course, but they
seemed musty and even wrong-headed compared to the exciting
modernity of the cognitive object analysis espoused by Ransom
and his circle, and by the even more theoretical W. K. Wimsatt.

The idea of influence in particular seemed rigid and mechanical,
and even mistaken, suited only for doctoral dissertations and signi-
fying nothing. As I wrote in 1969, " 'Influence,' once the dominat-
ing theme of scholarship, is rapidly drying up as a meaningful line
of approach; titles beginning 'Der Einfluss . . . ' today command
only a small and restive audience."[2] My dismissal was no doubt
conditioned not only by my training in New Critical procedures,
but also by a residual effect of Romanticism, whereby the demand
for uninfluenced originality outweighed the claims of neoclassical
imitation, and where the creative imagination was at once free and
unfathomable. Wordsworth asks:

> . . . But who shall parcel out
> His intellect by geometric rules,
> Split like a province into round and square?
> Who knows the individual hour in which
> His habits were first sown, even as a seed?
> Who that shall point as with a wand and say
> 'This portion of the river of my mind
> Came from yon fountain'? . . . [3]

After asking these questions, Wordsworth hails Coleridge.

> . . . No officious slave
> Art thou of that false secondary power
> By which we multiply distinctions, then
> Deem that our puny boundaries are things
> That we perceive, and not that we have made.
> To thee, unblinded by these formal arts,
> The unity of all hath been revealed. . . .
> Hard task, vain hope, to analyse the mind.[4]

[1]Ransom, p. 342.
[2]McFarland, *Coleridge,* p. 45.
[3]*Prelude,* 1805 version, II, 208–15 (pp. 82, 84).
[4]Ibid., 1850 version, II, 215–28 (p. 85).

Another formulator of the Romantic emphasis, Blake, for his part says

> I must Create a System, or be enslav'd by another Mans
> I will not Reason & Compare: my business is to Create[5]

and he says that "we do not want either Greek or Roman Models if we are but just & true to our own Imaginations" (p. 94).

Such denials of the pertinence of influence existed side by side with another way of freeing the imagination: namely, simply obliterating distinctions by saying that *all* cultural formation is influence. Influence thus became, to use the words of Hegel from another context, a night in which all cows are black. Goethe most definitively urged this defense. He denounces as "ridiculous" the "doubting of this or that famous man's originality and the seeking to trace his sources." One might "just as well question a well-nourished man about the oxen, sheep and hogs that he ate and that gave him strength. We bring abilities with us, but we owe our development to a thousand workings of a great world upon us, and we appropriate from these what we can and what suits us. I owe much to the Greeks and the French; I am infinitely indebted to Shakespeare, Sterne and Goldsmith. But the sources of my culture are not thereby established; it would be an unending and also an unnecessary task to do so. The main thing is that one have a soul that loves the truth and takes that truth where it finds it."[6]

The relation of influence to originality is thus paradoxical. I had realized this in my work published in 1969, even as I had dismissed the concept of influence, explaining there that "the paradox is not of my making, but is inherent in the very existence of tradition in its relation to individual talent. 'It is not in Montaigne, but in myself,' said Pascal, 'that I find all that I see in him.'"[7] By 1974, however, I had elevated the principle of paradox to what I called "an inescapable cultural dilemma," revealed in twin phrases of Emerson now as the counsel to "insist on yourself; never imitate," and now as the insight that "there never was an original writer."[8]

My statements of 1969 and 1974 thus constitute a parataxis whose structure will serve to introduce the larger body of cultural concerns I am addressing at this juncture. On the one hand, the intensified statement of 1974 obviously arose from the statement of 1969 and in a certain sense can be fully accounted for simply as a

[5]*Blake*, p. 151.
[6]*Gedenkausgabe*, XXIV, 300–301.
[7]McFarland, *Coleridge*, p. 44.
[8]See above, chap. 1, "The Originality Paradox."

broadening of a current of thought—as a widening of the river of my mind. On the other hand, the intervening five years had seen the beginning of the revolution I noted above. In particular, two books had appeared that were already changing the critical scene and that generated lateral currents that flowed into my own, or perhaps, to improve the metaphor, lateral winds that caused my own coals to glow more brightly. The two books were Paul de Man's *Blindness and Insight; Essays in the Rhetoric of Contemporary Criticism,* which appeared in 1971, and Harold Bloom's *Anxiety of Influence; A Theory of Poetry,* which appeared in 1973. Though departing from different premises and points of view, together they laid the foundation for what has since become known as the Yale School of criticism.

De Man's book was important in that it mediated to the American critical scene the deconstructionist theory of Derrida, which in its turn was an outgrowth of slightly earlier structuralist theories quarried out of Lévi-Strauss and Saussure, out of Husserl, out of Marx and Freud. In structuralist conception the literary or other cultural event, far from being an object of isolated purity, is merely a pressure point on an entire network of cultural meanings and relationships. And if in structuralism the cultural object tends to disappear into the dynamics of cultural interrelationship, in Derrida even the author's intent is dismantled. Wimsatt had screened out intent as interfering with our contemplation of the purity of the diamond; Derrida deconstructed that intent to make its sublative structure even more important than the text.

But I am not so much interested on this occasion in the European foundations of the Yale School as in the contribution of Bloom, who seems to me both more important and more challenging than does Derrida or other contemporary French theorists, all of whom I might somewhat dismissively characterize as being less important than their sources. Bloom, however, is another matter. He metabolizes a deep and idiosyncratic erudition into a powerful, detailed, and exceptionally dynamic re-formation of the theory of influence. Just as staid figures like George Washington and King George the Third, with other worthies of the American Revolution, are invested in Blake's *America* with apocalyptic rhetorical dynamic—

> Fiery the Angels rose, & as they rose deep thunder roll'd
> Around their shores: indignant burning with the fires of Orc
> and Bostons Angel cried aloud as they flew thro' the dark night

—just so do the inert alignments of historical influence become transformed in Bloom's work.

They become transformed both rhetorically and structurally. Indeed, one must understand how definitively Blakean Bloom's entire enterprise is. Bloom creates his own system so as not to be enslaved by Frye's. He elaborates it so tenaciously that one thinks not only of Blake but of Blake's prolix predecessor Swedenborg. He encloses himself in the system; in it giant forms struggle in shadowy and portentous configuration. Where Blake constructs recurrent energic personifications called by such idiosyncratic names as Orc and Rintrah and Palamabron and Bromion and Theotormon, Bloom presents recurrent dynamisms called in his own private mythology Clinamen, Tessera, Kenosis, Daemonization, Askesis, and Apophrades. Where Blake projects his godlike Zoas, personified as Urthona, Luvah, Urizen and Tharmas, Bloom elevates rhetorical tropes into his own version of Platonic first forms: irony, metonymy, metaphor, synecdoche; and over them all, like Blake's divine humanity, there broods metalepsis. Like Blake, too, Bloom's utterance can sometimes become overemphatic babble, most notoriously, perhaps, in the statement in *The Anxiety of Influence* that "the meaning of a poem can only be another poem," a hyperbole so absolute that Bloom returns to it a trifle nervously in *Kabbalah and Criticism,* where he says, "I recall venturing the apothegm that the meaning of a poem could only be another poem. Not, I point out, the *meaning* of another poem, but the other poem itself, indeed the *otherness* of the other poem."[9] This perhaps illuminates matters even less than does the earlier statement, but at least the hyperbole is reined in a bit.

To sum up, like Blake's system, Bloom's is apocalyptic, increasingly oblique as he continues to construct midrash on it, and like Blake's it chews up and digests public and external materials and recasts them into visionary forms dramatic. Like Blake's too, it is uttered in prophetic tones.

I have been at some pains to characterize Bloom's mode of theoretical criticism, because I shall in my consideration of certain interrelations in German and English culture be attempting to make theoretical points that define themselves by contrast to his arguments and yet can be taken as in some sense complementary to them.

Specifically, where Bloom is interested above all in what he calls "strong" poets and "strong" precursors, with the relations between them cast into lurid apocalypse as mortal struggle and oedipal combat, with metaphors of warfare and other dynamic of power howling through the scene, I am interested in minimal and

---

[9]*Anxiety,* p. 94; *Kabbalah,* p. 108.

almost imperceptible relationships. My readers may recall that one of Leibniz's most telling points against Locke's description of the provenance and structure of the human mind was that Locke's clear and distinct data[10] entirely failed to take into account all kinds of twilight phenomena of consciousness that Leibniz called "minute perceptions" ("petites perceptions")—such things as dreams and reverie and other indistinct perceivings.[11] We must not, said Leibniz, neglect "τό μικρὸν, the insensible progressions."[12] Leibniz's "petites perceptions," indeed, when they were called to the attention of the intelligentsia by Raspe's publication of the *Nouveaux essais* in 1765, were a major formative influence leading to the advent of Romanticism. The distinctions I shall propose can hardly anticipate such high historical effect, and very probably Harold Bloom would not be unequivocally enthusiastic about being projected into the role of a Locke of criticism; I am myself, however, rather placidly content, if only for the moment, to step into the role of Leibniz.

For Bloom the writing of a strong poem involves a struggle to clear imaginative space, for it must always be a shifting of the

[10]Or rather, "determinate data." Cf. Locke: *"Clear and distinct Ideas* are terms, which though familiar and frequent in Men's Mouths, I have reason to think every one, who uses, does not perfectly understand. . . . I have therefore in most places chose to put *determinate* or *determined,* instead of *clear* and *distinct,* as more likely to direct Men's thoughts to my meaning in this matter" (Locke, pp. 12–13).

[11]Leibniz's own favorite example of the existence of "minute perceptions" below or on the borderline of the conscious was that in walking beside the sea he heard a single roar of waves made up of the sounds of many individual waves that were not discernible in their particularity (*Leibniz,* V, 47; VI, 515). It is an interesting triple chapter in the history of ideas that (1) in order to give formal grounding to the doctrine of "minute perceptions" Leibniz distinguished *perceptions* from *apperceptions* and thereby instituted the division between the unconscious and the conscious mind (e.g., "Il y a mille marques qui font juger qu'il y a à tout moment une infinité de *perceptions* en nous, mais sans apperception et sans reflexion, c'est à dire des changements dans l'ame même dont nous ne nous appercevons pas, parce que les impressions sont ou trop petites et en trop grand nombre ou trop unies" [V, 46]), a distinction that, transmitted through Schelling and Romanticism to Schopenhauer and Eduard von Hartmann, eventuated in Freud's psychoanalytical doctrine that now has penetrated all interstices of modern assumption; (2) that it specifically was criticism of the doctrine of "clear and distinct ideas" that led to the division of the conscious and the unconscious; and (3) that inasmuch as the requirement of "clear and distinct ideas" as components in a theory of knowledge was initiated by Descartes ("quicquid clare distincteque percipio, verum est"), Leibniz developed the distinction of conscious and unconscious in opposition to the Cartesian tradition before he employed it in opposition to Locke, e.g.,: "Ainsi il est bon de faire distinction entre la *Perception* qui est l'état interieur de la Monade representant les choses externes, et l'*Apperception* qui est la *Conscience,* ou la connoissance reflexive de cet état interieur, laquelle n'est point donnée à toutes les Ames, ny tousjours à la même Ame. Et c'est faute de cette distinction, que les Cartesiens ont manqué, en comptant pour rien les perceptions dont on ne s'appercoit pas" (VI, 600).

[12]*Leibniz,* V, 50.

weight of a prior strong poem from the poet's mind and therefore a "misprision" or "misreading" of that poem. "The father is met in combat, and fought to at least a stand-off, if not quite to a separate peace." Even Bloom's sacred tropes are embattled; they "are defenses against other tropes." The characteristic images of combat and embattlement in Bloom's discourse, however, are not mere idiosyncrasy; on the contrary, they serve to define his theory's full range. Paul Valéry, writing a half-century earlier, points out that "influence is clearly distinguishable from imitation," for "*what a man does* either repeats or rejects *what someone else has done*—repeats it in another tone, refines or amplifies or simplifies it, loads or overloads it with meaning, or else rebuts, overturns, destroys and denies it, but thereby assumes it and has invisibly used it."[13]

In testing his theory in terms of one poem, Browning's *Childe Roland*, Bloom relies wholly on the vocabulary of combat. "Shelley is the Hidden God of the universe created by *Childe Roland to the Dark Tower Came*. His is the presence that the poem labors to void, and his is the force that rouses the poem's force. Out of that struggle between forces rises the form of Browning's poem, which is effectively the *difference* between the rival strengths of poetic father and poetic son."[14]

Curiously enough, Bloom's performance on his own chosen ground is here one of his least impressive; he does not even really relate Browning's poem to Shelley's "Triumph of Life," where the comparative materials are so persuasively rich. Indeed, this is a recurring feature of Bloom's actual critical practice: he frequently overlooks the richest illustrations for his own theory. He might have written an entire brief book on the compelling topic of *Childe Harold* as a misprision of *The Ancient Mariner*—we recall that Byron actually lifts phrases from the precursor poem—and of *Don Juan* as another misprision, this time with the double struggle to free itself from *Childe Harold* as well as *The Ancient Mariner* (from which it too openly borrows). But I do not recall any place where he mentions these matters.

To criticize Bloom's trope of strong poets struggling in giant combat is, however, not to dismiss it, and I have found my own understanding fecundated by Bloom's insistences even when I am not convinced by his rhetoric or by his examples. But at a conference on "English and German Romanticism, Cross-Currents and Controversies," where this chapter was first presented, and

[13]*Misreading,* p. 80, 74; *Valèry,* VIII, 241.
[14]*Misreading,* p. 116.

with a paper topic for that occasion called "Patterns of Parataxis in Anglo-German Cultural Currents," other urgencies presented themselves. First of all, we might note that both the title of the conference and my own title presuppose a field anterior to any particular works in it. Such, too, is Bloom's own presupposition; he begins *The Anxiety of Influence,* for instance, by saying that he "offers a theory of poetry by way of a description of poetic influence, or the story of intra-poetic relationships," and that "poetic history" is "indistinguishable from poetic influence, since strong poets make that history by misreading one another, so as to clear imaginative space for themselves." Then he inserts the proviso that his "concern is only with strong poets, major figures with the persistence to wrestle with their strong precursors, even to the death."[15] But where does he find his strong poets? The answer is that they are given to him under the rubric of English literature. He never questions the canon, nor does he question the use of poetry as such, as Keats does in "The Fall of Hyperion." Bloom's primary urge is to create his own system, and he sets about it posthaste, without wondering about his materials. Aside from such personally generous gestures by which he includes his own friends— John Ashbery, A. R. Ammons, Angus Fletcher, Paul de Man—in his listings of canonical figures, he is docile in accepting the valuations already given by literary history, as is strikingly apparent in his book called *The Visionary Company,* which is simply a résumé of the canon of English Romantic poetry.

But perhaps even more indicative of Bloom's acceptance of the priority of established field is a locus at the beginning of *Kabbalah and Criticism,* where after vatic musings on theological origins— "When the Holy One entered the Garden, a herald called out," and so forth—he says that "the first chapter of this book offers an account of that primordial scheme" (that is, of the Kabbalah's view of the origin of all things), and "in the second chapter, the scheme is related, in detail, to a theory of reading poetry."[16] In one step we have descended from the "primordial scheme" to "reading poetry": the mountain labors and brings forth the concerns of a graduate student in English.

Poetry has had many defenders and apologists, but only a radical withdrawal from primary realities can see it as among the most truly urgent of human activities. Much of human culture, to say nothing of human life as such, has little to do with poetry, as do

---

[15]*Anxiety,* p. 5.
[16]*Kabbalah,* pp. 11–12.

many of the finest spirits that that culture has produced. For Bloom, however, the realm of poetry constitutes an *epoché*, or a cessation, of the complexities of human awareness. Everything is translated into the concerns of poetry. "I find it curious," he says, "that many modern theorists actually talk about poems when they assert that they are talking about people" (p. 108). Again: "I question also the grand formula that Poetry is a man speaking to men. Poetry is poems speaking to a poem, and is also that poem answering back with its own defensive discourse" (p. 108). Still again: "I knowingly urge critical theory to stop treating itself as a branch of philosophical discourse. . . . A theory *of* poetry must belong *to* poetry, must *be* poetry, before it can be of any use in interpreting poems" (p. 109). The thought of the psychoanalyst Freud is reduced to poetry, as Bloom, following Lacan, transmogrifies the Freudian unconscious into merely a metaphorical ground for rhetorical figures. The thought of the philosopher Nietzsche is also reduced to poetry. "Nietzsche," explains Bloom, "speaks of ideas as if they were poems. In the following excerpt, I have changed only one word, substituting 'poem' for 'ideal'" (p. 112); and he then calmly appropriates Nietzsche's discourse for the Bloomean system. It is scant wonder, in this wholesale funneling into poetry, that the forms of tropes—metonymy, irony, synecdoche, and the rest—become the Thrones, Dominations, and Powers of a new angelology.

These evidences of Bloom's *epoché* all witness what I shall henceforth term the *anteriority of field.* So too do those conceptions called English Romanticism and German Romanticism. My knowledge is certain only with regard to myself, but I assume that my situation extends to us all, when I say that my command of the specific content of either English Romanticism or German Romanticism is radically incomplete; indeed, it would be difficult to say in which of the two cultural regions are more things missing from my awareness. Yet, fortified by the anteriority of field, I have no hesitation in speaking and writing in both realms.

It is the anteriority of field that allows us to see how vulnerable historically is the object analysis espoused by the New Criticism. I began this chapter with the image of a blue-white diamond laid upon a black velvet cloth as illustrative of the critical stance of Wimsatt and other New Critical theorists. From their standpoint no enquiry is demanded as to who wove or dyed the cloth or who quarried and polished the diamond. Since such contexts are void, the trope of diamond and velvet can be transumed; in the resulting metalepsis we are not justified in saying that the velvet is cloth, or that the diamond is a diamond: we see only a bright object twinkling against a dark field. If we draw back a little, we see more such objects and then still more; but no matter how many bright objects we view, there is still the same dark field.

The sense of uniqueness in the original isolated object is therefore something like the result of a zoom closeup in photography, whereby the object is enhanced by eliminating the original dimension of the field. The field in its unmagnified perspective, on the other hand, is like Kant's starry heavens above. To look at cultural events is like looking at stars in the night sky.

We look up with unaided vision and see stars, more than we can count, and of varying brightness and no immediately discernible pattern. When we undergo cultural education we as it were look at the sky through a telescope. We see more stars and we see them in more detail; but there are still more than we can count, and we infer that there are many more we do not see. When we look at the sky in different hemispheres, we seem to see the same thing, stars against a field. Only after study and reflection do we realize that the stars seen from the differing perspectives are not identical.

After more study, we begin to ascribe pattern to the seemingly random configuration of the stars. We begin to outline constellations, although only from the anteriority of field is this process possible. Hume points out that "there is no object, which implies the existence of any other if we consider these objects in themselves." "Objects have no discoverable connexion together; nor is it from any other principle but custom operating upon the imagination, that we can draw any inference from the appearance of one to the existence of another."[17] So from the unity supplied by the anteriority of field we begin to connect constellations of cultural patterns, by which with deeper observation we can locate whole galaxies: classical Greek culture, or German Romanticism, or English Romanticism. When the zoom effect of Wimsattian object analysis takes place, the constellational location of the object is denied; and yet the constellational location is necessary to isolate the object in the first place. Apart from his theories as to critical orientation, Wimsatt was the academic master of several cultural fields.

The rule derived thus seems invariable: first there is field, then constellation, and only as a third awareness is there object considered as focus of observation. Even when as children we ask our fathers to tell us a story, the objectification presumes the anteriority of field and the parataxis of constellation.

[17]Hume, pp. 86, 103.

Furthermore, though our primary intuition of the stars is of number and brightness and scattering, and only our secondary view, enhanced by meditation and magnification, begins to find pattern and interrelationship, that enhanced secondary view reveals to us that starry events differ in more ways than mere brightness or proximity. When Bloom sees only strong poets wrestling for imaginative space, it is as though he would limit the starry heavens to double stars of the first magnitude. But there are stars of differing intensity and size, and there are planets and moons; and what look like stars sometimes turn out to be whole galaxies, which again take different shapes: pinwheels, blobs, rings—there is even one identified as the "sombrero" galaxy. There are in addition quasars and pulsars and black holes. In the same way, the actual content of cultural field in its constellational groupings is not limited to poetry and strong poets but reveals other cultural configurations as well.

The galactic shape of English Romanticism is significantly different from that of German Romanticism in that much of the German achievement came to realization in the form of philosophical systems, which are largely absent from English Romanticism. Indeed, philosophy and music are the true vehicles of German genius. Hegel and Beethoven are each assuredly of greater cultural magnitude than even Hölderlin. Again, a contour of German Romanticism only faintly apparent in English Romanticism is *Gelehrsamkeit*. Matthew Arnold criticized the English Romantics, with the exception of Coleridge, for not knowing enough. One would not dream of making such a charge against the Schlegel brothers or Schleiermacher, or even against Tieck or Goethe, not to speak of Hegel. There are no Hegels in English Romanticism, and Coleridge, who comes the closest in aim and interest, is more like the Crab Nebula, a remnant of a supernova, than a churning Hegelian star.

Whatever the constellational differences may be, however, the metalepsis of starry heavens holds good for all aspects of cultural comprehension. I earlier suggested that much of life has little to do with poetry; much indeed has little to do with any form of high culture. But from antiquity onward, cultural events have always been there, like the stars overhead, even though not everyone heeds them, and others attend to them only sporadically. Still, they are always there; they are seen by every man, whether reflected upon or not; and we all intuitively realize that in cultural constellations, as in the starry heavens, our ultimate possibilities of transcendence lie.

It is interesting to note that in cultural awareness there need be

no specific quantity of objects; the starry heavens are still themselves whether we conjecture a thousand visible stars or ten thousand, or for that matter merely a hundred: all we need is field,
plurality, and, as prerequisite for examination, constellation. Indeed, Bloom's whole thrust is a corrective to his teacher, Wimsatt,
in that whereas the final magnification of Wimsattian object analysis negates the plurality that determines the field, Bloom restores
to poetic objects their defining plurality. "We need to stop thinking
of any poet as an autonomous ego," he says in *The Anxiety of
Influence*, "however solipsistic the strongest of poets may be. Every
poet is a being caught up in a dialectical relationship . . . with
another poet or poets."[18] And he says in *A Map of Misreading* that
he "studies poetic influence, by which I continue *not* to mean the
passing-on of images and ideas from earlier to later poets. Influence, as I conceive it, means that there are *no* texts, but only relationships *between* texts."[19]

Yet, though I accord with Bloom's restoration of plurality as
preceding the object, his actual assessment of pluralities seems to
me to be locked into something rather closer to a critical astrology
than a critical astronomy.

> Antithetical criticism as a practical discipline of reading begins with
> an analysis of misprision or revisionism, through a description of
> revisionary ratios, conducted through examination of tropes, imagery
> or psychological defenses, depending upon the preferences of an
> individual reader. An application of literary history, though greatly
> desirable, is not strictly necessary for the study of misprision. But as
> soon as one attempts a deeper criticism, and asks what is the
> interpretation that a poem offers, one is involved with the precursor
> text or texts as well as with the belated poem itself.[20]

The methodology seems cumbersome when confronted with the
caveat of Virginia Woolf, "But let us always remember—influences
are infinitely numerous; writers are infinitely sensitive; each writer

[18]*Anxiety*, p. 91.

[19]*Misreading*, p. 3. As to why "poetic influence" would *not* mean "the passing-on
of images and ideas from earlier to later poets," Valéry supplies the enlightening
illustration of Baudelaire. "He reached manhood at a time when . . . a dazzling
generation had appropriated the empire of Letters. Lamartine, Hugo, Musset, Vig-
ny were the masters of the moment. Let us put ourselves in the place of a young
man who is about to begin working in 1840. He has been brought up on artists
whom an imperious instinct commands him to blot out. His literary vocation has
been awakened and nourished by them, inspired by their glory, shaped by their
works, yet his survival necessarily calls for the denial, overthrow, and replacement
of the same men who appear to him to occupy the whole expanse of fame" (*Valéry*,
VIII, 195).

[20]*Misreading*, p. 116.

has a different sensibility."[21] I shall attempt the rudiments of a description of influence study more consonant with the elements noted by Woolf.

To that end I begin by substituting the neutral word *parataxis* for *influence*. In my discussion of 1969, I had noted that originality is "an error-freighted and ill-defined concept," as is the label *influence*: "such labels are crude and makeshift; they arise from no genuine understanding of the symbolic functions of literary activity, and history itself is not long content with any of them."[22] Bloom, too, is not entirely happy with the word *influence*. "My motive," he says at one point, "is to distinguish once for all what I call 'poetic influence' from traditional 'source study.'"[23] Elsewhere, he feels it necessary to define the term in a special way. "What I mean by 'influence' is the whole range of relationships between one poem and another, which means that my use of 'influence' is itself a highly conscious trope, indeed a complex sixfold trope that intends to subsume six major tropes: irony, synecdoche, metonymy, hyperbole, metaphor, and metalepsis, and in just that ordering." Again, he says that "if we consider 'influence' as the trope of rhetorical irony that connects an earlier to a later poet . . . then influence is a relation that means one thing about the intra-poetic situation while saying another." Still again, in *The Anxiety of Influence*, he says that "influence is *Influenza*—an astral disease."[24]

Bloom is here playing with the literal meaning of the word as an influx, which in its turn is linked metaleptically with the idea of current. The designation of the conference as recognizing "Cross-Currents" was taken up into the title of my own address, which for that occasion spoke of "Cultural Currents." What I have hitherto been saying reveals why I substituted *parataxis* for *influence*, and *cultural* for *poetical*; but I left *currents* as an offering to the aspiration of the conference. It is a trope, however, that has no legitimacy in

[21]Woolf, p. 163.

[22]McFarland, *Coleridge*, p. 45.

[23]*Misreading*, p. 116. Again: "Poetic influence, in the sense I give it, has almost nothing to do with the verbal resemblances between one poet and another" (p. 19). Still again: "Only weak poems, or the weaker elements in strong poems, immediately echo precursor poems, or directly allude to them. The fundamental phenomena of poetic influence have little to do with the borrowing of images or ideas, with sound-patterns, or with other verbal reminders of one poem by another. A poem is a deep misprision of a previous poem when we recognize the later poem as being absent rather than present on the surface of the earlier poem, and yet still being in the earlier poem, implicit or hidden *in* it, not yet manifest, and yet *there*." (*Kabbalah*, pp. 66–67).

[24]*Misreading*, pp. 70, 71; *Anxiety*, p. 95.

terms of the parataxis of aesthetic objects. If we look up into the
night sky, we do not see the drift of stars: we see stars in simple
juxtaposition. Conceptions of current are derived from the anteriority of field, not from the parataxes themselves. The river, as
Wordsworth says, is our own mind. I bridle at a certain fashion of
music criticism that speaks of, say, Mozart's D-minor piano concerto as looking forward to Beethoven. On the contrary, Mozart's
concerto looks forward to nothing: it simply is. In our historical
sense of field alone can it be related to subsequent compositions by
Beethoven. The work as a work is aesthetically complete and
would not change were all memory of Beethoven suddenly to be
obliterated from our cultural consciousness.

Still, the trope of current does pertain to the chronological sche-
matisms with which we demarcate the sense of field, as does
Bloom's insistence upon the word *precursor*. In that sense, indeed,
Bloom's own ideas are the downstream in a continuing current.
Some of his basic arguments were adumbrated in Walter Jackson
Bate's volume of 1970 called *The Burden of the Past and the English
Poet*.[25] Further upstream, in 1957, was the important prefiguration
of Northrop Frye's *Anatomy of Criticism*, where it is pointed out that
"poetry can only be made out of other poems; novels out of other
novels," a statement that finds its echo everywhere in Bloom, as,
for instance, in his formula that "poetry begins, always, when
someone who is going to become a poet *reads a poem*." But Frye,
too, has precursors. As Virginia Woolf notes in 1940, "books descend from books as families descend from families. Some descend
from Jane Austen; others from Dickens. They resemble their parents, as human children resemble their parents; yet they differ as

[25]A choice illustration of the convolutions of the originality paradox, however,
and of the power of *Zeitgeist*, is the fact that though Bate's *Burden of the Past* prefigures Bloom's *Anxiety of Influence* even with regard to the concept of "anxiety" (see
above, chap. 1), Bloom's theory was already full-formed in its essentials at the time
Bate's work appeared. Bloom's *Anxiety* was published in 1973, Bate's *Burden of the
Past* in 1970; but in his *Yeats*, which also appeared in 1970, Bloom is already speaking at length of the "line of poetic influence that led to Yeats"; of the "revisionary
readings of precursors that are involved in Yeats's poems"; of revisionary readings
as "a series of swerves away from the precursors, swerves intended to uncover the
Cherub, to free Yeats from creative anxieties." Bloom says that he will call these
swerves "by the Lucretian term *clinamen*"; and he states that "one purpose of the
analyses of Yeats's poems and plays offered by this volume is to suggest a newer
kind of practical criticism, one which results directly from an awareness of each
poet's own relation to his precursors. It is perhaps inevitable that Yeats, the conscious heir of the Romantics, compels us to a new kind of critical study of Romantic
influence" (*Yeats*, p. 7). In the same volume, Bloom says that "poetic influence, as I
conceive it, is a variety of melancholy or an anxiety-principle. It concerns the poet's
sense of his precursors, and of his own achievements in relation to theirs. Have
they left him room enough, or has their priority cost him his art?" (p. 5).

children differ, and revolt as children revolt." The insistence is identical with those of Frye and Bloom, as is the metaphor of the struggle of children with parents. Frye even says that "the new poem, like the new baby, is born into an already existing order of words, and is typical of the structure of poetry to which it is attached. The new baby *is* his own society appearing once again as a unit of individuality, and the new poem has a similar relation to its poetic society."[26]

But the line of precursorship could be traced almost endlessly into the past. Indeed, even a doctrine so seemingly original as psychoanalysis is involved in indebtedness, belatedness, and influence of various kinds, as Josef Breuer conceded in one of the earliest treatises in the psychoanalytical movement.

> No one who attempts to put forward today his views on hysteria and its psychical basis can avoid repeating a great quantity of other people's thoughts which are in the act of passing from personal into general possession. It is scarcely possible always to be certain who first gave them utterance, and there is always a danger of regarding as a product of one's own what has already been said by someone else. I hope, therefore, that I may be excused if few quotations are found in this discussion and if no strict distinction is made between what is my own and what originates elsewhere.[27]

What Breuer is here conceding is raised to general formulation in Valéry's observation that "we say that an author is *original* when we cannot trace the hidden transformations that others underwent in his mind; we mean to say that the dependence of *what he does* on *what others have done* is excessively complex and irregular."[28]

Breuer's concession and Valéry's formulation tend to subvert Bloom's conception of culture as the struggle of strong poets. For Breuer speaks of "a great quantity of other people's thoughts," an awareness that undermines the idea of a single strong precursor, and the dramatic wrestling with influence is further undermined by Breuer's statement about the "danger of regarding as a product of one's own what has already been said by someone else." It is, I think, the regarding as one's own what has already been said by someone else that leads, in successive layers and imperceptible repetitions, to the formation of that mysterious entity called a *Zeitgeist*, and of which a choice example is that elusive essence we call Romanticism. A cultural breath such as Romanticism, or if one wishes, Victorianism or the hippiedom of the 1960s, or Florentine

---

[26]Frye, *Anatomy*, p. 97; *Kabbalah*, p. 107; Woolf, p. 163; Frye, *Anatomy*, p. 97.
[27]*Freud*, II, 185–86.
[28]*Valéry*, VIII, 241.

culture of the Renaissance, or any other *Zeitgeist* is not formed by the struggles of ephebes with strong precursors, though they wrestle into eternity; it is formed rather by the minimal and dispersed influences Breuer invokes, and which I earlier suggested may be thought of as Leibniz's "τὸ μιϰϱὸν, the insensible progressions" that undermine Locke's building blocks of consciousness.

Perhaps a most trivial incident from my own experience can serve to illustrate these minimal influences. A few years ago I invented, or in my complacent conviction thought I had invented, the phrase "have a good day" that we all constantly hear. I would offer this benediction to taxi drivers in New York, and it only added to my complacency when I began to hear them intoning the same formula to me. Their own use of the words simply fortified my fantasy that I was enormously influential on others, although even I was impressed by the speed and thoroughness with which my influence had worked itself into the popular culture. It was not until I happened to fly out to Chicago and saw on a billboard the exhortation, in letters thirty feet high, to "have a good day" that my self-congratulation on my creative individuality gave way to an understanding of the true situation. As Karl Mannheim insists, "isolated discoveries" are for the sociologist "expressions of general social trends." He goes on to say that "it is not important for us whether the dynamic logic which was achieved at about the same time by Hegel, Schelling and Müller, was arrived at independently or under mutual influence. What is important is to find the sources in the social and intellectual life of the time from which arose the impulse to search for a dynamic logic."[29]

Mannheim, of course, has his own cultural axe to grind no less than does Bloom; what he says, however, presumes the importance of the minimal influences I have just invoked. It is these minimal influences or "insensible progressions" rather than the influence of strong precursors that build the coral reefs of a *Zeitgeist*, or, to use Hazlitt's rubric (and Shelley's phrase), the spirit of an age. To revert to the starry heavens of our metaleptic field, therefore, closer observation reveals not only strong poems and their juxtaposition, but philosophical systems, novels, journals, and other cultural formation, as well as clouds and streams of astral debris: dispersed metaphorical clusters, emotional solar winds of almost imperceptible effect, cosmic rays of doctrine detectible only by special examination, and so forth (it would be very difficult, for instance, to show that the influence of Milton's precursorship on the English Romantic poets was stronger than the influ-

[29]*Mannheim*, p. 209, n. 1.

ence of the political upheaval called the French Revolution). The streamings of this variegated astral matter can doubtless exist in many forms, but in their eddying between German and English culture I wish to call attention here to only five.

Our first awareness, if we adjust our sights so as to locate German and English culture within the same field of view, is that the joint structure seems to be a kind of streaming in the shape of the figure H, with a detour of currents at the joining bar. That is to say, from about 1700 to the Romantic era cultivated Germans read and were profoundly influenced by things English (and in the context of languages used, we may include Scottish writers under the term), but the British did not read the Germans in return. It was Hume who woke Kant from his dogmatic slumber, but the only foreign culture Hume himself was interested in was French. After the advent of Romanticism, the stream of influence almost completely reversed its direction of flow. Except for a fascination with Byron (and of course with Scott), it is astonishing how little the German intelligentsia after 1800 were aware of any of the English Romantic writers. By this time, however, the cultivated English were virtually scrambling to imbibe German culture. Shelley embarked on a translation of Goethe's *Faust* even though he did not know German; Coleridge translated Schiller's *Wallenstein*, though he made mistakes and found the labor "soul-destroying." Carlyle built the greater part of his reputation as a mediator of German culture to the English, and his angry reaction to Coleridge was at least in part conditioned by his unwillingness to accept him as a competitor priest in the ministration of German sacraments.

> Coleridge sat on the brow of Highgate Hill [wrote Carlyle] . . .
> looking down on London and its smoke-tumult, like a sage escaped
> from the inanity of life's battle; attracting towards him the thoughts
> of innumerable brave souls still engaged there. His express contri-
> butions to poetry, philosophy, or any specific province of human
> literature or enlightenment, had been small and sadly intermittent;
> but he had, especially among young inquiring men, a higher than
> literary, a kind of prophetic or magician character. He was thought
> to hold, he alone in England, the key to German and other Trans-
> cendentalisms. . . . The practical intellects of the world did not much
> heed him, or carelessly reckoned him a metaphysical dreamer: but to
> the rising spirits of the young generation he had this dusky sublime
> character; and sat there as a kind of *Magus*, girt in mystery and
> enigma; his Dodona oak-grove (Mr. Gilman's house at Highgate)
> whispering strange things, uncertain whether oracles or jargon.[30]

[30]*Carlyle*, XI, 52–53.

The prestige that attached to Coleridge's knowledge of things German was envied by others than Carlyle; indeed, the pursuit of German culture rapidly became not so much a cultural adornment as a cultural necessity. By 1841, for instance, an article in *Blackwood's Magazine* said that "German, in particular, we *must* study; for, like Goethe's magical apprentice, having set the imp agog after water-buckets, he threatens to swamp and drown us altogether unless we get hold of the word which he will obey."[31] In the succeeding year, 1842, Carlyle's friend and Coleridge's former disciple, John Sterling, wrote that "still more remarkably than in poetry, the philosophical speculations of all Europe are daily learning obedience to the example of Germany. . . . In that country,—poor as Germany is compared with England and France,—there may now probably be found the greater part of the generous knowledge and earnest meditation extant on earth."[32] In short, though the cultivated Briton of the Elizabethan age looked to Italy to improve his mind; and the cultivated Briton of Dryden's time and the Enlightenment looked to France; by Romantic and Victorian times he looked almost slavishly to Germany.

We need be in no doubt when the radical shift occurred. In the eighteenth century, a genius like Handel improved his position by moving from Germany to England. In the late 1750s Hamann could write that "it is pleasant and profitable to translate a page of Pope . . . but vanity and a curse to leaf through a part of [Diderot's] *Encyclopédie*."[33] In the 1770s and 1780s men like Herder and Lessing, Moritz and Lichtenberg, looked eagerly to England as a kind of spiritual home.[34] "At last I am in my beloved London," writes Lichtenberg in February 1775, "for which I have longed and schemed and pined"; and when it came time to return to Germany, he wrote: "I do not return willingly to Göttingen and scarce think that I shall ever be able to live there contentedly."[35] Elsewhere Lichtenberg produced a comparison of English and German schoolboys that dramatically highlights the German sense of English superiority.

---

[31]"Traits and Tendencies of German Literature," *Blackwood's Edinburgh Magazine*, 50 (1841), 160. The statement continues: "Nor is it from Germany only by external importation that the deluge floods in; we have a sort of indwelling Germanism at home, which is very powerful, and has many names. Undeniably, Coleridge was a German. . . . A German of the Germans was Percy Bysshe Shelley; a German in his pure incorporeal idealism; German in his pantheizing poetry and poetic pantheism; British only in his pride" (p. 160).

[32]Sterling, I, 385, 404.

[33]*Kant*, X, 8.

[34]Goethe too can be included here. See Strich, pp. 101–20. See further James Boyd, *Goethe's Knowledge of English Literature* (Oxford: Clarendon Press, 1932).

[35]*Lichtenberg's Visits*, pp. 79, 109.

> To amuse myself I sometimes imagine one of our learned fifteen-year-old German boys in company with a fifteen-year-old boy from Eton. The first in his wig, powdered, humble, and tensely anxious to let loose a mass of learning, in all his opinions nothing but an imitation of his papa or his preceptor, a mere reflection. . . . The English boy, his clean, curly hair hanging over his ears and forehead, his face glowing, his hands all scratched, with a cut on each knuckle; Horace, Homer and Virgil are always in his mind; he is definite and original in his opinions, makes a thousand mistakes, but always corrects himself.[36]

By the 1790s, however, the tide was streaming strongly the other way. As a single instance that also involves schoolboys, Coleridge, without even knowing German, proposed in 1796 to have "Robinson, the London bookseller" pay his way to and from

> Jena, a cheap German University where Schiller resides. . . . If I could realize this scheme, I should there study Chemistry & Anatomy, [and] bring over with me all the works of Semler & Michaelis, the German Theologians, & of Kant, the great german Metaphysician. On my return, I would commence a School for 8 young men at 100 guineas each—proposing to *perfect* them in the following studies in order as follows—1. Man as Animal: including the complete knowlege of Anatomy, Chemistry, Mechanics & Optics.—2. Man as an *Intellectual* Being: including the ancient Metaphysics, the systems of Locke & Hartley,—of the Scotch Philosophers—& the new Kantian S[ystem—]3. Man as a Religious Being: including an historic summary of all Religions & the arguments for and against Natural & Revealed Religion.[37]

Less apocalyptic than Coleridge's plan, with its proposed wrestling with Kant and other strong precursors, was a cross-cultural pattern whose special structure makes it the first of the five constellations to which I referred above. These five formations may be called, respectively, *epanados, diadromos, periodos, hyetos,* and *aphycton.* All take their figuration from the anteriority of field; all are parataxes; three of them can be discerned as influence relationships; two of them can be ascribed only to *Zeitgeist* progressions.

The first of these five patternings, *epanados,* is a parataxis whereby a typical but not great work exerts formative influence by repetition. Its effect need not be decisive for any given strong poem, but, itself a product of minimal influences, it contributes significantly to the spirit of the age. A choice illustration from the reversal of current in the 1790s is provided by Gottfried Bürger's *Lenore,* which, as both O. F. Emerson's study of 1915 and Evelyn Jolles's

[36]*Lichtenbergs Aphorismen,* III, 146.
[37]*Collected Letters,* I, 209.

volume of 1974 show, was of unmistakable effect in the deepening
of English Romantic colorations, and probably can be discerned in
some of the emphases of *The Ancient Mariner*, in *Christabel*, and
most specifically in the "woman wailing for her demon lover" of
Kubla Khan.[38] The ballad was, a commentator observes, "the first
real touch of the German romantic movement in England"; remarkably the German tributary to English Romanticism "over-
flowed in five translations and seven versions of Bürger's *Lenore*
during the single year 1796."[39] Bürger's ballad of unholy love is not
a "strong" poem as Bloom uses that term, neither were its first
English translators and revisers, with a single exception, what
Bloom calls "strong precursors" (they were J. T. Stanley, William
Taylor, H. J. Pye, W. R. Spencer, and Walter Scott), but the ballad
and its translations constitute an *epanados* that contributed significantly to characteristic motifs of English Romanticism.

A different though related kind of parataxis of current, *diadromos*, occurs when the effect of an important or "strong" author
or body of work is deflected from its obvious channel and runs
lastingly into that of another country. Perhaps the most immediately familiar example of this phenomenon is Poe's vastly greater
prestige in French culture than in English-speaking culture. Fully
as important, however, even if less well known, is the role of the
Englishman Shaftesbury in the stream of German culture. When
Shaftesbury's *Characteristics* was published in 1711 it was immediately taken up by German intellectuals, and just as Baudelaire's
enthusiasm hurled Poe into the French mainstream, so did the
enormous authority of Leibniz hurl Shaftesbury powerfully into
the eighteenth-century currents that led to German Romanticism.
"I thought I had penetrated deeply into the opinions of our illustrious author," writes Leibniz upon reading the *Characteristics*,

> until I came to the treatise that is unjustly called Rhapsody. Then I
> perceived that I had been in the forechamber only and was now
> entirely surprised to find myself in the . . . sanctuary of the most
> sublime philosophy. . . . The turn of the discourse, the style, the
> dialogue, the neo-Platonism . . . but above all the grandeur and
> beauty of the ideas, their luminous enthusiasm, the apostrophe to
> divinity, ravished me and brought me into a state of ecstasy. At the
> end of the book I finally returned to myself and had leisure to think
> about it. . . . I found in it all of my Theodicy before it saw the light

[38]See Oliver Farrar Emerson, *The Earliest English Translations of Bürger's* Lenore; *A
Study in English and German Romanticism* (Cleveland: Western Reserve University
Press, 1915). See further Evelyn B. Jolles, *G. A. Bürgers Ballade* Lenore *in England*
(Regensburg: Verlag Hans Carl, 1974).
[39]Emerson, pp. 9, 60.

of day. The universe all of a piece, its beauty, its universal harmony,
the disappearance of real evil. . . . It lacked only my preestablished
harmony, my banishment of death, and my reduction of matter or
the multitude to unities or simple substances.[40]

Impelled by this kind of rapturous assessment, the work of
Shaftesbury assumed a central place in the minds of young German intellectuals, especially Herder and Goethe, and many mono-
graphs and specialized articles have detailed the broad course of
the Shaftesburian current in eighteenth-century German thought.
Indeed, Eduard Spranger says at one point in his magisterial
study, *Wilhelm von Humboldt und die Humanitätsidee:* "Here, as so
often, all lines and threads lead back to Shaftesbury, who, without
being a thinker in the strictest sense, sowed seeds on all sides that
sprout up in the metaphysics, ethics, and aesthetics of the eighteenth century. In universality of effect he is like the very great:
Socrates, Kant, or Leibniz."[41]

Such was not at all the case in English culture leading into Romanticism. One well-known scholar even says that Coleridge did
not know Shaftesbury at all. The scholar is in error; but it is certainly true that Shaftesbury does not loom large in English Romanticism.[42] He commanded little enthusiasm among his later English
readers, and the blocking effect of such lack of enthusiasm can be
experienced in Thomas Gray's words as quoted by Dr. Johnson.

> You say you cannot conceive how Lord Shaftesbury came to be a
> philosopher in vogue; I will tell you: first, he was a lord; secondly,
> he was as vain as any of his readers; thirdly, men are very prone to
> believe what they do not understand; fourthly, they will believe any
> thing at all, provided they are under no obligation to believe; fifthly,
> they love to take a new road, even when that road leads no where;
> sixthly, he was reckoned a fine writer, and seems always to mean
> more than he said. Would you have any more reasons? An interval
> of above forty years has pretty well destroyed the charm. A dead
> lord ranks with commoners; vanity is no longer interested in the
> matter; for a new road is become an old one.[43]

A third kind of paratactic figure is formed when the effect of a
cultural stress is deflected into another culture and then returns to
its original one further downstream. This figure we may call *periodos*, and it is well illustrated by A. D. Lindsay's observation. "It is

[40]*Leibniz*, III, 429–30.
[41]Spranger, p. 156.
[42]Thus Wordsworth can point out in 1815 that Shaftesbury is "an author at present unjustly depreciated" (*Prose*, III, 72).
[43]Johnson, III, 432.

a most interesting episode in the international exchange of ideas—how the thought of Locke, that most English of all philosophers, with his supreme commonsense, his acceptance of facts, his toleration and his love of liberty, and along with all this his dislike of working out principles to their logical consequences, fructified in France in clear consistent systems, and came back in its French form to inspire Bentham and his successors." Or, to take our illustration from English and German rather than English and French currents, *periodos* can be illustrated from Hume in Britain to Friedrich Jacobi in Germany, and then from Jacobi in Germany back to Coleridge in Britain. While writing *The Friend* and the *Biographia Literaria*, Coleridge had busied himself with Jacobi's philosophical writings, and at one point in a marginal notation he defends Jacobi's *Glaubensphilosophie* in these words: "This is not a fair Criticism on Jacobi. What was his Object? To prove, that FAITH, which the Philosophers of his Day, held in contempt, was sensuous Evidence? . . . No! But to prove that the sensuous Evidence itself was a species of Faith and Revelation." Coleridge correctly recognized in Jacobi an ally in his attempt to save Christian guarantees of soul from the assault of the Enlightenment, and especially of scoffers like Hume. But Jacobi's argument that faith was necessary to all perception whatever ("das Element aller menschlichen Erkenntnis und Wirksamkeit ist Glaube") was itself, in a notable *periodos*, almost certainly suggested by the analysis of belief in Hume's *Enquiry Concerning Human Understanding* and in his *Treatise of Human Nature*.[44]

The near-certainty is reinforced because Jacobi somewhat later, in 1787, wrote a treatise called *David Hume über den Glauben, oder Idealismus und Realismus,* where he defends his faith-philosophy by enlisting Hume on his side. One of the interlocutors in the dialogue says that he has been reading Hume's essays. The other says, "Against faith, therefore?" and the first one replies unexpectedly, "For faith," whereupon the second interlocutor challenges the first to make him "acquainted with Hume as teacher of faith" (II, 128–29). Hume had specifically been talking of belief, whereas Jacobi uses the ambiguity of *Glaube* in German to change the emphasis to faith, which emphasis was the one taken up by Coleridge. But we are further pointed to Hume as formative for Jacobi's faith-philosophy by a statement of his close friend Hamann to Kant in 1759, which shows how carefully the German literati were heeding the writings of the British philosopher. "The Attic philosopher,

[44]Lindsay, p.v.; Schrickx, pp. 815–16; *Jacobi*, IV:I, 223.

Hume," says Hamann, "needs faith if he is to eat an egg and drink a glass of water."[45]

A fourth pattern of cross-cultural parataxis, which I term *hyetos*, occurs when a theme is widely dispersed in the *Zeitgeist*, without necessarily being connected by overt influences. The Wandering Jew is a prime example. This mythic figure plods through the most diverse Romantic contexts, from *The Monk* by M. G. Lewis to Nikolaus Lenau's heartfelt *Ahasuer, der ewige Jude*. Indeed, though we are not at all surprised to find the Wandering Jew in Shelley and Byron, we are perhaps startled to find that even the least exotic and most tied to daily life of all Romantic poets—I refer of course to Wordsworth—composed in 1800 a poem called *Song for the Wandering Jew*, of which the seventh and last stanza runs

> Day and night my toils redouble,
> Never nearer to the goal;
> Night and day, I feel the trouble
> Of the Wanderer in my soul.

But even more revelatory of the *Zeitgeist* than the *hyetos* of the Wandering Jew is the *hyetos* of Prometheus. Goethe, as we know, returned repeatedly to the myth, and no less a critic than Georg Brandes says of his hymn on this subject that "everything that Spinoza had taught . . . everything that Ludwig Feuerbach later proclaimed is assembled—or anticipated—in this youthful, beautiful, profound poem. A greater poem of rebellion has never been written. It is eternal. Each line is moulded for all time. Each line stands like so many letters of fire in the nocturnal sky of humankind. Few verses that have ever been written on this earth can be compared to it." In a well-known passage in *Dichtung und Wahrheit*, Goethe talks of his near-obsession with the Prometheus myth, and he compares the character of Prometheus with that of Milton's Satan. Remarkably enough, Shelley too makes the same comparison in the preface to his own *Prometheus Unbound*. "The only imaginary being resembling in any degree Prometheus," says Shelley, "is Satan; and Prometheus is, in my judgment, a more poetical character than Satan, because, in addition to courage, and majesty, and firm and patient opposition to omnipotent force, he is susceptible of being described as exempt from the taints of ambition, envy, revenge, and a desire for personal aggrandisement, which, in the Hero of Paradise Lost, interfere with the interest."[46] But where Shelley's sources were Aeschylus and Byron, Goethe's

[45]*Kant*, X, 15.
[46]Brandes, I, 152–53; *Gedenkausgabe*, X, 699–700; *Shelley*, II, 171–72.

were Wieland and Hederich's *Mythologisches Lexikon*. The two great
realizations of the Prometheus myth by major poets in German and
English, though similar in structure and emphasis, had no discernible relationship of cause and effect upon one another.

The hyetic dispersal of the theme of the Wandering Jew has
been documented by George Anderson, and that of Prometheus by
Raymond Trousson.[47] No such documentation exists for the fifth
and concluding paratactic constellation, which I call *aphycton*.
Aphycton exists when the inner logic of an intellectual emphasis
leads to a similar disposition of metaphorical materials even when
no influence is present. It differs from *hyetos* in that the latter relates
to characteristics of the *Zeitgeist* as such—the Wandering Jew to Romantic homelessness and alienation, Prometheus to Romantic rebellion—while *aphycton*, though dispersed in much the same way
as *hyetos*, relates primarily not to a thematic coloring but to a logical
operation. I shall take as a fairly extended example the metaphor of
sand, and I shall begin with a notable collocation in a brief poem by
Blake.

> Mock on Mock on Voltaire Rousseau
> Mock on Mock on 'tis all in vain
> You throw the sand against the wind
> And the wind blows it back again
>
> And every sand becomes a Gem
> Reflected in the beams divine
> Blown back they blind the mocking Eye
> But still in Israels paths they shine
>
> The Atoms of Democritus
> And Newtons Particles of Light
> Are sands upon the Red sea shore
> Where Israels tents do shine so bright[48]

The common experience of a common substance, sand, being
blown back into the face of one who throws it, becomes in Blake's
beautiful progression an experience of gems, and finally an experience of a sacred situation, "the sands upon the Red sea shore."
The sacred sands are conversions of mechanical and lifeless particles, "the Atoms of Democritus / And Newtons Particles of Light,"
which Blake's visionary physics were concerned to refute as inim-
ical to the imaginative life of man.

[47]George Anderson, *The Legend of the Wandering Jew* (Providence, R.I.: Brown
University Press, 1965); Raymond Trousson, *Le Thème de Prométhée dans la littérature
européenne* (Genève: Librairie Droz, 1976), 2 vols.
[48]*Blake*, pp. 468–69.

The wonderful transformation of sand from atoms and particles to gems and sacred ground arises directly from the logical collocation, for Blake, who uses sand frequently in his writings, does not always use it honorifically, as we see, for instance, in his statement that "Abstinence sows sand all over," where sand metaphorically equals desiccation (p. 465). But where sand metaphorically equals irreducible particles or atoms, Blake gives it a vast charge of significance.

> To see a World in a Grain of Sand
> And a Heaven in a Wild Flower
> Hold Infinity in the palm of your hand
> And Eternity in an hour (p.484)

In those lines from *Auguries of Innocence,* Blake presents a complex logical operation as an intuitive poetical surface. His connecting the infinitely small with the infinitely large rests upon the logical fact that infinity cannot be assigned predicates and is therefore identical in all its aspects, and his "Heaven in a Wild Flower" not only sounds like Tennyson's flower in the crannied wall, but also builds on the same logical truth.

The necessity of this logic is aphyctically invoked by Coleridge when he says that "one thought includes all thought, in the sense that a grain of sand includes the universe." Fichte aphyctically expands the same metaphor by the same logic: "In every moment of her duration nature is one connected whole; in every moment each individual part must be what it is, because all the others are what they are; and you could not remove a single grain of sand from its place without thereby, although perhaps imperceptibly to you, changing something throughout all parts of the immeasurable whole." Fichte goes on to argue that "you cannot conceive even the position of a grain of sand other than it is at the present," and after discussion he concludes "that you might never have been at all and all that you have ever done, or ever hope to do, must have been obstructed in order that a grain of sand might lie in a different place."[49]

Fichte's argument about sand metaphorically transliterates an argument in Leibniz about atoms: the smallest body, urges Leibniz, "is affected by all other things in the entire world . . . an effect in the atom must result from all the impressions of the universe and, conversely, the entire state of the universe can be gathered from the atom." And if Blake's connection of sand to world encloses an aphyctic inevitability, so too does the connection of sand

[49]*Table Talk*, p. 315; *Fichte*, II, 274–75.

to the infinitely small and thereby the infinite itself. When Leeuwenhoek reported to the Royal Society his discovery of protozoa,
which he called *"animalcula* or living Atoms," he says that he
judged "that if 100 of them lay by another, they would not equal
the *length* of a grain of course Sand; and according to this estimate,
ten hundred thousand of them could not equal the dimensions of a
grain of such course Sand." Hume finds the invocation of sand
equally inevitable when talking of the infinitely small. " 'Tis therefore certain that the imagination reaches a *minimum.* . . . When
you tell me of the thousandth and ten thousandth part of a grain of
sand . . . the images, which I form in my mind to represent the
things themselves, are nothing different from each other . . . the
idea of a grain of sand is not distinguishable, nor separable into
twenty, much less into a thousand, ten thousand, or an infinite
number of different ideas."[50]

Finally, we may note that the sand topos is a true *aphycton* and
not an influence, for Hegel, in the *Wissenschaft der Logik,* terms a
world in a grain of sand a philosophical tautology, and we can see
that the metaphorical usage arose aphyctically in his mind and not
by way of influence by his using the idiosyncratic but synonymous
Stäubchen—little piece of dust—rather than sand. "A determinate
or finite being," says Hegel, "is such as refers itself to another; it is
a content that stands in a relation of necessity with other content or
with the whole world. In view of the mutually determinant connection of the whole, metaphysics could make the assertion (which
is really a tautology) that if the least grain of dust were destroyed
the whole universe must collapse."[51]

The parataxis of *aphycton,* which casts into relief the constant
renewal of individual discovery within the stream of tradition,
defines one kind of limit for Bloom's radical suppression of poetic
individuality. Despite the acuteness of his insight and the plangency of his formulations, Bloom's system is, not metaphorically but
literally, one of half-truths. Most advancements of our understanding occur incrementally, by holding on to what we already know
and extending its perimeter. Bloom radically varies this procedure
by mortgaging what we already know to lay claim to what we have
not previously seen. The new insights are exciting, but they cannot
join on to prior knowledge to form a whole, because prior knowledge has been denied in order to gain the insight. The resulting
half-truths necessarily occur within a system, for they can be vi-
talized only by reference back to their role in that system, not by
reference to our common experience. A single example should

---

[50]Couturat, p. 522; *Philosophical Transactions* 12 (1677), 828; Hume, p. 27.
[51]*Hegel*, V, 87.

make the contention clear. "Influence, as I conceive it," says Bloom, in one of the formulations that shower like sparks from his pen, "means that there are no *texts*, but only relationships *between* texts."[52] The statement is vulnerable to the same logic by which Marx destroyed Proudhon's "property is theft": the existence of *texts* (or property) must be granted prior to any possibility of relationships *between* texts (or the conception of theft). The new understandings about influence relationships that Bloom proffers us are all too often purchased at the cost of logic and ineluctable experience.

It is precisely this hypothecation of our common sense to new insight that characterizes Bloom's devaluation of individual experience as the basis of poetry. His half-truth is that poems take shape as resonances from earlier poems, and that no one would become a poet were there not prior poets to serve as models. But the other half of the truth, which his system cannot accommodate, is that it is an individual's unique experience that makes him feel like a poet in the first place, and that it is his distillation of that experience that provides him the essence of his poetry. The entire course of Keats's development, poetic, intellectual, emotional, documents this truth, and indeed demonstrates that the uniqueness of individual awareness must always occur and be distilled before there can supervene the phenomena of intra-poetic relationships.[53]

[52]*Misreading*, p. 3.

[53]It was not prior poems, but intensity of experience, that generated the poetic genius of Keats. "Keats was in his glory in the fields!", testifies Haydon. "The humming of the bee, the sight of a flower, the glitter of the sun, seemed to make his nature tremble! his eyes glistened! his cheek flushed! his mouth positively quivered & clentched!" (*Haydon*, II, 316). The unity and intensity of experience that precede and give meaning to the discursive techniques of poetry are signalized by Leibniz, who of all philosophers most unequivocally asserts the fullness and priority of individual knowledge. Even before Locke's essay appeared, Leibniz urged almost mystically that "it is a bad habit we have of thinking as if our souls received certain forms as messengers and as if it had doors and windows. We have all these forms in our own minds, and even from all time, because the mind always expresses all its future thoughts and already thinks confusedly of everything of which it will ever think distinctly. Nothing can be taught us the idea of which is not already in our minds, as the matter out of which this thought is formed. This Plato has excellently recognized when he puts forward his doctrine of reminiscence. . . . Aristotle preferred to compare our souls to tablets that are still blank but upon which there is a place for writing and maintained that there is nothing in our understanding that does not come from the senses. This conforms more with popular notions, as Aristotle usually does, while Plato goes deeper" (*Leibniz*, IV, 451–52). Compare Proclus: "According to the tradition, the Pythagoreans recognized that everything we call learning is remembering, not something placed in the mind from without, like the images of sense pictured in the imagination, nor transitory, like the judgments of opinion. Though awakened by sense-perception, learning has its source within us, in our understanding's attending to itself. They realized too that, although evidences of such memories can be cited from many areas, it is especially from mathematics that they come, as Plato also remarks" (*Proclus*, p. 37).

Yet Bloom often speaks as though poems were generated solely from other poems, rather than from personal, monadic experience.[54] On the contrary, though it may have been the reading of earlier poems that made Wordsworth write verses, it was his personal experience of the orange sky of evening that made him a great poet. Moreover, "every great poet," as John Stuart Mill insists, "has had his mind full of thoughts, derived not merely from passive sensibility, but from trains of reflection, from observation, analysis, and generalization." This monadic fullness, urges Mill, actually works against the flow of tradition. It makes no difference, he says, that something was known by others before one was born. "The question is, how is *he* to know it. There is one way; and nobody has ever hit upon more than one—by *discovery.*" Monadic experience, even more than the influence of strong precursors, generates the content of great poetry. "Each person's own reason must work upon the materials afforded by that same person's own experience," says Mill. "Knowledge comes only from within."[55]

So the full truth is a tension of opposites. There is tradition, and tradition is extraordinarily important; but there is also such a reality as individual talent. Even after all respect is paid to the power and ingenuity of Bloom's conception of poetry's genesis and development, a truer accounting of cultural process would seem to be that rendered by Herder, who observes that two principles underlie intellectual history. "They are *tradition* and *organic powers.* All education arises from imitation and exercise, by means of which the model passes into the copy. What better word is there for this transmission than *tradition?* But the imitator must have powers to receive and convert into his own nature what has been transmitted to him, just like the food he eats. Accordingly, what and how much he receives, where he derives it from, and how he applies it to his own use are determined by his own receptive powers." Herder's specification of personal "receptive powers" refers to an individual's placement in cultural history; Mill's specification of personal "discovery" refers to his unique selfhood. Their combined weight rests in the scales against Bloom. Eloquence, says Mill in a famous distinction, is designed to be heard; poetry, on the contrary, can only be "*over*heard." "Poetry," he urges, "is feeling confessing itself to itself in moments of solitude." "All poetry is of the nature of soliloquy."[56] For the poet, in the lyric instant, is

[54]E.g., "Every poem we know begins as an encounter *between poems*" (*Misreading*, p. 70). "Poetry is poems speaking to a poem, and is also that poem answering back with its own defensive discourse" (*Kabbalah*, p. 108).

[55]*Mill*, I, 413, 330, 332.

[56]Herder, *Ideen*, I, 337; *Mill*, I, 348, 349.

addressing neither us nor other poets; he is speaking to himself alone, in an utterance that participates in the structure of rumination. And what is lastingly valuable in that utterance arises from the depths of his own life and his awareness of the real world in which he lives, moves, and has his being.

· 3 ·

The Best Philosopher

*T*hough *"originality" is treasured as* an emblem of individuality, it can hardly claim any other reality. Paradoxical at best, its status has been further eroded by the influence theories of Bloom, which themselves, if the contentions of the preceding chapter are accepted, can be supplemented readily by demonstrations of other kinds of precedence.

To those formally identified, moreover, such as Bloom's six revisionary ratios or the five cross-cultural forms of influence just propounded, can be added many that either fall as single instances outside such forms or have not yet been arranged into new categories. In Romanticism itself, with its extraordinary emphasis on originality, and even in the deepest, most powerful, and most characteristic works of individual Romantic authors, the equivocal nature of originality, along with other permutations of the creative impulse, reveal themselves in any analytical examination.

Take Wordsworth's "Immortality Ode" as object of such examination. The poem stands in the acknowledged forefront of all his endeavor; in my own judgment, indeed, it constitutes, along with the first two books of "The Prelude," "Tintern Abbey," "The Ruined Cottage," and "Michael," one of the five ultimate poetic statements by the greatest poet of the nineteenth century. Strangely enough, however, the "Immortality Ode" has bothered critics in a way that its closest counterpart, "Tintern Abbey," has not. The murmuring cadences of the limpid blank verse of "Tintern Abbey" here give way to a venturesome and chance-taking alternation of long and short lives, all as part of the rough-hewn effect that an ode provides and that was cherished by Romantic poets in much the same way that untamed nature was preferred to the formal gardens of the eighteenth century. If one stands at Rydal Hall near Ambleside, the view from the terrace is of mountains and fields and water in picturesque symmetry. If one moves a few score yards over to Rydal Mount, the view loses all such symmetry and instead provides a wild and irregular prospect that makes the earlier vista seem insipid.

Such too was the aspiration of the odal form. But in attaining his irregular and natural effect in the "Immortality Ode," Wordsworth skirted and sometimes crossed the boundary of the ineffective and the banal, especially in some of his shorter lines. We cringe at the "six years' Darling of a pigmy size"; we wince at "The little Actor cons another part." "The Pansy at my feet" seems incongruous; the rhyme of "hither" and "thither" seems impoverished in the lines that run "Which brought us hither / Can in a moment travel thither."

An interesting aspect of the rhyme of "hither" and "thither" is that it occurs in the very center of one of the three or four greatest passages Wordsworth ever wrote.

> Hence in a season of calm weather
> Though inland far we be,
> Our souls have sight of that immortal sea
> Which brought us hither,
> Can in a moment travel thither,
> And see the Children sport upon the shore,
> And hear the mighty waters rolling ever more.[1]

The onomatopoetic splendor of the cadence here, and the thalassic depths of primal experience sounded by the images, authenticate the lines as one of the touchstones of world poetry. But still there is the briskly banal "hither" and "thither."

Such dead spots occur frequently in Wordsworth, and in fact they often occur precisely in his greatest moments, as though there is some unconscious blocking agent at work in the movement of his verse, an unconscious reluctance to allow the ultimate to happen.[2] An example of this that every Wordsworthian notices sooner or later is the frequency with which he interrupts great currents of statement with parenthetical expressions. For a single example, consider the passage in "Tintern Abbey" that runs this way:

> Though changed, no doubt, from what I was when first
> I came among these hills; when like a roe

[1]Wordsworth, *Poems*, IV, 284.

[2]Curiously enough, these blocking moments or dead spots, though they sometimes occur in proximity to passages that might be termed sublime, do not seem to relate to Kant's requirement for "the feeling of the sublime," that it be "brought about by the feeling of a momentary check ("das Gefühl einer augenblicklichen Hemmung") to the vital forces followed at once by a discharge all the more powerful." (*Kant*, V, 245). See further Neil Hertz, "The Notion of Blockage in the Literature of the Sublime," in *Psychoanalysis and the Question of the Text; Selected Papers from the English Institute, 1976–77*, ed. Geoffrey H. Hartman (Baltimore: The Johns Hopkins University Press, 1978), pp. 62–85.

> I bounded o'er the mountains, by the sides
> Of the deep rivers, and the lonely streams,
> Wherever nature led: more like a man
> Flying from something that he dreads than one
> Who sought the thing he loved. For nature then
> (The coarser pleasures of my boyish days,
> And their glad animal movements all gone by)
> To me was all in all.—I cannot paint
> What then I was. The sounding cataract
> Haunted me like a passion: the tall rock,
> The mountain, and the deep and gloomy wood,
> Their colours and their forms, were then to me
> An appetite; a feeling and a love,
> That had no need of a remoter charm,
> By thought supplied, nor any interest
> Unborrowed from the eye.—That time is past,
> And all its aching joys are now no more,
> And all its dizzy raptures.[3]

I have quoted the passage with some fullness in order to recall to our minds that it constitutes another of Wordsworth's supreme poetic testaments. And yet right in its middle is the blocking and distracting statement, set off in parentheses, "The coarser pleasures of my boyish days, / And their glad animal movements all gone by." What he should have written was "For nature then / To me was all in all.—I cannot paint / What then I was." Indeed, when reading these lines aloud, one may sustain their current by simply skipping the parenthetical statement. It would be hard to imagine a statement more intrusive and less welcome than the parenthetical assurance, which is a choice illustration of what Coleridge termed one of the "characteristic defects" of Wordsworth's poetry, that is, "an *anxiety* of explanation and retrospect."[4]

A different kind of example of Wordsworth's unconscious penning back of the flow of ultimate emotion is supplied by his reaction to Mont Blanc and the crest of the Alps. For Romantics in general mountains tended to excite apocalyptic realizations, as Wordsworth had already shown by his early lines on the climbing of Mount Snowdon, which he eventually inserted into the last book of "The Prelude."[5] Mont Blanc, as the greatest of the Euro-

[3]Wordsworth, *Poems*, II, 261.

[4]*Biographia*, II, 129.

[5]For the remarkable change by which an endemic dislike of mountains began to be replaced in the eighteenth century by rapture see the standard work by Marjorie Nicolson, *Mountain Gloom and Mountain Glory; The Development of the Aesthetics of the Infinite* (Ithaca, N.Y.: Cornell University Press, 1959). See also *Romanticism and Consciousness: Essays in Criticism*, ed. Harold Bloom (New York: W. W. Norton & Co., 1970), pp. 62–63.

pean mountains, was particularly likely to arouse apocalyptic awareness, as we can see, for instance, in Shelley's awed report to Peacock.

> Pinnacles of snow, intolerably bright, part of the chain connected with Mont Blanc shone thro the clouds at intervals on high. I never knew I never imagined what mountains were before. The immensity of these aerial summits excited, when they suddenly burst upon the sight, a sentiment of extatic wonder, not unallied to madness. . . . This vast mass of ice has one general progress which ceases neither day nor night. It breaks & rises forever; its undulations sink whilst others rise. From the precipices which surround it the echo of rocks which fall from their aerial summits, or of the ice & snow scarcely ceases for one moment. One would think that Mont Blanc was a living being & that the frozen blood forever circulated slowly thro' his stony veins.[6]

The awe conveyed by Shelley's prose is also conveyed by his great poem on that same mountain:

> Far, far above, piercing the infinite sky,
> Mont Blanc appears,—still, snowy, and serene—
> Its subject mountains their unearthly forms
> Pile around it, ice and rock; broad vales between
> Of frozen floods, unfathomable deeps, . . .
>   . . . Below, vast caves
> Shine in the rushing torrents' restless gleam, . . .
> Mont Blanc yet gleams on high:—the power is there—
>   . . . The secret Strength of things
> Which governs thought, and to the infinite dome
> Of Heaven is as a law, inhabits thee![7]

And yet Wordsworth, faced by that same stupendous mountain, and with the ascent of Snowdon already behind him, hails Mont Blanc not with awe but with its opposite; and his disappointment constitutes a notable blocking dead spot:

>   That very day,
> From a bare ridge we also first beheld
> Unveiled the summit of Mont Blanc, and grieved
> To have a soulless image on the eye
> That had usurped upon a living thought
> That never more could be. . . .[8]

Shortly further on, he again declines a natural invitation to apocalypse, and his description of the crossing of the crest of the Alps is a sort of absolute in anticlimax:

[6]Shelley, *Letters*, I, 497, 500.
[7]*Shelley*, I, 230–33.
[8]*Prelude*, VI, 523–28 (p. 235).

> . . . our future course, all plain to sight,
> Was downwards, with the current of that stream.
> Loth to believe what we so grieved to hear,
> For still we had hopes that pointed to the clouds,
> We questioned him again, and yet again;
> But every word that from the peasant's lips
> Came in reply, translated by our feelings,
> Ended in this,—*that we had crossed the Alps.*
>   (VI, 584–91)

It is not until the ultimate moment has passed, when he is descending on the other side, that Wordsworth can unloose the images of apocalypse inherent in the confrontation of the mountains. When he does so, we realize that we again confront a supreme moment in a context of blockage, for his downhill passage transcends even the apprehensions of Shelley's great poem. "The immeasurable height / Of woods decaying, never to be decayed," writes Wordsworth in soul-shaking evocation,

> The stationary blasts of waterfalls,
> And in the narrow rent at every turn
> Winds thwarting winds, bewildered and forlorn,
> The torrents shooting from the clear blue sky,
> The rocks that muttered close upon our ears,
> Black drizzling crags that spake by the wayside
> As if a voice were in them, the sick sight
> And giddy prospect of the raving stream,
> The unfettered clouds and region of the Heavens,
> Tumult and peace, the darkness and the light—
> Were all like workings of one mind, the features
> Of the same face, blossoms upon one tree;
> Characters of the great Apocalypse,
> The types and symbols of Eternity,
> Of first, and last, and midst, and without end.
>   (VI, 626–40)

Wordsworth's screening of the ultimate intrudes in a different form in a fourth of his supreme statements. There are some lines in the twelfth book of the 1850 "Prelude" that I believe I should have to put forward if some higher power asked me to select one and only one passage that summed up all Wordsworth was and aspired to be. The other passages are touchstones of world poetry, but this one, I think, is the *ne plus ultra:*

> Oh! mystery of man, from what a depth
> Proceed thy honours. I am lost, but see
> In simple childhood something of the base

> On which thy greatness stands; but this I feel,
> That from thyself it comes, that thou must give,
> Else never canst receive. The days gone by
> Return upon me almost from the dawn
> Of life: the hiding-places of man's power
> Open; I would approach them, but they close.
> I see by glimpses now; when age comes on,
> May scarcely see at all; and I would give,
> While yet we may, as far as words can give,
> Substance and life to what I feel, enshrining,
> Such is my hope, the spirit of the Past
> For future restoration. . . .
>   (VI, 272–86)

And yet right in the middle of this great Wordsworthian current there occurs a statement that constitutes an anxiety of explanation and a block to the current. I refer to the statement that "this I feel, / That from thyself it comes, that thou must give, / Else never canst receive." Actually, this assurance forms an incoherence in the larger statement. Peruse it again. If we leave out the anxious explanation, the meaning flows more naturally; indeed, the passage dovetails beautifully.

>   . . . I am lost, but see
> In simple childhood something of the base
> On which thy greatness stands. . . . The days gone by
> Return upon me almost from the dawn
> Of life: the hiding-places of man's power
> Open. . . .

Not only does the anxious explanation about giving to receive constitute an incoherence in the passage as it stands, but the sentiment it contains is so anomalous in relation to what Wordsworth says in his profoundest moments in other parts of his poetic production that one is tempted to respond to his assurance that "this I feel" with the retort, "I beg your pardon, sir, but you feel nothing of the sort, as is amply attested by other statements you have made." Far from feeling that "from thyself it comes, that thou must give, / Else never canst receive," what Wordsworth instinctively felt was that one should "Let Nature be your Teacher," that

> One impulse from a vernal wood
> May teach you more of man,
> Of moral evil and of good,
> Than all the sages can,

that

. . . there are Powers
Which of themselves our minds impress;
That we can feed this mind of ours
In a wise passiveness.[9]

To be sure, these testimonies to wise passiveness occur here in near doggerel verse, but they are elsewhere repeated again and again, in different contexts, some of which are very great poetic moments.

A child, I held unconscious intercourse
With the eternal beauty, drinking in
A pure organic pleasure from the lines
Of curling mist, or from the level plain
Of waters colour'd by the steady clouds.[10]

Again:

From Nature and her overflowing soul
I had received so much, that all my thoughts
Were steeped in feeling; I was only then
Contented, when with bliss ineffable
I felt the sentiment of Being spread
O'er all that moves and all that seemeth still;
    (II, 416–21)

And again:

Thus deeply drinking-in the soul of things,
We shall be wise perforce;[11]

And again:

Far and wide the clouds were touched,
And in their silent faces could he read
Unutterable love. Sound needed none,
Nor any voice of joy; his spirit drank
The spectacle: sensation, soul, and form,
All melted into him; they swallowed up
His animal being; in them did he live,
And by them did he live; they were his life.
    (V, 15)

And still again:

I was as wakeful, even, as waters are
To the sky's motion; in a kindred sense
Of passion, was obedient as a lute
That waits upon the touches of the wind.[12]

[9]Wordsworth, *Poems*, IV, 57, 56.
[10]*Prelude*, 1805 version, I, 589–93 (p. 66).
[11]Wordsworth, *Poems*, V, 149.
[12]*Prelude*, 1805 version, III, 135–38 (p. 108).

If it was not from his own instinctive feelings that Wordsworth found his formula that "from thy self it comes, that thou must give, / Else never canst receive," where then did he find it? The answer is clear: he found it in Coleridge, who in 1802 had specifically rebuked Wordsworth for "wise passiveness."

> I may not hope from outward Forms to win
> The Passion & the Life, whose Fountains are within.
>
> O Wordsworth! we receive but what we give,
> And in our Life alone does Nature live:[13]

This view, indeed, as stated in Coleridge's "Dejection: An Ode," is as irreducible a component of Coleridge's view of the world as "wise passiveness" is for that of Wordsworth. Thus in 1807, in his poem "To William Wordsworth," Coleridge said that Wordsworth's "moments awful, / Now in thy inner life, and now abroad" were actually moments

> When power streamed from thee, and thy soul received
> The light reflected, as a light bestowed.[14]

Again, it was "not from any external impulses, not from any agencies that can be sought for" that human life and meaning derived; for to Coleridge "man comes from within, and all that is truly human must proceed from within." "That which we find in ourselves is . . . the substance and the life of *all* our knowledge. Without this latent presence of the 'I am,' all modes of existence in the external world would flit before us as colored shadows." To his philosophical collaborator, J. H. Green, Coleridge said in 1829, "We behold our own light reflected from the object as light bestowed *by* it."[15] In short, in his formula that says "that from thyself it comes, that thou must give, / Else never canst receive," Wordsworth not only blocks the poetic flow of his ultimate statement, but also introjects an alien element of thought into his most typical utterance.

That it is alien, however, paradoxically for Wordsworth means that in a sense it is typical. Take, for instance, a very minor example later in the same ultimate passage:

> I see by glimpses now; when age comes on,
> May scarcely see at all; and I would give,
> While yet we may, as far as words can give,
> Substance and life to what I feel. . .

---

[13]*Collected Letters*, II, 817.
[14]Coleridge, *Poems*, I, 404, 405.
[15]*Philosophical Lectures*, p. 226; *Lay Sermons*, p. 78; *Collected Letters*, VI, 813.

The *we* is alien to the discourse: it is *I* who see by glimpses; it is *I* who would give substance and life by words, and it is *I* who feel; so where does the *we* come from? "I would give, while yet we may," is not even good grammar in that *we* has no antecedent, specific or implied.

The same kind of alien grammatical element is introduced into the great pantheistic passage in "Tintern Abbey." The presence that disturbs the poet with the joy of elevated thoughts, the something far more deeply interfused, does not have its dwelling *in* the light of setting suns but *is* that light:

> . . . a sense sublime
> Of something far more deeply interfused,
> Whose dwelling is the light of setting suns,
> And the round ocean and the living air,
> And the blue sky, and in the mind of man[16]

Had the dwelling been *in* the setting sun, *in* the round ocean, *in* the living air, *in* the blue sky, then it would also be fitting to have it *in* the mind of man. But Wordsworth has deliberately set up a current of expectation that dispenses with *in*, which is not only alien but more banal than the statements without the preposition.

I have been at some pains to establish the variety and pervasiveness of Wordsworth's tendency to introduce blocking elements into the flow of his greatest passages because this characteristic is more prevalent in the "Immortality Ode" than in any other of his major statements. Indeed, it may be that its prevalence, though not noticed by critics, is the common factor in the widespread and usually unspecified or misspecified discontent that inheres in so much of the commentary to the poem. It is interesting to realize how various the statements of this discontent have been. Thus Arnold observes restively that the ode is "not wholly free from something declamatory." A. C. Bradley notes of Wordsworth that "where his metrical form is irregular his ear is uncertain. The Immortality Ode, like *King Lear*, is its author's greatest product, but not his best piece of work." Still again, Trilling comments that "the Ode is not wholly perspicuous. . . . The difficulty does not lie in the diction, which is simple, or even in the syntax, which is sometimes obscure, but rather in certain contradictory statements which the poem makes, and in the ambiguity of some of its crucial words." Fiercer critics speak more fiercely. "Ode: Intimations of Immortality is loosely associational in method," says Yvor Winters contemptuously: "Wordsworth gives us

16Wordsworth, *Poems*, II, 262.

bad oratory about his own clumsy emotions and a landscape that he has never really perceived." Leavis, again, charges the poem with "empty grandiosity" and "general factitiousness," and with "falsity" and "rhythmic vulgarity." More specific is Coleridge's comment on the lines in stanza 8, "Thou, over whom thy immortality / Broods like the day, a master o'er the slave," where he says that "without examining the propriety of making a 'master *brood* o'er a slave,' or the *day* brood *at all*; we will merely ask, what does all this mean?"[17]

If we think of the "Immortality Ode" in comparison to its counterpart, "Tintern Abbey," which in a sense is the same poem written from a different perspective, we see that the greater anxiety apparent in the "Immortality Ode" seems to stem from two sources: the first, which we have already noted, and which Bradley notes also, is that the irregular stanzaic form of the "Immortality Ode" does not allow Wordsworth so much control as does the limpid blank verse of "Tintern Abbey." The second is that the Platonic framework adopted in the "Immortality Ode," no doubt under the influence of Coleridge, is an alien element in Wordsworth's own experience of reality and tends to displace nature from its primary position in the poem. Though both poems dwell on nature and on childhood, and though both present strategies for coping with Wordsworth's characteristic fear of loss of being in the progression from childhood to adulthood and adulthood to old age, the adoption in the "Immortality Ode" of the Platonic fiction of the lapse of the soul from a prior existence tends to relegate the nurturing function of nature to a secondary role. In "Tintern Abbey," nature is

> The anchor of my purest thoughts, the nurse,
> The guide, the guardian of my heart, and soul
> Of all my moral being,

whereas in the "Immortality Ode" that function is seriously adulterated:

> The homely Nurse doth all she can
> To make her Foster-child, her Inmate Man,
> Forget the glories he hath known,
> And that imperial palace whence he came.[18]

Still another of the differences between "Tintern Abbey" and the "Immortality Ode" resides in the progression of emotion. In

---

[17]Arnold, *Essays*, p. 159; Bradley, p. 117; Trilling, p. 130; Winters, pp. 171–72; Leavis, *Revaluation*, pp. 184–85; *Biographia*, II, 138.
[18]Wordsworth, *Poems*, IV, 281.

"Tintern Abbey," the poem is somewhat restless and uncertain at its beginning, settles down to a broad and deep current of Wordsworthian certainty, and concludes, with the benediction to Dorothy, in some of the most pure and limpid verse Wordsworth ever wrote.

> Therefore let the moon
> Shine on thee in thy solitary walk;
> And let the misty mountain-winds be free
> To blow against thee . . .
> . . . .
>   . . . Nor, perchance—
> If I should be where I no more can hear
> Thy voice, nor catch from thy wild eyes these gleams
> Of past existence—wilt thou then forget
> That on the banks of this delightful stream
> We stood together; and that I, so long
> A worshipper of Nature, hither came
> Unwearied in that service: rather say
> With warmer love—oh! with far deeper zeal
> Of holier love. Nor wilt thou then forget,
> That after many wanderings, many years
> Of absence, these steep woods and lofty cliffs,
> And this green pastoral landscape, were to me
> More dear, both for themselves and for thy sake!
>   (II, 263)

In the "Immortality Ode" the progression is reversed. The poem begins quietly—"There was a time"—but encounters increasingly choppy waters. It begins again, quite unmistakably, at stanza 5, with the great statement about the lapse of the soul:

> Our birth is but a sleep and a forgetting:
> The Soul that rises with us, our life's Star
>   Hath had elsewhere its setting,
>   And cometh from afar:
>   Not in entire forgetfulness,
>   And not in utter nakedness,
> But trailing clouds of glory do we come
>   From God, who is our home:
> Heaven lies about us in our infancy!
>   (IV, 281)

Though these lines and the remainder of the stanza are supremely successful poetry, turgidity and incoherence again begin to characterize the poem's movement, especially in stanzas 7, 8, 9, and the concluding stanza, stanza 11. Stanza 10, in fact, seems to attempt to clear the movement by recapitulating the entirety of"Tintern Abbey's" survey of childhood, adulthood, and youth, with the loss of childhood's being, as in the earlier poem, compensated by a greater sense of human community, and with old age compensated by a more philosophical understanding of the human situation.

What though the radiance which was once so bright
Be now for ever taken from my sight,
   Though nothing can bring back the hour
Of splendour in the grass, of glory in the flower;
    We will grieve not, rather find
    Strength in what remains behind;
    In the primal sympathy
    Which having been must ever be;
    In the soothing thoughts that spring
    Out of human suffering;
    In the faith that looks through death,
In years that bring the philosophic mind.
   (IV, 284)

The passage is a duplicate in microcosm of "Tintern Abbey." The poet will here, "grieve not, rather find / Strength in what remains behind," which restates the transition in "Tintern Abbey" from the aching joys and dizzy raptures of childhood, which are no more, to the "abundant recompense" of human community.

          . . . Not for this
Faint I, nor mourn nor murmur; other gifts
Have followed; for such loss, I would believe,
Abundant recompense. For I have learned
To look on nature, not as in the hour
Of thoughtless youth; but hearing oftentimes
The still, sad music of humanity,
   (II, 261)

The "years that bring the philosophic mind" of the "Immortality Ode's" tenth stanza correspond to the "after years" of "Tintern Abbey," when the "mind / Shall be a mansion for all lovely forms," and the memory "a dwelling-place / For all sweet sounds and harmonies."

If stanza 10 recapitulates the statement of "Tintern Abbey," however, stanzas 7, 8, 9, and 11 go on their own track. The calmness of the close of "Tintern Abbey" rests, as I have suggested, upon its blank verse cadence, and also upon its security in the idea that "Nature never did betray / The heart that loved her," and upon the soothing presence of Dorothy. None of these factors is present in the "Immortality Ode," and as a consequence Wordsworth must cope with his customary dread of the loss of being in time's process by another means. He does so by flooding the poem with the philosophy of joy. It is this process of flooding that results in the deep emotional power of the final stanzas, but it is also this flooding that introduces turgidity and incoherence.

A prime illustration is stanza 9, which in the course of its statement wins through to the supreme lines about the immortal sea with the children sporting on the shore, but wins through only after being almost swamped by turgidity and incoherence. The stanza begins this way:

> O joy! that in our embers
> Is something that doth live,
> That nature yet remembers
> What was so fugitive!
> The thought of our past years in me doth breed
> Perpetual benediction: not indeed
> For that which is most worthy to be blest;
> Delight and liberty, the simple creed
> Of Childhood, whether busy or at rest,
> With new-fledged hope still fluttering in his breast:
> (IV, 283)

The specification "whether busy or at rest" is pointless; it merely serves to fill the line in the same way that the redundant "late and soon" fills the line in "The world is too much with us; late and soon, / Getting and spending we lay waste our powers" (III,18)— which would mean quite the same if the poet simply said: "The world is too much with us, / Getting and spending we lay waste our powers."

Another kind of turgidity arises from the statement that "The thought of our past years in me doth breed / Perpetual benediction," which not only does not follow from the preceding statement but indeed more or less cancels its necessity. The preceding statement itself seems almost a paradigm for the Freudian mechanism of denial. To find the flame of life replaced by embers calls for gloom, not joy. The poem has moved bleakly enough from the idea that "Heaven lies about us in our infancy" to the idea that "Shades of the prison-house begin to close / Upon the growing Boy," from the idea that though the boy still beholds the light, "At length the Man perceives it die away, / And fade into the light of common day." The logical burden of the poem, therefore, is depression at this loss of being, at the haunted sense that "The things which I have seen I now can see no more," at the certain knowledge "That there hath past away a glory from the earth."

The bleaker the present and future situation, however, the more Wordsworth floods it with the philosophy of joy, and this kind of emotional drenching reaches inundating levels in the concluding stanza, where both great emotional power and absolute incoherence obtain. To say, as Wordsworth does in the last stanza,

> I love the Brooks which down their channels fret,
> Even more than when I tripped lightly as they

is quite simply an impossibility in terms of the profound and repeated statements at the beginning of the poem. The enormously powerful lines that conclude the Ode are a kind of absolute in their disconnectedness and incoherence.

> Another race hath been, and other palms are won.
> Thanks to the human heart by which we live,
> Thanks to its tenderness, its joys, and fears,
> To me the meanest flower that blows can give
> Thoughts that do often lie too deep for tears.
>   (IV, 285)

Our comment to such lines can be to repeat the question Coleridge asked about another collocation in the same poem: "What does all this mean?"

If Wordsworth must embark on the ultimate testimony of the "Immortality Ode" without the support of blank verse, of nature as primary benefactor, and of Dorothy as human companion ministering to him through the succession of the years, a fourth bulwark of Wordsworthian security, which is extensively present in the poem, must thereby accept a hugely augmented burden. I refer to the simple creed of childhood. In response to the greater demands placed upon it here, childhood is raised to the ideological formulation by which the child is termed "best Philosopher." "Thou," says Wordsworth to the child,

> whose exterior semblance doth belie
>   Thy Soul's immensity;
> Thou best Philosopher, who yet dost keep
> Thy heritage, thou Eye among the blind,
> That, deaf and silent, read'st the eternal deep,
> Haunted for ever by the eternal mind,—
>   Mighty Prophet! Seer blest!
>   On whom those truths do rest,
> Which we are toiling all our lives to find,
> In darkness lost, the darkness of the grave;
>   (IV, 282)

It is the idea of the child as "best Philosopher" that constitutes the most idiosyncratic emphasis of the "Immortality Ode," just as the idea of the poet as "worshipper of Nature" constitutes that of"Tintern Abbey."

To be sure, Wordsworth paid a price for the augmented emphasis in each case. The fervent confession, "that I, so long / A worshipper of Nature, higher came / Unwearied in that service," which seems so right in the context of "Tintern Abbey," caused him considerable embarrassment later. As he writes in 1815, after a reader had criticized the expression as pantheistic and anti-Christian: "I have alluded to the Ladys errors of opinion—she talks of my being a worshipper of Nature—a passionate expression uttered incautiously in the Poem upon the Wye had led her into this mistake, she reading in cold-heartedness and substituting the letter for the spirit. . . . She condemns me for not distinguishing between nature as the work of God and God himself. But where does she find this doctrine inculcated? Where does she gather that the Author of the Excursion looks upon nature and God as the same?" As Wordsworth's need for the sustenance of nature causes him to escalate his statement in the one instance to "worshipper of Nature," so his great emphasis on childhood in the "Immortality Ode" in that instance escalates the simple creed of childhood to the nomination of the child as "best Philosopher."

But here too Wordsworth encounters criticism. Arnold says, "the idea of the high instincts and affections coming out in childhood, testifying of a divine home recently left, and fading away as our life proceeds,—this idea, of undeniable beauty as a play of fancy, has itself not the character of poetic truth of the best kind; it has no real solidity." Arnold, whose own childhood was not particularly happy, is rather bothered by Wordsworth's apotheosis of that state and returns to attack it worriedly. "In general we may say of these high instincts of early childhood, the base of the alleged systematic philosophy of Wordsworth, what Thucydides says of the early achievements of the Greek race: 'It is impossible to speak with certainty of what is so remote; but from all that we can really investigate, I should say that they were no very great things.' "[19]

Coleridge, too, whose childhood was even less happy than Arnold's, is bothered by the idea of the child as "best Philosopher." "In what sense is a child of that age a *philosopher?*," asks Coleridge,

In what sense does he *read* 'the eternal deep?' In what sense is he declared to be *'for ever haunted'* by the Supreme Being? or so inspired

[19]*Middle Years*, II, 188; Arnold, *Essays*, pp. 151–52.

as to deserve the splendid titles of a *mighty prophet*, a *blessed seer?* By reflection? by knowledge? by conscious intuition? or by *any* form or modification of consciousness? These would be tidings indeed; but such as would pre-suppose an immediate revelation to the inspired communicator, and require miracles to authenticate his inspiration. Children at this age give us no such information of themselves; and at what time were we dipped in the Lethe, which has produced such utter oblivion of a state so godlike? There are many of us that still possess some remembrances, more or less distinct, respecting themselves at six years old; pity that the worthless straws only should float, while treasures, compared with which all the mines of Golconda and Mexico were but straws, should be absorbed by some unknown gulf into some unknown abyss.[20]

Coleridge is so irked by the child as "best Philosopher" that even after this lengthy repudiation he is not satisfied. After a digression he returns to the attack. "In what sense can the magnificent attributes, above quoted, be appropriated to a *child*, which would not make them equally suitable to a *bee*, or a *dog*, or a *field of corn.* . . . The omnipresent Spirit works equally in *them*, as in the child; and the child is equally unconscious of it as they" (II, 140).

But if ever passages cried out for Derridean deconstruction, these passages from Coleridge do so; they are a choice example, in the great critic, of the blindness that in Paul de Man's words frequently accompanies insight. For where Coleridge seems to be, and indeed undoubtedly is, dissociating himself unequivocally from the idea that a child can be a philosopher, the ironic truth is that Wordsworth almost certainly has as his model for the "best Philosopher" Coleridge's own son Hartley. Charles Lamb, for instance refers to Hartley in 1797 as "the small philosopher, the minute philosopher" and from 1797 to 1800 repeatedly referred to him as "the young philosopher" and as the "Philosopher."[21] The irony is drawn still finer by the fact that Coleridge himself seems to have referred to his son Hartley as a philosopher, and did so in terms that answered all the questions he himself raised against Wordsworth's passage. Thus on 8 August 1811, Henry Crabb Robinson records in his diary that

Coleridge . . . related some curious anecdotes of his son Hartley, whom he represented as a most remarkable child—a deep thinker in his infancy; one who tormented himself in his attempts to solve the problems that would equally torment the full-grown man. . . . Hartley, when about five, was asked a question by someone con-

[20]*Biographia*, II, 138–39.
[21]*Lamb*, I, 105, 114, 221, 180.

cerning himself calling him "Hartley." "Which Hartley?" asked the
boy. "Why, is there more than one Hartley?" "Yes," he replied,
"there is a deal of Hartleys." "How so?" "There's Picture Hartley"
(Hazlitt had painted a portrait of him) "and Shadow Hartley, and
there's Echo Hartley, and there's Catch-me-fast Hartley," at the same
time seizing his own arm with the other hand very eagerly, an action
which shows that his mind must have been drawn to reflect on what
Kant calls the great and inexplicable mystery, viz. that man should
be both his own subject and object, and that these should yet be
one. At the same early age, says Coleridge, he used to be in an
agony of thought, puzzling himself about the reality of existence.[22]

Though Crabb Robinson's conversation was recorded in 1811, its
substance was being circulated by Coleridge well before the composition of the "Immortality Ode" in 1802. On Monday 9 February
1801, for instance, Coleridge writes to Dorothy Wordsworth:

> I had a very long conversation with Hartley about Life, Reality,
> Pictures, & Thinking, this evening. He sate on my knee for half an
> hour at least, & was exceedingly serious. . . . He pointed out
> without difficulty that there might be five Hartleys, Real Hartley,
> Shadow Hartley, Picture Hartley, Looking Glass Hartley, and Echo
> Hartley. . . . To morrow I am to exert my genius in making a paper-
> balloon / the idea of carrying up a bit of lighted Candle into the
> clouds makes him almost insane with Pleasure. As I have given you
> Hartley's Metaphysics I will now give you a literal translation of
> page 49 of the celebrated Fichte's Uber den Begriff der
> Wissenschaftslehre.[23]

So it was Coleridge himself who spoke of "Hartley's Metaphysics"
and thereby licensed the child as "best Philosopher."

In truth, Coleridge seemed almost obsessive on this issue. To
Sara Hutchinson in July 1802 he comments: "Dear Hartley—!—I
picked up a parcel of old Books at Wilkinson's which he gave me /
among them is an old System of Philosophy by some FANTASTIC or
other, with a large Print of Sun, Moon, & Stars, Birds, Beasts, &
Fishes—with Adam & Eve, rising out of a Chaos! . . . I asked
Hartley what he thought of it—& he said— . . . '*very* curious! A
Sea not in a World, but a World rising out of a Sea!' (these were his
own umprompted [*sic*] words, & entirely his own idea). . . . This
strikes me as a most happy image of the Creation" (II, 827). Coleridge's recountal continues, and at one point Hartley is repre-

---

[22]*Robinson*, I, 44. For the "great and inexplicable mystery" compare Zachary
Mayne in 1728. "*Self* is likewise the Subject, as well as the Object of *Consciousness*. . . . For most assuredly, in being Conscious of *Self*, it is nothing but *Self*
which is Conscious" (Mayne, p. 149).
[23]*Collected Letters*, II, 673.

sented as saying, " 'When I was a little Boy, I was frightened at the Monkey & the Dromedary in London . . . but now I am not frightened at them, *because they are like themselves.'* What do you mean Hartley?—'Don't ask me so many questions, Papa! I can't bear it. I mean, that I am frightened at men that are not like men / a Monkey is a monkey—& God made the Dromedary—but Peter is a crazy man' " (II, 828).

Earlier, on 17 March 1801, Coleridge confided to his notebook an entry that once again linked Hartley and the activity of a philosopher. "Hartley looking out of my study window fixed his eyes steadily & for some time on the opposite prospect, & then said—Will yon Mountains *always* be?—I shewed him the whole magnificent Prospect in a Looking Glass, and held it up, so that the whole was like a Canopy or Ceiling over his head, & he struggled to express himself concerning the Difference between the Thing & the Image almost with convulsive Effort.—I never before saw such an Abstract of *Thinking* as a pure act & energy, of *Thinking* as distinguished from *Thoughts*."[24] In sum, it was not for nothing that Coleridge named his son "David Hartley Coleridge, in honor of the great Master of Christian Philosophy."[25]

So much for the child Hartley as philosopher. There is unfortunately not space in the pages remaining here to enter into the delicious and hotly debated question of whether Wordsworth himself was or was not a philosopher. R. D. Havens says he was not; E. D. Hirsch says he was. John Jones says he was not; Melvin Rader says he was. Matthew Arnold says he was not; Samuel Taylor Coleridge says he was. Whether he was or was not, in any case, there can be no doubt that Coleridge thought he was. "Wordsworth is a Poet," he says, "and I feel myself a better Poet, in knowing how to honour *him*, than in all my own poetic Compositions, all I have done or hope to do—and I prophesy immortality to his *Recluse*, as the first & finest philosophical Poem." Again, he says that Wordsworth "will hereafter be admitted as the first & greatest philosophical Poet—the only man who has effected a compleat and constant synthesis of Thought & Feeling and combined them with Poetic Forms." Still again, of a portrait of his friend done by Hazlitt, he writes to Wordsworth, "Sir G[eorge Beaumont] & his wife both say, that the Picture gives them an idea of you as a profound strong-minded Philosopher, not as a Poet—I

---

[24]*Notebooks*, I, 923.
[25]*Collected Letters*, I, 247. Compare Lamb's question about the infant: "And how does little David Hartley? . . . does his mighty name work wonders yet upon his little frame, & opening mind?" (*Lamb*, I, 89).

answered (& I believe, truly—) that so it must needs do, if it were a good Portrait—for that you were a great Poet by inspirations, & in the Moments of revelation, but that you were a thinking feeling Philosopher habitually—that your Poetry was your Philosophy under the action of strong winds of Feeling—a sea rolling high."[26]

When Wordsworth calls the child "best Philosopher," therefore, he is accepting his friend's invitation to use a term most cordially and insistently offered to him to fill a role demanded by that friend. Though Coleridge was not particularly desirous of remembering his own childhood, there can be no doubt that childhood for Wordsworth was emotionally and conceptually central, whether or not philosophy was invoked. It is possible, indeed, to assemble passages running all the way from simple recognition of childhood's joy to an understanding that childhood must constitute a philosophical base of human meaning, under the aegis of the paradox that "the child is father of the man." In "To a Butterfly," for instance, Wordsworth speaks lightly.

> We'll talk of sunshine and of song,
> And summer days, when we were young;
> Sweet childish days, that were as long
> As twenty days are now.[27]

His statement becomes somewhat weightier in "Personal Talk."

> Children are blest, and powerful; their world lies
> More justly balanced; partly at their feet,
> And part far from them. . . .
>   (IV, 74)

The statement becomes overtly philosophical in "The Prelude," where he has, as he says, yearned "toward some philosophic song, / Of Truth that cherishes our daily life,"[28] for in book 2 he looks toward the child, in pre-Freudian insight, as the key to life's meaning.

>   Blest the infant Babe,
> (For with my best conjecture I would trace
> Our Being's earthly progress,) blest the Babe,
> Nursed in his Mother's arms. . . .

[26]See Havens, *The Mind of a Poet; Volume One; A Study of Wordsworth's Thought* (Baltimore: The Johns Hopkins Press, 1941); Hirsch, *Wordsworth and Schelling; A Typological Study of Romanticism* (New Haven, Conn.: Yale University Press, 1960); Jones, *The Egotistical Sublime; A History of Wordsworth's Imagination* (London: Chatto & Windus, 1954); Rader, *Wordsworth: A Philosophical Approach* (Oxford: Clarendon Press, 1967); *Collected Letters*, II, 1034, 957.

[27]Wordsworth, *Poems*, II, 23.

[28]*Prelude*, I, 229–30 (p. 47).

. . . .
Along his infant veins are interfused
The gravitation and the filial bond
Of Nature that connects him with the world.
    (II, 232–35, 242–44)

It is interesting to note that Wordsworth does not here speak of the child growing up, but rather uses the philosopher's term, *being*— he would trace "Our Being's earthly progress." The sense that childhood is ontologically central is still stronger in the supreme passage in book 12.

Oh! mystery of man, from what a depth
Proceed thy honours. I am lost, but see
In simple childhood something of the base
On which thy greatness stands.
    (XII, 272–75)

Again, in book 5, he asserts that

. . . Our childhood sits,
Our simple childhood, sits upon a throne,
That hath more power than all the elements.
    (V,507–9)

And the asseveration in the "Immortality Ode" that on the child rest those truths that we are toiling all our lives to find is echoed in the statement of "It is a Beauteous Evening, Calm and Free," written in the same year, where his illegitimate daughter is hailed,

Dear Child! . . .
. . . .
Thou liest in Abraham's bosom all the year;
And worshipp'st at the Temple's inner shrine,
God being with thee when we know it not.[29]

Furthermore, Wordsworth's reverence for what he called "the sacred light of Childhood"[30] echoed a deep if subliminal motif in Romanticism as such. "The feeling by which we are attached to nature," said Schiller, "is closely related to the feeling with which we mourn the lost age of childhood and childlike innocence. Our childhood is the only undisfigured nature that we still encounter in

[29]Wordsworth, *Poems*, III, 17.
[30]*Prose*, II, 16. He continues, "We have been discoursing . . . of Infancy, Childhood, Boyhood, and Youth—of pleasures lying upon the unfolding Intellect plenteously as morning dew-drops—of Knowledge inhaled sensibly like a fragrance—of dispositions stealing into the Spirit like Music from unknown quarters—of images uncalled for and rising up like exhalations—of hopes plucked like beautiful wild flowers."

civilized mankind; hence it is no wonder if every trace of the nature outside us leads us back to our childhood."[31]

Wordsworth was not, therefore, as Coleridge and Arnold and other commentators have misconceived, utilizing a perverse metaphor in elevating the state of childhood. He was, on the contrary, speaking the simple truth as he knew and felt it.[32] He was one of those—I, your author, am another—who had experienced what Freud has described as "the oceanic feeling," although in analyzing this feeling Freud confessed that he himself had not felt it.[33]

Certainly neither Coleridge nor Arnold felt it. Dickens did not feel it. St. Augustine preferred death itself to the state of childhood. But others attest to different experiences. Freud's oceanic feeling lies behind Vaughan's "Happy those early dayes! when I / Shin'd in my Angell-infancy," when he "felt through all this fleshly dresse / Bright *shootes* of everlastingnesse."[34] It is the same feeling that Traherne memorializes in a passage of great rapture.

> The Corn was Orient and Immortal Wheat. . . . I thought it had stood from everlasting to everlasting. The Dust and Stones of the Street were as Precious as GOLD. The Gates were at first the End of the World, The Green Trees when I saw them first through one of the Gates Transported and Ravished me. . . . Boys and Girls Tumbling in the Street, and Playing, were moving Jewels. . . . Eternity was Manifest in the Light of the Day, and som thing infinit Behind evry thing appeared. . . . The Streets were mine, the Temple was mine, the People were mine. . . . The Skies were mine, and so were the Sun and Moon and Stars, and all the World was mine.[35]

[31]*Schiller*, XII, 180–81. Again, Berta, in Tieck's *Der blonde Eckbert*, dies when she loses imaginative touch with her childhood.

[32]Wordsworth said of the "Immortality Ode": "This poem rests entirely upon two recollections of childhood, one that of a splendour in the objects of sense which is passed away, and the other an indisposition to bend to the law of death as applying to our own particular case. A Reader who has not a vivid recollection of these feelings having existed in his mind in childhood cannot understand that poem" (*Middle Years*, II, 189). Elsewhere he observes that "forlorn, and cut off from communication with the best part of nature, must that man be, who should derive the sense of immortality, as it exists in the mind of a child, from the same unthinking gaiety . . . with which the lamb in the meadow . . . is endowed; who should ascribe it, in short, to blank ignorance in the child . . . or to an unreflecting acquiescence in what had been instilled into him! . . . If we had no direct external testimony that the minds of very young children meditate feelingly upon death and immortality, these enquiries, which we all know they are perpetually making concerning the *whence*, do necessarily include correspondent habits of interrogation concerning the *whither*" (*Prose*, II, 50–51).

[33]*Freud*, XXI, 64–68.

[34]*De civitate Dei*, Lib. XXI, Cap. 14; *Vaughan*, pp. 169–70.

[35]Traherne, I, 111.

That is the "oceanic feeling"; that is what Wordsworth felt; that is what the specification of the child as "best Philosopher" means, not metaphorically, but simply, literally, and in fact.[36]

But where does Hartley Coleridge fit in with this great apprehension? The answer is that he, as a child much in Wordsworth's view, and as the son of a philosopher Wordsworth enormously respected, became the vehicle by which Wordsworth raised himself from the emotional feeling of the supremacy of childhood to its philosophical formulation. If one is correct in thinking that Wordsworth elevates the role of the child in the "Immortality Ode" in part because he has been obliged somewhat to mute the role of nature, it is in this context interesting to recall that Blake did not much care for Wordsworth's poetry in that it relied too much on nature. "Natural Objects," writes Blake, "always did & now do Weaken deaden & obliterate Imagination in Me. Wordsworth must know that what he Writes Valuable is Not to be found in Nature." But Blake was enthusiastic about the apotheosis of childhood, and in fact the poem he seemed to value most in Wordsworth is "To H. C. Six Years Old," of which he says, "This is all in the highest degree Imaginative & equal to any Poet." H. C. is Hartley Coleridge; the specification "six years old" accords with Wordsworth's "Six years Darling of a pigmy size"; the fear in the poem that Hartley will lose being as he grows older is the same one more deeply explored in the "Immortality Ode." Furthermore, the poem "To H. C. Six Years Old" was probably begun in the same month and possibly even the same day as the "Immortality Ode"—27 March 1802.[37]

If the passage about the "best Philosopher" contains none of the blockings that we associate with the intrusion of Coleridgean emphasis into Wordsworth, or with the attainment of elevated moments in Wordsworth—and the "best Philosopher" passage is an elevated moment indeed—it owes its freedom from such obstruction, I think, to two factors. The first is the one just presented, by

---

[36]That Traherne and Wordsworth are testifying to the same experience, and that it is an experience and not a poetic strategy, is apparent from another passage, where Traherne hails the child's knowledge of truth in terms closely similar to those with which Wordsworth invokes the child as "best Philosopher." "All appeared New, and Strange at the first, inexpressibly rare, and Delightfull, and Beautifull. I was a little Stranger which at my Enterance into the World was Saluted and Surrounded with innumerable Joys. My Knowledg was Divine. I knew by Intuition those things which since my Apostasie, I Collected again, by the Highest Reason. . . . Is it not Strange, that an Infant should be Heir of the World, and see those Mysteries which the Books of the Learned never unfold?" (Traherne, I, 110–11).

[37]*Blake*, pp. 655, 654; *Chronology*, p. 156.

which Coleridge's conversations about Hartley's philosophical
prowess, along with his proselytizing of the role of philosophical
poet for Wordsworth, conjoined with rather than worked against
emphases already existing in Wordsworth's own experience and
tendency. The second is that the preceding stanza in the "Immortality Ode" acts almost as a lightning rod for such blockings, and
then Wordsworth frees himself from their effect there by a radical
shift in perspective.

The preceding stanza, stanza 7, is, indeed, one of the most
strained and obstructed in any great poem.

> Behold the Child among his new-born blisses,
> A six years' Darling of a pigmy size!
> See, where 'mid work of his own hand he lies,
> Fretted by sallies of his mother's kisses,
> With light upon him from his father's eyes!
> See, at his feet, some little plan or chart,
> Some fragment from his dream of human life,
> Shaped by himself with newly-learned art;
>   A wedding or a festival,
>   A mourning or a funeral;
>   And this hath now his heart,
>   And unto this he frames his song:
>   Then will he fit his tongue
> To dialogues of business, love or strife;
>   But it will not be long
>   Ere this be thrown aside,
>   And with new joy and pride
> The little Actor cons another part;
> Filling from time to time his 'humorous stage'
> With all the Persons, down to palsied Age,
> That Life brings with her in her equipage;
>   As if his whole vocation
>   Were endless imitation.[38]

Not only do we encounter here the combined sentimentality and
grotesquerie of the notorious specification, "A six years' Darling of
a pigmy size," or labor through the little Actor conning a Shakespearean part from Jaques's Seven Ages of Man speech, but we
also have to contend with rhymes such as "humorous stage" and
"equipage."

Immediately following this near-chatter, however, we hear, in
astonishing reversal, the organ-tones of Wordsworthian grandeur:

> Thou, whose exterior semblance doth belie
>   Thy Soul's immensity;

[38]Wordsworth, *Poems*, IV, 281–82.

Thou best Philosopher, who yet dost keep
Thy heritage, thou Eye among the blind,
That, deaf and silent, read'st the eternal deep,
Haunted for ever by the eternal mind,—
    Mighty Prophet! Seer blest!
    On whom those truths do rest,
Which we are toiling all our lives to find.
    (IV, 282)

What has happened, I suggest, is that the preceding stanza cloys because the adult is looking down on and patronizing the child, who is virtually chucked under the chin: he becomes a "six years' Darling," his concerns are "some little plan or chart," he himself is a "little Actor." In the stanza that follows, however, Wordsworth suddenly alters this patronizing perspective and looks directly across at the child: the "little Actor" becomes "Thou, whose exterior semblance doth belie / Thy Soul's Immensity / Thou best Philosopher," "Mighty Prophet! Seer Blest!"

Wordsworth has done here what he does in another of his great moments, his sonnet about the death of his three-year-old daughter Catharine, in which there is no specification that in any way indicates that she could not be a lover of thirty years of age. And yet she is a three-years' child:

Surprised by joy—impatient as the Wind
I turned to share the transport—Oh! with whom
But Thee, deep buried in the silent tomb,
That spot which no vicissitude can find?
Love, faithful love, recalled thee to my mind—
But how could I forget thee? Through what power,
Even for the least division of an hour
Have I been so beguiled as to be blind
To my most grievous loss!—That thought's return
Was the worst pang that sorrow ever bore,
Save one, one only, when I stood forlorn,
Knowing my heart's best treasure was no more;
That neither present time, nor years unborn
Could to my sight that heavenly face restore.
    (III, 16)

Just as his "heart's best treasure" in this poem bridges all gap of age between adult and child, and the deeply serious perspective of equality releases enormous currents of feeling, so in the passage about the child as "best Philosopher" does Wordsworth's shift from the patronizing perspective of adulthood to the perspective of equality allow him the grandeur of his great apostrophe to simple childhood.

Thus we may conclude that one of Wordsworth's greatest and most characteristic moments in one of his greatest poems was directly indebted on several levels to the insistences of Coleridge. The argument of this chapter has threaded its way across terrain heavily mined with paradox, from that inhering in the proximity of Wordsworth's dead spots and his great statements, to that inhering in Coleridge's own contradictory attitudes toward the child as philosopher. In this same line, it seems fitting to terminate the chapter with a final burst of paradox, this one inhering in the very nature of originality and indebtedness. Wordsworth in the "best Philosopher" passage is directly indebted to Coleridge, as he is at other places in his poetry to Coleridge, to Milton, to Spenser, to Shakespeare, and to others. And yet Coleridge himself always insisted on Wordsworth's originality. Wordsworth's poetry, says Coleridge, is of a kind "perfectly unborrowed and his own." A critic of all but equal authority, Hazlitt, concurs. "Mr. Wordsworth," he says in his *Lectures on the English Poets,* "is the most original poet now living."[39]

How can such judgments be true, if the indebtedness we have just described be also true? One answer might be developed from a phenomenon we have all experienced that Nietzsche calls being "always in our own company". "Whatever in nature and history is of my own kind speaks to me, spurs me on, and comforts me; the rest I do not hear or forget right away. We are always in our own company." But perhaps a more compelling resolution of the paradox lies in a closer questioning of the nature of originality itself. Hazlitt, in one of his profound formulations, writes of Wordsworth that "his mind is . . . coeval with the primary forms of things." Wordsworth's "Thoughts and Sentiments," writes Coleridge in another version of the same perception, "are *fresh* and have the dew upon them."[40]

It is, I suggest, the presence or absence of those characteristics rather than the existence of formal priority that generates judgments as to originality or its lack. To return to John Stuart Mill, whom we invoked at the end of the preceding chapter, we find individuality, not priority, to be the validating factor in originality. "Philosophic genius," writes Mill, "is said to be the discovery of new truth. But what is new truth? That which has been known a thousand years may be new truth to you or me." He continues, "Now, the capacity of extracting the knowledge of general truth

---

[39]*Biographia,* II, 151; *Hazlitt,* V, 156.
[40]*Nietzsche,* II, 142; *Hazlitt,* IV, 112; *Biographia,* II, 144–45.

from our own consciousness, whether it be by simple *observation*, by that kind of self-observation which is called *imagination*, or by a more complicated process . . . is *originality;* and where truth is the result, whosoever says Originality says Genius. . . . Whoever thinks at all, thinks to that extent, originally."[41]

Those things that Wordsworth valued occupied his mind with a special intensity, and it is from our awareness of intensity, not from our awareness of priority, that we derive our conviction as to his originality. In a second apprehension of that originality, this one in *The Spirit of the Age,* Hazlitt specified the Wordsworthian intensity.

> To the author of the *Lyrical Ballads* nature is a kind of home; and he may be said to take a personal interest in the universe. There is no image so insignificant that it has not in some mood or other found the way into his heart: no sound that does not awaken the memory of other years. . . . The daisy looks up to him with sparkling eye . . . a linnet's nest startles him with boyish delight: an old withered thorn is weighed down with a heap of recollections: a grey cloak, seen on some wild moor, torn by the wind, or drenched in the rain, afterwards becomes an object of imagination to him: even the lichens on the rocks have a life and being in his thoughts. He has described all these objects in a way and with an intensity of feeling that no one else had done before him. . . . He is in this sense the most original poet now living, and the one whose writings could least be spared: for they have no substitute elsewhere.[42]

In the light of such insistence, the idea of originality reveals itself as a direct witness to the unique individuality of an author. Originality symbolizes the mystery of *principium individuationis*, which in its most idealized form is the concept of soul; ultimately that is its only function. Originality is concerned to attest not the priority, but rather, to use a term favored by medieval writers, the "authority" of an author. Edward Said argues that "beginnings" should be distinguished from "origins": "beginning and beginning-again are historical whereas origins are divine." Harold Bloom, noting that "the prestige of origins is a universal phenomenon," says that "the original Time is both strong and sacred, whereas its recurrences progressively become weaker and less holy." Edward Said, again, speaks of "the empty fact of priority," and he points to Vico's "initial distinction between the gentile or

---

[41]*Mill*, I, 330, 332.
[42]*Hazlitt*, XI, 89.

historical and the sacred or original—paralleling my distinction between beginning and an origin."[43]

The distinctions are just. Origin is not a definable precedence but an ineffable numinous. "How shall I seek the origin?," asks Wordsworth despairingly, "where find / Faith in the marvellous things which then I felt?"[44] To value origin is to value a qualitative state, not an event of priority. John Hollander, in an article entitled simply "Originality," cites George Eliot's epigraph to *Daniel Deronda*. "Men can do nothing without the make-believe of a beginning. . . . [But] no retrospect will take us to the true beginning; and whether our prologue be in heaven or on earth, it is but a fraction of that all supposing fact with which our story sets out." Again, Heidegger insists on the radical paradoxicality of any appeal to origins. "Origin . . . means that from and by which something is what it is and as it is. What something is, as it is, we call its essence or nature. The origin of something is the source of its nature. . . . On the usual view, the work arises out of and by means of the activity of the artist. But by what and whence is the artist what he is? By the work; for to say that the work does credit to the master means that it is the work that first lets the artist emerge as a master of his art. The artist is the origin of the work. The work is the origin of the artist."[45]

Coleridge liked to argue (perhaps heeding the ninth of the Thirty-nine Articles of his church) that "original" sin referred not to an ultimately prior event, from which guilt then was inherited by all succeeding that priority, but was instead the capacity of each individual, as an individual, to originate sin. Such, mutatis mutandis, is the buried truth about the treasuring of the concept of originality in cultural matters. Priority as requisite for cultural originality is necessarily a kind of illusion: the past must always be prologue for any achievement whatever. Priority as defining factor in originality can accordingly seem pertinent only in segmented observations of historical flow; it seems relevant only in the relationship of small

[43]Said, p. xiii; Bloom, *Misreading*, pp. 46, 47; Said, pp. 316, 357. Again, Foucault points out that "it is always against a background of the already begun that man is able to reflect on what may serve for him as origin. For man, then, origin is by no means the beginning—a sort of morning of history from which his ulterior acquisitions would have accumulated. Origin, for man, is much more the way in which man in general, any man, articulates himself upon the already begun of labor, life, and language; it must be sought for in that fold where man in all simplicity applies his labor to a world that has been worked for thousands of years" (Foucault, p. 341).

[44]*Prelude*, II, 346–47 (p. 93). For an extended discussion centering upon this passage see Leslie Brisman, *Romantic Origins* (Ithaca, N.Y.: Cornell University Press, 1978), pp. 276–361.

[45]Hollander, p. 25; Heidegger, p. 17.

cultural groups not widely separated in time and context, where the fiction of an absolute first need not be challenged. But whenever we are able to supply historical magnification to seemingly prior events, we invariably see that they are as much encrusted by antecedent conditioning facts as the most influence-laden cultural creation in the foreground of our attention. In the matrix of priority, the deep truth is that enunciated by Valéry. "We say that an author is *original* when we cannot trace the hidden transformations that others underwent in his mind."[46]

Northrop Frye enunciates the same truth in different words. "Any serious study of literature soon shows that the real difference between the original and the imitative poet is simply that the former is more profoundly imitative." Indeed, almost everyone with close experience of cultural creation has glimpsed this fundamental truth in one form or another. "As to imitation," says Shelley, "poetry is a mimetic art . . . one great poet is a masterpiece of nature which another not only ought to study but must study. He might as wisely and as easily determine that his mind should no longer be the mirror of all that is lovely in the visible universe, as exclude from his contemplation the beautiful which exists in the writings of a great contemporary." Wordsworth, for his part, notes that "the predecessors of an original Genius of a high order will have smoothed the way for all that he has in common with them;—and much he will have in common." Shelley, agains, states that "poets, not otherwise than philosophers, painters, sculptors, and musicians, are, in one sense, the creators, and, in another, the creations, of their age. From this subjection the loftiest do not escape. There is a similarity between Homer and Hesiod, between Aeschylus and Euripides, between Virgil and Horace, between Dante and Petrarch, between Shakespeare and Fletcher, between Dryden and Pope; each has a generic resemblance under which their specific distinctions are arranged."[47]

If priorities, hidden or evident, relate only to cultural occurrences seen from the outside by an observer aligning figures in historical groupings, from inside, from within the individual, originality is the moment of fullness and intensification in living experi-

---

[46]*Valéry*, VIII, 241.

[47]Frye, *Anatomy*, p. 97; *Shelley*, II, 173–74; *Prose*, III, 80; *Shelley*, II, 174. Cf. James Beattie. "Virgil imitates many poets, and particularly Homer, from whom he has borrowed the plan, and many of the sentiments, images, and phrases, of the Eneid: but Virgil's style, and manner, and the numbers of his verse, are altogether his own. . . . Tasso imitates Homer in his plan, and Virgil in his style. Pope imitates Boileau and Dryden. . . . In fact all good poets imitate one another more or less" (Beattie, pp. 158–59).

ence that erupts in self-realization (Max Weber). It erupts, it leaps;
as Heidegger emphasizes for the German *Ursprung* (origin):

> Art lets truth originate. Art, founding preserving, is the spring that
> leaps to the truth of what is, in the work. To originate something by
> a leap, to bring something into being from out of the source of its
> nature in a founding leap—this is what the word origin means.
>
> The origin of the work of art—that is, the origin of both the
> creators and the preservers, which is to say of a people's historical
> existence, is art. This is so because art is by nature an origin: a
> distinctive way in which truth comes into being, that is, becomes
> historical.[48]

Originality is a numinous term; accordingly, its value and function can be transposed into other terms sharing its numinous
effulgence, as the value and function of those terms can be substituted back into those of originality. Such is the situation with
regard to the relation of originality and imagination. If we take the
terms in their strict meaning, disregarding their numinous aura,
originality and *imagination* do not refer to the same things. But
neither term is much used without its aura. By Romantic times, as
Wordsworth pointed out, "IMAGINATION" had become "a word
which has been forced to extend its services far beyond the point to
which philosophy would have confined" it.[49] The same holds true
for *originality*.

Indeed, if originality, as argued above, indicates the sacredness
of origins, and thus in its reciprocity with the work means not
priority but the holiness of individuation, such too is the numinous
ascent of imagination. "The word, Imagination," says Wordsworth, "has been overstrained, from impulses honourable to mankind, to meet the demands of the faculty which is perhaps the
noblest of our nature" (III, 81). This overstraining, as with originality, lifts itself from the *principium individuationis* to the highest
principle of self, which is soul. Wordsworthian "imagination," as
Geoffrey Hartman defines it, is "consciousness of self raised to
apocalyptic pitch."[50]

Because both terms, *originality* and *imagination*, historically accumulated value in inverse ratio to their clear and distinct definition,
they tended not only to share a common aura but also to restore
that numinous which by the eighteenth century was increasingly
divested from *soul* as a term in its own right. This doubling of effect

[48]Heidegger, pp. 77–78.
[49]*Prose*, III, 81.
[50]Hartman, p. 17.

is repeatedly apparent. For instance, Alexander Gerard, in his discussion of *genius,* which was still another of the numinous terms that accepted some of the burden that *soul* could no longer bear, said in 1774 that "GENIUS is properly the faculty of *invention;* by means of which a man is qualified . . . for producing original works of art." But imagination is interchangeable with originality in this complex. Imagination can present "ideas, not as copies, but as originals." To the "imagination, invention is accordingly referred, even by the generality of mankind. If a poet . . . only repeat the sentiments of others . . . every person imputes this defect of invention, to the barrenness of his *fancy.* All genuine productions in the arts, are marked with strong signatures of a bright and lively imagination: and every original work in science, will be found, on examination, to proclaim a force and vigour of the same power."[51]

In the foregoing passage, the term *imagination* is not differentiated from the term *fancy.* But Coleridge, as we all know, did discriminate them, and in fact, in still finer calibration, further distinguished *primary imagination* from *secondary imagination.* The threefold distinction bears directly upon Kant's three final objects of human reason: the freedom of the will, the immortality of the soul, and the existence of God. Indeed, from the very first Coleridge's conceivings about imagination issued from a theological matrix. As early as 1795, in a lecture on the slave trade, recently printed in the first volume of his *Collected Works* (1971), he departs directly from the Biblical assurance that "God created man in his *own* image, in the image of God created he him" (*Gen.* 1:27). For he says that "to develope the powers of the Creator is our proper employment—and to imitate Creativeness by combination our most exalted and self-satisfying Delight. . . . Our Almighty Parent hath therefore given to us Imagination that stimulates to the attainment of *real* excellence by the contemplation of splendid Possibilities. . . . Such and so noble are the ends for which this restless faculty was given us" (pp. 235–36). Though at this time there is no threefold distinction of *primary imagination, secondary imagination,* and *fancy,* the later distinction elaborates rather than replaces or rejects this initial theological formulation. It is to that later distinction that we shall now turn, to trace further permutations of the numinous aura of soul.

[51]Gerard, *Essay,* pp. 8, 30, 31–32.

• 4 •

The Origin and Significance of Coleridge's Theory of Secondary Imagination

*C*oleridge *refers to the secondary* imagination only once in his published writings. The place is, of course, the end of the thirteenth chapter of the *Biographia Literaria*.

> The IMAGINATION then, I consider either as primary, or secondary. The primary IMAGINATION I hold to be the living Power and prime Agent of all human Perception, and as a repetition in the finite mind of the eternal act of creation in the infinite I AM. The secondary I consider as an echo of the former, co-existing with the conscious will, yet still as identical with the primary in the *kind* of its agency, and differing only in *degree*, and in the *mode* of its operation. It dissolves, diffuses, dissipates, in order to re-create; or where this process is rendered impossible, yet still at all events it struggles to idealize and to unify. It is essentially *vital*, even as all objects (*as* objects) are essentially fixed and dead.
>
> FANCY, on the contrary, has no other counters to play with, but fixities and definites. The Fancy is indeed no other than a mode of Memory emancipated from the order of time and space; and blended with, and modified by that empirical phenomenon of the will, which we express by the word CHOICE. But equally with the ordinary memory it must receive all its materials ready made from the law of association.[1]

It is probably fair to say that this is both one of the most famous passages in all of English prose and one of the least satisfactorily understood. Up until about the middle of this century or shortly afterward, indeed, scholars usually approached it with an almost reverential regard, at the same time that a feeble and redundant gloss was all they could supply by way of commentary. A favorite

---

[1]*Biographia*, I, 304–5.

question on viva voce examinations was a request to distinguish Coleridge's conceptions of primary imagination, secondary imagination, and fancy; and the ritual answer, which invariably satisfied the examiners in full, was simply to repeat the puzzling words.

Where there was not merely ritualistic citation, there was apt to be a certain disgruntlement. To cite a single instance, W. J. Bate, in 1950, said that "this rather artificial distinction between 'primary' and 'secondary' imagination is not among Coleridge's more lucid contributions to aesthetics. . . . The passage may be regarded as simply a cryptic phrasing of what one may discover in other ways to be Coleridge's general theory of the imagination. . . . Whatever its meaning, Coleridge does not dwell upon it elsewhere. As it now stands, it is neither clear nor particularly helpful."[2]

It is easy to sympathize with such objections. Not only is there no preparation for the threefold distinction of chapter 13 in Coleridge's previous writings, there is none even in the *Biographia*. In chapter 4 of that work Coleridge states his conviction that "fancy and imagination" are "two distinct and widely different faculties," illustrates the difference by the examples of Cowley and Milton, and says that it is his object "to investigate the seminal principle" of the distinction. Nowhere is there any mention of, or preparation for, any additional differentiation. When, in chapter 12, he comes nearer to the promised discussion, it is to assert that he will "now proceed to the nature and genesis of the imagination"—still with no foreshadowing of a "secondary" imagination. And in chapter 13 itself, in an astonishing volte-face, he writes himself a letter in which he says: "I see clearly that you have done too much, and yet not enough. You have been obliged to omit so many links, from the necessity of compression, that what remains, looks . . . like the fragments of the winding steps of an old ruined tower." While the reader who has lasted thus far is still bemused by the phrase about the "necessity of compression," Coleridge proceeds simply to dump upon him the threefold distinction, or as the book more elaborately puts it, to "content myself for the present with stating the main result of the Chapter, which I have reserved for that future publication"—that is, for the magnum opus.[3]

Not having the magnum opus to clarify matters, we must accordingly supply our own account of the "nature and genesis of the imagination," and such an account must necessarily be a trac-

[2]Levin, *Perspectives*, pp. 144, 145–46.
[3]*Biographia*, I, 82, 84, 88, 293, 302–3, 304.

ing backward more than a forward progression from first principles. I shall attempt here to supply the essentials of such an account by addressing myself to three questions. First of all, why is
the threefold distinction simply deposited rather than deduced?
Secondly, where in Coleridge's thought or reading does the secondary imagination originate? And thirdly, what is the context in
which we should consider the secondary imagination?

We need not linger over the answer to the first of our questions,
that is, Why is the threefold distinction deposited rather than deduced? Briefly, the matter seems to stand this way: Coleridge had
been following Schelling's line of reasoning, found himself unable
to reconcile it with the threefold distinction—which neither comes
from nor is paralleled by anything in Schelling—and so wrote
himself a letter promising a later rethinking, while leaving as a
down payment, as it were, the statements about primary imagination, secondary imagination, and fancy.

Coleridge had been involved in chapter 12 with an attempt to
reconcile the subjective and the objective, which, transposed into
his own terms of "I am" and "it is," was the consuming goal of his
philosophical activity. To this end he had translated substantial
passages from Schelling's *System of Transcendental Idealism*, which
seemed to promise such a reconciliation. Coleridge had here accepted the thoroughly Schellingian notion that "the true system of
natural philosophy places the sole reality of things in an ABSOLUTE
. . . in the absolute identity of subject and object, which it calls
nature, and which in its highest power is nothing else than self-
conscious will or intelligence."[4]

In chapter 13, still following Schelling, who had been following
Kant, Coleridge says that "the transcendental philosophy demands; first, that two forces should be conceived which counteract
each other by their essential nature."[5] He goes on to speak of "this
one power with its two inherent indestructible yet counteracting
forces, and the results or generations to which their inter-penetra-
tion gives existence" (I, 299), and moves ever closer to Schelling's
own, pantheistic, theory of imagination. Coleridge's last state-

[4]See McFarland, *Coleridge*, especially pp. 148–60; ibid., pp. 24–26, and Shawcross, I, 268–71; and *Biographia*, I, 285.

[5]Ibid., p. 299. Cf. Schelling, e.g., "Die Philosophie geht aus von einer un-
endlichen Entzweiung entgegengesetzter Thätigkeiten" (*Schelling*, III, 626). This
frequently expressed fundamental of Schelling's thought was largely derived from
Kant's analysis of the metaphysical foundations of the dynamic (see *Kant*, IV, 511).
Cf. Goethe's comment: "Since our excellent Kant says in plain words that there can
be no material without attraction and repulsion (that is, without polarity), I am
much reassured to be able, under this authority, to proceed with my view of the
world according to my earliest convictions, in which I have never lost confidence"
(*Gedenkausgabe*, XIX, 732).

ment, before breaking off and writing himself his explanatory letter, trembles on the very brink of pantheism. "Now this tertium aliquid can be no other than an interpenetration of the counteracting powers, partaking of both."[6] Coleridge is here only a step from Schelling's openly pantheistic theses that "the system of Nature is at the same time the system of our Spirit,"[7] and that "one might explain imagination as the power of transposing itself through complete self-activity into complete passivity" (I, 332n).

To Coleridge, whose entire intellectual life was bound up with the necessity of avoiding pantheism, such a reconciliation of subjective and objective came at too high a price. And so he abruptly refuses to press forward. "Thus far had the work been transcribed for the press," he interrupts, "when I received the following letter from a friend."[8]

There is perhaps an additional reason for Coleridge's merely depositing the threefold distinction. By doing so he makes his description, as Bate says, "cryptic"; and he probably was almost as content with this effect as he would have been with a clear demonstration. In any event, his letter's reference to the "many to whose *unprepared* minds your speculations on the esemplastic power would be utterly unintelligible" (I, 303) seems almost to imply the Plotinian view that "holy things may not be uncovered to the stranger."[9] In general, by Coleridge, as by other Romantic thinkers, the faculty of imagination was treasured as something mysterious and unfathomable. Wordsworth refers to it as an "awful Power" that rises "from the mind's abyss." Schelling calls it a "wonderful faculty." Baader says that it is "a wonder of wonders," which is "no mere word, but a microcosmos of secret forces within us."[10] Coleridge, for his part, calls it a "magical power"[11] and says

---

[6]Ibid., pp. 299–300. The "tertium aliquid" would metaphysically have to be God, so the solution would be pantheistic. I suspect, however, that Coleridge did not see this until the last moment because his mind was set on "finite generation." Schelling had said that the "infinite opposition" could be resolved through "each individual representation of art." "What," he asks, "is that wonderful power" that can resolve an infinite opposition? "We have until now not been able to make this mechanism completely understandable, because it is only the power of art that can fully reveal it. That productive faculty is the same by which art also attains the impossible, that is, resolves an infinite opposition in a finite product. It is the faculty of poetry [*Dichtungsvermögen*] . . . it is the only thing by which we are able to think and unify the contradictory—that is, the imagination" (*Schelling*, III, 626).

[7]*Schelling*, II, 39.

[8]*Biographia*, I, 300.

[9]Plotinus, *Enneads*, VI.ix.11. It is interesting to note that Coleridge has just mentioned Plotinus in the preceding sentence of the *Biographia*.

[10]*Prelude*, VI, 592–94 (p. 239); *Schelling*, I, 332n, III, 626; *Baader*, XI, 85.

[11]*Biographia*, II, 16. We may see the same mysteriousness in Jean Paul's rubric of 1795: "Über die natürliche Magie der Einbildungskraft."

that his investigation of its principle will follow the faculty to its "roots" only "as far as they lift themselves above ground, and are visible to the naked eye of our common consciousness."[12]

Such imprecision and emotional loading of the term in the late eighteenth and early nineteenth centuries were results of a protest against the mechanism and rationalism of Newton, Locke, and what Coleridge calls the "impious and pernicious tenets" of the "French fatalists or necessitarians."[13] As a principle that stood against the passivity of mind, and against the soul's domination by dead outer things, the imagination possessed an importance that seemed actually to be enhanced by a certain obscurity.[14] For obscurity allowed a sense of vastness, mysteriousness, and incommensurability that precision and demonstration tended to reduce. Coleridge honors such predilection for a *je ne sais quoi* in the concept of imagination when he says that "Imagination, Fancy &c." are "all poor & inadequate Terms" for "the sensuous Einbildungskraft."[15] We see the same sense of mysterious expansion, coupled with imprecision, in Herder's reference to *"die Einbildungskraft, or whatever we want to call this sea of inner sensibility."* Indeed, Kant himself was content to be vague on this issue. Jacobi rightly notes that Kant's *Einbildungskraft* is "a blind forward and backward connecting faculty" that rests upon "a spontaneity of our being, whose principle is entirely unknown to us."[16] As De Vleeschauwer says:

---

[12]*Biographia*, I, 88.

[13]Ibid., p. 291. To make headway against the school of Locke, one needed to exploit all possibilities. In the words of one commentator, Locke was a "writer whose influence pervades the eighteenth century with an almost scriptural authority. . . . Surely never has a secular writer obtained such universal recognition or been received with such unquestioning faith as Locke" (Cobban, p. 16). Moreover, "the French fatalists or necessitarians" opposed by Coleridge were still more insistent than was their master upon the chief point of Lockian thought: the theoretical diminution of the soul's autonomy. For instance Condillac, in the words of another commentator, "was a professional Lockian, more Lockian in his final system even than Locke himself" (Gay, II, 178). In general, as Ernst Cassirer emphasizes, "the development of empirical philosophy from Locke to Berkeley and from Berkeley to Hume represents a series of attempts to minimize the difference between sensation and reflection, and finally to wipe it out altogether. French philosophical criticism of the eighteenth century hammered at this same point also in an attempt to eliminate the last vestige of independence which Locke had attributed to reflection" (Cassirer, *Enlightenment*, p. 100).

[14]Cf. Coleridge in 1803: "Mix up Truth & Imagination so that the Imag. may spread its own indefiniteness over that which really happened" (*Notebooks*, I, 1541). Cf. Wordsworth: "Imagination . . . recoils from every thing but the plastic, the pliant, and the indefinite" (*Prose*, III, 36).

[15]Note on the flyleaf of J. G. E. Maass, *Versuch über die Einbildungskraft*, rev. ed. (Halle and Leipzig, 1797), now in the British Library.

[16]*Herders Werke*, VIII, 190; *Jacobi*, II, 306.

Kant complicates the solution, so simple in its dualistic structure, by introducing imagination as an intermediary and mediating factor. It is the third element between the two original elements. It is capable of adopting this role because its nature is itself uncertain: Kant brings it into relation sometimes with sensibility, sometimes with understanding, and the schematism erects this confusion into a principle by making imagination participate both in sensibility and in understanding. Because of its confused nature the function delegated to it is not everywhere the same.[17]

Coleridge shows both his understanding of Kant's position and his ready acceptance of obscurities in the imagination by saying that "Fancy and Imagination are Oscillations, *this* connecting Reason and Understanding; *that* connecting Sense and Understanding."[18]

The word *connecting* in this last statement is significant both for Coleridge's breaking off of argument and for the function of imagination itself. For it seems clear that to Coleridge the imagination is less necessary as an element in an a priori theory of poetry than as a means of connecting poetic, philosophical, and theological interests. Most of all, it connects the inner world of "I am" with the outer world of "it is."[19]

The importance of systematic connection for Coleridge can scarcely be overemphasized. Indeed, as L. C. Knights has observed, "in the Coleridgean world everything is connected with everything else." So in chapter 9 of the *Biographia Literaria* Coleridge asserts his need for an "abiding place for my reason," and it is evident that this could be found only in system. "I began to ask myself; is a system of philosophy, as different from mere history and historic classification, possible?" To abandon the concept of system was, he then says, a "wilful resignation of intellect" against which "human nature itself fought." And at the end of chapter 12, just before a reference to "the imagination, or shaping and modifying power; the fancy, or the aggregative and associative power," he speaks against those who dismiss "not only all system, but all

---

[17]De Vleeschauwer, *Kantian Thought*, pp. 83–84.

[18]Brinkley, p. 694. For a critical application of the principle of imagination's oscillatory nature see the report of Coleridge's statement about a passage from *Romeo and Juliet*. "There is an effort in the mind, when it would describe what it cannot satisfy itself with the description of, to reconcile opposites, and to leave a middle state of mind more strictly appropriate to the imagination than any other when it is hovering between two images: as soon as it is fixed on one it becomes understanding, and when it is waving between them, attaching itself to neither, it is imagination" (Foakes, p. 82).

[19]See McFarland, *Coleridge*, p. 157 n.1. "Broadly speaking the function of the imagination for Coleridge was to connect the 'I am' with the 'it is,' while maintaining the primacy and independence of the 'I am.'"

logical connection." "This, alas!," Coleridge continues, "is an irre-
mediable disease, for it brings with it, not so much an indisposition
to any particular system, but an utter loss of taste and faculty for all
system and for all philosophy."[20]

Imagination is therefore primarily a connective developed because of Coleridge's commitment to systematic philosophizing. It
would not appear to be rewarding, accordingly, to try to make very
much critically of its presence in particular poems. But that is not to
say that knowledge of the threefold distinction is wholly without
value in the understanding of Coleridge's poetry. As a single illustration, which I shall try not to labor unduly, the widely held
view that "Kubla Khan" is a poem about poetic or imaginative
creation,[21] in which the major images are symbolic, would, in the
light of the threefold distinction and Coleridge's systematic concerns, seem to be an un-Coleridgean reading, or at least only a
partial reading.

"Kubla Khan" is, to be sure, an outstanding example of the
secondary imagination at work. Furthermore, not only does the
poem possess an unconscious but to us unmistakable undercurrent
of sexual reference, but it would also certainly be Coleridgean to
think of it as containing a consciously symbolic statement.[22] In-

---

[20]*The New York Review of Books* 16 (22 April 1971), 55; *Biographia*, I, 141, 293, 292.

[21]Thus George Watson: "What is 'Kubla Khan' about? This is, or ought to be, an
established fact of criticism: 'Kubla Khan' is a poem about poetry" (Watson, p. 122).
Cf. W. J. Bate: "The theme . . . is the hope and precarious achievement of the
human imagination" (Bate, *Coleridge*, p. 78); Marshall Suther: "More integral than
any of these readings . . . is that which sees the poem as an introspective account of
the elements of personality involved in the poetic experience, an anatomy, as it
were, of the poetic experience. . . . Then we have the *poem* as symbol, partaking of
the reality it would render intelligible, *being* what it is *about*" (Suther, p. 287); Harold
Bloom "*Kubla Khan*, a poem about poetry [is] . . . not quite a 'poem about the act of
poetic creation,' for it contains that theme as one element in a more varied unity"
(*Visionary Company*, pp. 211, 218); Humphry House: " 'Kubla Khan' is a poem about
the act of poetic creation" (House, p. 115); Virginia L. Radley: "Coleridge attempts
in 'Kubla Khan' to portray the world of Imagination pictorially in terms of sunlit
caverns and floating pleasure-domes"; " 'Kubla Khan' becomes clearly a recapitula-
tion in poetry of Coleridge's concept of the secondary Imagination" (Radley, pp. 78,
80).

[22]In aid of the point, consider the testimony of a companion who had been in
Germany with Coleridge: "He frequently recited his own poetry, and not unfre-
quently led us rather farther into the labyrinth of his metaphysical elucidations,
either of particular passages, or of the original conception of any of his productions,
than we were able to follow him. . . . At the conclusion of . . . the first stanza of
Christabel he would perhaps comment at full length upon such a line as 'Tu whit!—
Tu whoo!' that we might not fall into the mistake of supposing originality to be its
sole merit." Of the *Ancient Mariner* the same companion reports that he "could not
fully appreciate the mysteries of the Albatross" but that his pleasure in reperusals of
the poem "was not the less from my being able to enter, unattended by the author
and his bewildering metaphysics" (Carlyon, I, 138, 141). Again, on 10 September

deed, as Coleridge says in *The Statesman's Manual*, the imagination, "incorporating the Reason in Images of the Sense," gives birth to "a system of symbols."[23]

Bate has argued, however, in his sensitive volume in the Masters of World Literature series, that theological preoccupations subsume all Coleridge's other concerns.[24] It is not merely idle chatter for Coleridge to say that "the primary IMAGINATION" is "a repetition in the finite mind of the eternal act of creation in the infinite I AM." The controlling symbolism of "Kubla Khan" is, I think, anagogic; it refers to the "eternal act"—which alone, in Coleridge's scheme, could be called an idea of "reason"—not to the repetitive act in the finite mind nor to the echoes of that act. A poem written by Coleridge that ends with the word "Paradise" and begins with the creation of a garden should be interpreted, I believe, as a poem about God and Eden. The loss of the garden affirms, as Coleridge said in 1815 that he had wanted Wordsworth's poetry to affirm, "a Fall in some sense, as a fact . . . the reality of which is attested by Experience & Conscience."[25] The Khan, wonderful, powerful, remote in space and time, heard about rather than seen, is what

---

1802 Coleridge, in urging a symbolic reading for the "haemony" passage in Milton's *Comus*, speaks of Milton's "platonizing Spirit" and says that he "wrote nothing without an interior meaning" (*Collected Letters*, II, 866). The same might be claimed for Coleridge himself.

[23]*Lay Sermons*, p. 29. "An IDEA," notes Coleridge elsewhere, "in the *highest* sense of that word, cannot be conveyed but by a *symbol*" (*Biographia*, I, 156).

[24]Theology was even more important to Coleridge than was poetry. As Bate says, "to begin with, no other poet . . . has devoted so little time and effort to his poetry. Second, and more important, none has considered it so incidental to his other interests, hopes, or anxieties. Failure to recognize these two facts alone . . . has led to misinterpretations . . . that are still accepted and passed on without examination. Most common among them is the stock premise that one of the major modern poets . . . hit his true stride in the 'Ancient Mariner,' 'Christabel,' and 'Kubla Khan,' and then, because of opium and general weakness of will, was forced to fritter away the next thirty-five years in chasing philosophical and theological will-of-the-wisps" (Bate, *Coleridge*, pp. 40–41). Cf. Coleridge in 1804: "When my Triplets you see / Think not of my Poesy / But of the holy Trinity" (*Notebooks*, II, 1904). The subordinate position of poetry in Coleridge's scheme of things is further implied by his "early study" of "the illustrious Florentine"—that is, Ficino (*Biographia*, I, 144); for, Eugenio Garin emphasizes, "in Ficino's view, poetry loses its intrinsic value, for it becomes solely an incarnation of the truth, a sensuous image of the One. But at the same time it is clear that the whole of cosmic reality is seen as a poem by God" (Garin, p. 95). Coleridge's criticism too was subordinate to his philosophical and theological concerns. J. R. de J. Jackson maintains that "there can be little doubt that philosophy was his central activity, and that the criticism . . . was a digression from it . . . his criticism was in fact . . . in the nature of an inspired aside" (Jackson, p. 15).

[25]*Collected Letters*, IV, 575. Cf. *Table Talk*, p. 65 (1 May 1830): "A Fall of some sort or other—the creation, as it were, of the non-absolute—is the fundamental postulate of the moral history of Man. Without this hypothesis, Man is unintelligible."

Sidney might call "a notable *prosopopeias*" that represents God himself.[26] Although the words in Purchas say that *"In Xamdu did Cublai
Can* build *a stately* Palace,"[27] Coleridge's Khan does not build,
rather he creates by decree—that is, by a word, or divine fiat. And
the garden, like Milton's Eden, is menaced from its beginning by
conflicts arising from an ancestral past.[28]

Such a reading could be bulwarked by considerations drawn
from the extensive literature of commentary on the poem. Geoffrey
Yarlott, for instance, suggests that "Alph, the sacred river," instead of being the Nile or the Alpheus, could "derive from 'Alpha,'
the beginning—the sacred source of all things." And the part of
the poem that does seem to be about poetic creation, that is, where
the speaker will revive within him the Abyssinian maid's "sym-
phony and song" so as to rebuild the dome in air, and thereby
show that he had "drunk the milk of Paradise," is, as Elisabeth
Schneider has pointed out, an echo of the *Ion*, which is the *locus
classicus* for the connection of poetic act with divine things.[29]

In any case, and whether one agrees or disagrees with an interpretation of the poem that transfers the emphasis from imaginative creation to theology, it should be evident that the imagination,
though it cannot be dismissed in the consideration of Coleridge's
poetry, is a tool of only limited critical use. To a considerable extent
it functions simply as another name for that which is poetic about a
poem. Whatever that may happen to be, however, can be ap-

[26]I cannot agree with John Beer that "Kubla Khan is the Tartar king of tradition:
fierce and cruel, he bears the brand of Cain," or that "Kubla Khan may seem a
peaceful and prosperous ruler, but his garden is not and cannot be the garden of
Eden" (Beer, pp. 222, 228). Nor do I agree with House that the Khan is "the
Representative Man, or Mankind in general" (House, p. 120). Nor again with Bate
that "Kubla . . . is man as he in general would be, . . . placed in an enviable position of power" (Bate, *Coleridge*, p. 79). I am more nearly in agreement with G.
Wilson Knight's view that Kubla is a symbol of "God: or at least one of those 'huge
and mighty forms,' or other . . . intuitions of . . . mountainous power in Wordsworth," although I disagree with other points in Knight's interpretation (Knight,
p. 93).

[27]As quoted in Lowes, p. 358.

[28]Elisabeth Schneider emphasizes the extent to which Milton "hovers over Coleridge's poem" (Schneider, p. 264 and passim). Cf. House: "Of course we have in
'Kubla Khan' a fruit of Coleridge's Miltonising" (House, p. 119). Kubla Khan's
decreeing of the pleasure dome in a spot "where Alph, the sacred river ran"
underground, where "there were gardens bright with sinuous rills," and where "A
mighty fountain momently was forced" seems unmistakably a misprision or at least
a descendant of the locus in the fourth book of *Paradise Lost*, where Milton says that
"God had thrown / That Mountain as his Garden mould," which was "high
rais'd / Upon the rapid current" that rose as "a fresh Fountain, and with many a
rill / Water'd the Garden; thence united fell / Down the steep glade," and met "the
nether Flood, / Which from his darksome passage now appears" (*Paradise Lost*, IV,
225–32).

[29]Yarlott, p. 138, n.1; Schneider, pp. 245–46.

proached by general methods available to any critic. In the *Biographia Literaria*, a book that is largely about poetry, the definition of the secondary imagination emphasizes and honors poetic creation. But it operates more as a link between its author's poetic and his systematic theological and philosophical interests than as a program for how poetry should be written.

Perhaps this role can be more fully understood if we turn to the second of our stipulated questions, that is, Where in Coleridge's thought or reading did the secondary imagination originate? With regard to the answer, a passage published by Ernest Hartley Coleridge in the *Anima Poetae* in 1895 is instructive, both in its own right and for what it indicates about the textual difficulties that have hindered Coleridgean interpretation.

> In the preface of my metaphysical works, I should say—"Once for all, read Kant, Fichte, &c., and then you will trace, or, if you are on the hunt, track me." Why, then, not acknowledge your obligations step by step? Because I could not do so in a multitude of glaring resemblances without a lie, for they had been mine, formed and full-formed, before I had ever heard of these writers, because to have fixed on the particular instances in which I have really been indebted to these writers would have been hard, if possible, to me who read for truth and self-satisfaction, and not to make a book, and who always rejoiced and was jubilant when I found my own ideas well expressed by others—and, lastly, let me say, because . . . I seem to know that much of the *matter* remains my own, and that the *soul* is mine. I fear not him for a critic who can confound a fellow-thinker with a compiler.[30]

The statement, written in 1804, is clearly central to the whole question of Coleridge's intellectual indebtedness and constitutes both a proud testament to his own mental vitality and also, more am-

---

[30]*Anima Poetae*, ed. Ernest Hartley Coleridge (London: Heinemann, 1895), p. 106. Though Coleridge considered Kant as merely "preparatory philosophy" to "Christianity the one true Philosophy" (*Collected Letters*, III, 533), he nevertheless felt his debt to Kant to be very great. "The writings of the illustrious sage of Königsberg, the founder of the Critical Philosophy, more than any other work, at once invigorated and disciplined my understanding. The originality, the depth, and the compression of the thoughts; the novelty and subtlety, yet solidity and importance, of the distinctions; the adamantine chain of the logic; and I will venture to add . . . the *clearness* and *evidence*, of the 'CRITIQUE OF THE PURE REASON': of the 'JUDGMENT'; of the 'METAPHISICAL ELEMENTS OF NATURAL PHILOSOPHY'; and of his 'RELIGION WITHIN THE BOUNDS OF PURE REASON,' took possession of me as with a giant's hand" (*Biographia*, I, 153). For Coleridge's debt to Fichte see Daniel Stempel, "Revelation on Mount Snowdon: Wordsworth, Coleridge, and the Fichtean Imagination," *Journal of Aesthetics and Art Criticism*, 29 (1971), 371–84. See also Gian N. G. Orsini, *Coleridge and German Idealism; A Study in the History of Philosophy* (Carbondale: Southern Illinois University Press, 1969), pp. 172–91.

bivalently, perhaps something of a license to engage in the borrowings or plagiarisms that he embarked upon during his period of dejection.

But the editor of *Anima Poetae* did not transcribe the passage correctly. When it was republished in 1961, in the second volume of Kathleen Coburn's monumental edition of the *Notebooks,* numerous changes in punctuation and spelling appeared. More importantly, an interloper appeared as well. Where earlier "Kant, Fichte, &c." had been acknowledged by Coleridge as the masters of his thought, the opening sentence now read,

> In the Preface of my Metaphys. Works I should say—Once & all read Tetens, Kant, Fichte, &c—& there you will trace or if you are on the hunt, track me.[31]

We almost sympathize with Ernest Hartley Coleridge's discarding of the name. For who on earth was Tetens? And what conceivably did he have to do with Coleridge?

To answer the latter question first, Tetens was the thinker to whom we may trace or track Coleridge's theory of secondary imagination. For the rest, he was the most important German psychologist of the *Aufklärung,* exerted a major influence on the formation of Kant's *Critique of Pure Reason,*[32] was for a time professor at the University of Kiel, and from there was given in 1789 a royal commission as a high official of state finance in Copenhagen. He was born, according to varying accounts, on 16 September 1736, or 5 November 1738, and he died in 1807 on 15 August (Danish reckoning) or 19 August (German reckoning).[33]

Although Tetens wrote a number of treatises, some of them in Latin, his fame and significance rest almost exclusively upon a two-volume work published in Leipzig in 1777 and entitled *Philosophische Versuche über die menschliche Natur und ihre Entwickelung.* Coleridge, the "library-cormorant," annotated both volumes, and his

---

[31] *Notebooks,* II, 2375.

[32] Kant's *Dissertatio* of 1770 influenced Tetens, and then Tetens's *Philosophische Versuche* of 1777 exerted influence back on Kant's *Kritik der reinen Vernunft* of 1781. See, e.g., Gustav Störring, *Die Erkenntnistheorie von Tetens: Eine historisch-kritische Studie* (Leipzig: Verlag von Wilhelm Engelmann, 1901), p. 159. See further Arthur Seidel, *Tetens' Einfluss auf die kritische Philosophie Kants* (Würzburg: Buchdruckerei Konrad Triltsch, 1932); Max Brenke, *Johan Nicolas Tetens' Erkenntnistheorie vom Standpunkt des Kriticismus* (Rostock: C. Boldt'sche Hofbuchdruckerei, 1901); Arthur Apitzsch, *Die psychologischen Voraussetzungen der Erkenntniskritik Kants dargestellt und auf ihre Abhängigkeit von der Psychologie C. Wolfs und Tetens' geprüft* (Halle a. d. S.: Druck der C. F. Post'schen Buchdruckerei in Kolberg, 1897); Otto Ziegler, *Johann Nicolaus Tetens' Erkenntnistheorie in Beziehung auf Kant* (Leipzig: Druck von Hesse & Becker, 1888). See also n. 87 below.

[33] For details of Tetens's career see Uebele, pp. 5–25.

copies are at present in the British Library. It seems likely that he studied Tetens over a considerable time, for the notebook entry in 1804 indicates enough enthusiasm to suggest a substantial period of prior reading, and a crossed-out statement on the flyleaf of the first volume, in which he laments his separation from the Wordsworths, seems to have been written not only during his Malta sojourn but also after he learned, in the spring of 1805, of John Wordsworth's death. "O shall I ever see them again?" he asks, and then he exclaims, "O dear John! Would I had been thy substitute!"[34]

Indeed, such is the length of Tetens's volumes that reading them over a substantial period of time would be a normal procedure. Kant, who, according to De Vleeschauwer, delayed his first *Critique* in order to complete a study of Tetens,[35] says in a gentle gibe that Tetens, in his "long essay on freedom in the second volume," was hoping as he wrote that with the aid of uncertainly sketched ideas he would find his way out of "this labyrinth," but "after he had wearied himself and his reader," the matter remained the same as before.[36] And Coleridge, in a friendly note on the last page of the preface, seems obliquely to record as much dismay as anticipation about the rest of the work. "Would to Heaven," he writes, "that all Folios & Quartos contained in their 7 or 800 pages as much meaning & good sense, as these 36 pages octavo in large type."[37] As Tetens's first volume, exclusive of preliminary material, is 784 pages, and his second 834 pages, Coleridge's statement about "7 or 800" pages seems to apply very much to matters at hand.

But I suspect he read every word. Both volumes are annotated, although not copiously; the subject of freedom in the second volume, which elicited Kant's gibe to Markus Herz, receives a Coleridgean comment; most of all, however, I trust my own sense of how Coleridge read, built up from tracing or tracking him through numerous treatises. Quite in opposition to earlier views that had him dipping and skimming through works he barely understood, we must see him now as a man who was able to read when he was

---

[34]The note has been printed in Coburn, p. 40.

[35]De Vleeschauwer, *Kantian Thought*, p. 69.

[36]Letter to Markus Herz, April 1778, in *Kant*, X, 232. The criticism is tempered by Kant's preceding statement that "Tetens, in his vast and prolix work on human nature, has said much that is acute." Tetens, for his part, frequently refers to Kant's achievements, calling him, for instance, "the profound philosopher who observes the understanding so keenly" (*Über die allgemeine speculativische Philosophie* [Bützow and Wismar: In der Berger- und Boednerschen Buchhandlung, 1775], p. 56n).

[37]Note at p. xxxvi of vol. I of Tetens, now in the British Library.

able to do nothing else.[38] He read the works of Kant, for instance, with an almost unholy attentiveness, and was able to do so straight through the most severe periods of his opium addiction.[39]

In any event, what he needed in Tetens he could find within the first quarter of the first volume. And what was there to be found was not only the formulation of the theory of secondary imagination, but also the entire threefold division of the imaginative faculty that he deposits at the end of the thirteenth chapter of the *Biographia Literaria.*

The significance of this aspect of Coleridge's use of Tetens has not, I believe, been fully realized as yet. E. L. Stahl, in an article on Coleridge and Goethe that appeared in 1952 in the *Festgabe* for Fritz Strich, broached the possibility of Tetens (along with Maass) as an influence on Coleridge's theory of imagination. In 1955, René Wellek likewise mentioned the possibility. And although Stahl did not see the full situation, and Wellek contented himself with part of a single sentence, an article by Walter Greiner, which appeared in *Die neueren Sprachen* in 1960, identified both the secondary imagination and the threefold distinction of chapter 13 as stemming from Tetens.[40] Greiner, however, could not know the passage in the *Notebooks* that so conclusively points to Tetens as a Coleridgean source, nor was he, as a doctoral candidate, equipped to assess the meaning of his discovery. His article made no impression on established Coleridge scholarship.

Now Tetens, like Coleridge, and indeed almost everyone who has thought about the matter, initially dichotomizes the power of representation. He explains that "we ascribe to the psyche (*Seele*) not only a power to produce representations in themselves . . . but also a power of calling them forth again, a re-representing power, which is customarily termed fancy [*Phantasie*] or imagination [*Einbildungskraft*]."[41] As to these two latter terms, although Tetens

[38]Compare Dorothy Wordsworth's testimony, in a letter to Catherine Clarkson on 28 February 1810, during a time of virtual collapse on Coleridge's part. "As to Coleridge, . . . I hope that you are sufficiently prepared for the worst. We have no hope of him. . . . If he were not under our Roof, he would be just as much the slave of stimulants as ever; and his whole time and thoughts, (except when he is reading and he reads a great deal), are employed in deceiving himself, and seeking to deceive others. He will tell me that he has been writing, that he *has* written half a Friend; when I *know* that he has not written a single line" (*Middle Years*, I, 398–99). Again, on 2 June 1810: "Coleridge is still at Keswick where, as at Grasmere, he has done nothing but read" (p. 412).

[39]Cf. *Notebooks*, I, 1517. See further Whalley, p. 338.

[40]Stahl, pp. 101–16, especially p. 103; Wellek, II, 164; Walter Greiner, "Deutsche Einflüsse auf die Dichtungstheorie von Samuel Taylor Coleridge," *Die neueren Sprachen*, n.f., 9 (1960), 57–65.

[41]Tetens, I, 24.

says that *imagination* more truly indicates the re-representing power "in so far as it renews imagistic representations of sensation" (I, 24), the words remain for him synonymous, and in his actual practice he seems to prefer the word *fancy*. He is not satisfied, however, with the twofold division of *perceiving faculty* and *fancy*. In a radical departure from previous psychologizing, he adds a third entity, which he calls *Dichtungsvermögen*—that is, the power of joining together, and also, ambivalently, the power of poetry. "The activities of representation," he now says,

> can be conceived under three headings. *First* we produce original representations out of the sensations within us . . . this is *perception*. . . . *Secondly*, this power of sensation is reproduced even when those first sensations have ceased. . . . This effect is commonly ascribed to the . . . fancy. . . .
>
> *Thirdly*. This reproduction of the ideas is still not all, however, that the human power of representation does with them. It does not merely reproduce them, it does not merely alter their previous coexistence . . . but it also creates new images and representations. . . . The soul is able not only to arrange and order its representations, like the curator of a gallery of paintings, but is itself a painter, and invents and constructs new paintings.
>
> These achievements belong to the *Dichtungsvermögen*, a creative power, whose sphere of activity seems to have a great scope. . . . It is the self-active fancy . . . and without doubt an essential ingredient of genius. (I, 105–7)

Tetens's threefold division of the representing power or *Vorstellungskraft* into *Perceptionsvermögen, Dichtungsvermögen*, and *Phantasie*[42] is paralleled by Coleridges's threefold division of the imaginative powers into primary imagination, secondary imagination, and fancy. Moreover, there are striking similarities between Tetens's *Perceptionsvermögen* and Coleridge's primary imagination. To Coleridge, primary imagination is the "prime Agent of all human Perception"; to Tetens, the *Perceptionsvermögen* is the "facultas percipiendi" or faculty of perceiving (I, 24). Coleridge's faculty is a repetition of the "eternal act of creation"; Tetens's is called the "constituting power" ("Fassungskraft") (I, 105). It "produces the original representations out of the sensations in us, and maintains

---

[42] "The power of representation is a main branch that shoots out into the different faculties . . . as into so many twigs, that of receiving representations, that of drawing them forth again, and that of transforming them—that is, into the *Perceptionsvermögen*, into the *Einbildungskraft*, and into the plastic *Dichtungsvermögen*" (Tetens, I, 26).

them during after-perceiving, and we preserve these after-percep-
tions as reproductions of the sensed objects in us."[43]

The similarities extend also to Coleridge's fancy and Tetens's
fancy. For Coleridge, fancy "must receive all its materials ready
made from the law of association"; for Tetens, fancy operates
"nach der Regel der Association"—"according to the rule of association." For Coleridge, fancy is "the aggregative and associative
power"; for Tetens, fancy reproduces sensations either according
to "their previous coexistence in the senses" or according to the
rule that "similar representations group themselves with one another." This, he says, is "the law of the association of ideas."[44]

Tetens's new third entity, the *Dichtungsvermögen*, intrudes into
the activities of the law of association. Representations, says
Tetens, would occur strictly according to the "true association of
ideas," that is, according to their similarity or their coexistence, "if
nothing comes in between" (I, 112–13). But this "if," he says, is
"an if that permits exception" (I, 113). "The self-active *Dichtungsvermögen* comes between, and creates new representations
out of those already there, makes new points of union, new connections, and new series. The power of thought discovers new
relationships, new similarities, new coexistences, and new depen-
dences . . . and makes in this manner new channels of communication among ideas" (I, 112).

The intruding *Dichtungsvermögen* is the source of an activity that
Tetens calls *Dichtkraft*, and *Dichtkraft* seems to be neither more nor
less than Coleridge's secondary imagination. Chapter 14 of
Tetens's first essay is called "Concerning the Law of the Association of Ideas," and the rubric continues with the assurance that the
"law of association" is "only a law of the fancy in the reproduction
of sensations: it is no law for the combination of ideas in new
series" (I, 108). And then chapter 15 which is called "Von der
bildenden Dichtkraft"—that is, "On the plastic joining or poetic
power"—begins to discuss how new series are formed. The ten
sections of the discussion are indicated just below the title of the
chapter and include such headings as "laws of the creative *Dichtkraft*," "influence of the *Dichtkraft* on the order in which the reproductions of the fancy follow," and "the *Dichtkraft's* effecting
power extends through all classes of representations" (I, 115).

In the discussion itself are to be found repeatedly the exact

[43]Ibid. Tetens's curious technical word, "after-perceiving" ("*Nachempfinden*") is
the original, I suspect, of Coleridge's statement about "distinct recollection, or as
we may aptly express it, *after-consciousness*" (*Biographia*, I, 103). *Empfindung,
Nachempfindung, Reproduktion*, and *Dichtkraft* are the functions of *Vorstellungskraft*,
while *Apperception, Verstand*, and *Vernunft* are the functions of *Denkkraft*.
[44]Tetens, I, 140; *Biographia*, I, 293; Tetens, I, 106.

words used by Coleridge. Coleridge says that the secondary imagination "dissolves, diffuses, dissipates," that it struggles "to unify"; and elsewhere he says that imagination "blends, and (as it were) *fuses*." Tetens says that *Dichtkraft* is characterized by ac'tivities of "dissolving" ("Auflösen") and "reuniting" ("Wiedervereinigen"), "diffusing" in the sense of intermingling ("Ineinandertreiben") and "blending" ("Vermischen").[45]

The similarities do not end here. In chapter 13 of the *Biographia Literaria*, just before his threefold formulation, Coleridge refers to the imagination as *"the esemplastic power"*; and at the beginning of chapter 10 he opens with the famous statement: *"Esemplastic. The word is not in Johnson, nor have I met with it elsewhere."* Esemplastic, Coleridge then says, means "to shape into one," which is a "new sense" of the word "imagination."[46] The *Dichtkraft*, likewise, is not only a *bildende*—that is, shaping—power; it is also one whose "first law," Tetens says, is that "several simple representations" be "united into one" ("in Eine vereiniget").[47]

By way of illustrating the difference between fancy and *Dichtkraft*, Tetens invokes the example of Linnaeus, on the one hand, and of Milton and Klopstock, on the other. For Tetens, Linnaeus has, as Coleridge said of Cowley, a fanciful mind; the imagination of Linnaeus, says Tetens, "conceives a countless multitude of clear representations of sensation from bodily objects, and a like multitude of heard and gathered shades and tones; receives them in their clarity and reproduces them" (I, 159). The work of Milton, on the other hand, for Tetens as for Coleridge, is characterized by a different order of imagination—by *Dichtkraft*, which "with inner intensity reworks the imaginings, dissolves and blends, separates and draws together again, and creates new forms and appearances."[48]

---

[45]*Biographia*, I, 304; II, 16; Tetens, I, 117.

[46]*Biographia*, I, 303, 168, 168–70.

[47]Tetens, I, 136. Coleridge also knew Jean Paul's view by which "die Phantasie macht alle Teile zum Ganzen. . . . Sie totalisiert alles"—"imagination makes all parts a whole. . . . It totalizes everything" (*Jean Paul*, II, 38). This statement, however, was not even published until 1804, some two years after Coleridge had already defined *"Imagination"* as the *"modifying,* and *co-adunating* Faculty."* Moreover, Jean Paul considered *Einbildungskraft* as a power inferior to *Phantasie;* and his contexts are not so close to Coleridge as those of Tetens.

[48]Tetens, I, 160. Again: *"Dichtkraft* magnifies and reduces . . . it heaps up the similar and of one sort, or diminishes it, and makes magnitudes, grades, degrees which are over or under the magnitudes of sensation. It creates Brobdingnagians and Lilliputians" (I, 136). After citing three "laws" for *Dichtkraft*, Tetens says: "These are some of the laws and modes of action of *Dichtkraft*, which creates new simple representations. I have here intended to indicate only the first lines of this investigation. Are these all? I am not saying that" (I, 138). Such a statement constituted a virtual invitation for someone like Coleridge to make his own contribution.

Such passages could be adduced in great number, but perhaps these few serve to show that the plastic, shaping *Dichtkraft*, with its emphasis on dissolving, diffusing, blending, reuniting, and forming into one, and its introduction as a third entity into a spectrum made up of a psychological theory of perception and re-representation, is clearly an important source of the theory of secondary imagination.

We may approach the third and last of our stipulated questions from the perspective of this fact. What is the context in which we should consider the secondary imagination? Actually, the question might almost better be phrased: What is the context for the primary imagination? For the secondary imagination, although named as such only in chapter 13, seems really to be the imagination Coleridge customarily talks about elsewhere and to be called secondary only because of the primary imagination. The latter is the true newcomer. Coleridge's earliest invocation of the distinction between imagination and fancy, for instance, speaks of "Fancy, or the aggregating Faculty of the mind" and of "*Imagination*, or the *modifying*, and *co-adunating* Faculty."[49] The imagination here described seems to be the secondary imagination, and the date of the formulation, 10 September 1802, puts it interestingly close to the notebook entry of 1804 with its retrospective praise of Tetens. Furthermore, the phrase "co-adunating Faculty"—the faculty that makes many into one—could serve as a literal translation of the German *Dichtungsvermögen*, with the verb *dichten*, meaning "to join together" or "to caulk," serving as an ambivalent root along with *dichten* meaning "to compose poetry." In any event, our last question might be restated this way: What is the context in which we should consider Coleridge's use of Tetens's threefold distinction?

The answer to this question involves Coleridge's old nemesis, association psychology. The *Biographia Literaria* contains an intellectual history of Coleridge's concern to extricate himself from association psychology and at the same time attempts to elaborate a theory of imagination. Tetens, significantly, not only investigated the faculties of representation, but did so in the context of current theories of association psychology. He was, as J. H. Randall says, "in the thick of the crucial questions about knowledge raised in the 1760's."[50] The *Philosophische Versuche*, in other words, was very much a professional piece of psychological analysis, as those terms might apply to the situation in the late eighteenth century.

[49]*Collected Letters*, II, 865–66.
[50]Randall, p. 83.

This professionalism, or scientism, was extraordinarily important to Coleridge, in view both of his temperamental needs and of what he was trying to do in philosophy. The matter was, for Coleridge, not one of merely rejecting association psychology and affirming a theory of imagination against it. Blake, for instance, does that much. The attitudes of Locke and Newton were as repugnant to him as they were to Coleridge. He says, "Mans perceptions are not bounded by organs of perception, he percieves more than sense (tho' ever so acute) can discover." And he states that "to Me This World is all One continued Vision of Fancy or Imagination."[51] Imagination for Blake asserts the mind's freedom and is opposed to the hegemony of the external. "Natural Objects always did & now do Weaken deaden & obliterate Imagination in Me."[52] But Blake's opinions, though on these issues not very different from those of Coleridge, are formulated as insights, not as conclusions from argument or investigation. Instead of argument, Blake simply escalates, and indeed, exaggerates, his own statement:

> To cast off Bacon, Locke & Newton from Albions covering
> To take off his filthy garments, & clothe him with Imagination[53]

As Northrop Frye notes, "Bacon, Newton and Locke do not look very convincing in the role of three-headed hellish Cerberus which Blake assigns them." Blake, for his part, says with disarming candor that men and works such as "Locke on Human Understanding" inspire his "Contempt & Abhorrence"; "they mock Inspiration & Vision Inspiration & Vision was then & now is & I hope will always Remain my Element my Eternal Dwelling place. how then can I hear it Contemnd without returning Scorn for Scorn."[54]

Coleridge too looked on Locke with "Contempt & Abhorrence."[55] For him, however, it was important not merely to abuse Newton and Locke but to argue against them on their own cognitive terms. To use his own Phraseology, it was necessary to remove "the sandy Sophisms of Locke, and the Mechanic Dogmatists" by "demonstrating that the Senses were living growths and developements of the Mind & Spirit in a much juster as well as higher sense, than the mind can be said to be formed by the

---

[51]*Blake*, pp. 2, 677.
[52]Ibid., p. 655. See, e.g., Paley, pp. 200–260.
[53]Blake, p. 141.
[54]Frye, *Symmetry*, p. 187; *Blake*, p. 650.
[55]Henry Crabb Robinson, for instance, reports a typical conversation with Coleridge. "Of Locke he spoke as usual with great contempt. . . . He assented to my remark that atheism might be demonstrated out of Locke" (*Miscellaneous Criticism*, p. 390).

Senses." The important word here is *demonstrating*. "I can assert," says De Quincey, "upon my long and intimate knowledge of Coleridge's mind, that logic the most severe was as inalienable from his modes of thinking as grammar from his language."[56] Blake, on the other hand, dismissing both demonstration and logic, felt that

> Hes a Blockhead who wants a proof of what he Can't Percieve
> And he's a Fool who tries to make such a Blockhead believe[57]

But Coleridge, committed to a systematic reconciliation of all elements of experience, could not proceed in such a peremptory way. John Beer notes, in a passage that is increasingly recognized as going to the heart of Coleridge's interests, "Side by side with his visionary world of speculation, there is in his mind a positivist world of rationalist investigation, which he no doubt hoped would eventually be harmonized with it." And Coleridge himself said that the sum total of his convictions would constitute a system such "that of all Systems that have ever been presented, this has the least of *Mysticism*, the very Object throughout from the first page to the last being to reconcile the dictates of common Sense with the conclusions of scientific Reasoning."[58] Indeed, as Richard Haven has emphasized, Coleridge

> shared the respect of his age for science and scientific theories, the confidence that human experience could be explained as physical nature could be explained, that there were laws of human nature as well as laws of motion. While he was drawn to various earlier visionaries, he was also well aware of what seemed to be their inadequacy, their inability, that is, to meet the challenge of "enlightened" analysis and criticism. What he required was a means of reconciling the experience of the oasis [i.e., of visionary insight] with acceptable conceptions of physical and psychological reality.[59]

So Coleridge could hardly fail to be attracted by the most scientific and soberly professional psychologist of the German enlightenment. Tetens's two formidable tomes begin with a statement that seems to promise God's plenty. "The following essays concern the workings of the human understanding, its laws of thought and its basic powers; furthermore, they concern the active power of will, the fundamental character of humanity, freedom, the nature of the soul, and its development." Tetens immediately makes this comprehensiveness still more attractive by declaring

---

[56]*Collected Letters*, IV, 574; *De Quincey*, II, 153.
[57]*Blake*, p. 499.
[58]Beer, p. 287; *Collected Letters*, IV, 706.
[59]Haven, p. 81.

himself in favor of the most respectable scientific procedures. He states (following Newton) that he has "carefully sought to avoid the admixture of hypotheses among propositions of experience"; and he says that "concerning the method which I have utilized, I consider it necessary to explain myself at the beginning. It is the method of observation that Locke has pursued with regard to the understanding, and our psychologists have followed in the doctrine of psychic experience."[60]

Still another aspect of Tetens's procedure would doubtless have engaged Coleridge's attention. Tetens focuses not only on the tradition of Locke but specifically on Hartley and Priestley. Hartley's hypothesis, which Coleridge knew so well and from which he needed to free himself,[61] is brought forward almost at the outset. Tetens says: "The Hartleyan hypothesis that movements of the brain . . . consist in certain vibrations of the brain fibres or even of the aether in the brain, has been set forth by Mr. Priestley in a new, somewhat altered, well executed, and most praiseworthy exposition. Since then people have accustomed themselves to regard ideas as above all vibrations in the brain."[62] Coleridge, who was "much pleased . . . with everything that overthrows & or illustrates the overthrow of that all-annihilating system of explaining every thing wholly by association," would have been even more interested, however, in Tetens's further preliminary remarks about the "difficulties" of Hartley's view: for Tetens concludes, "It seems to me, nothing is less probable than that the whole sensible motion of the brain that constructs the material idea can consist purely and simply in vibration, as is hypothesized."[63]

If we inquire into the intellectual origin of this discontent on the part of Tetens with Hartley's psychology of association, we are led to a single source: Leibniz. Hartley's master, Locke, had supposed "the Mind to be, as we say, white Paper, void of all Characters, without any *Ideas*," and to be furnished by *"Experience."* "SENSATION" was the "great Source, of most of the *Ideas* we have." "External, Material things, as the Objects of SENSATION; and the Opera-

[60]Tetens, I, iii, xxix, iii–iv.

[61]Coleridge speaks in the *Biographia Literaria* of "Hartley's hypothetical vibrations in his hypothetical oscillating ether of the nerves" (I, 106). As early as November 1974, Coleridge writes of "a diligent, I *may* say, an intense study of Locke, Hartley and others who have written most wisely on the Nature of Man" (*Collected Letters*, I, 126). By December of that year he announces that he is "a compleat Necessitarian— and understand the subject as well almost as Hartley himself" (Ibid., p. 137).

[62]Tetens, I, viii–ix. Forty years later Coleridge says that "it is fashionable to smile at Hartley's vibrations and vibratiuncles; and his work has been re-edited by Priestley, with the omission of the *material* hypothesis" (*Biographia*, I, 110).

[63]*Notebooks*, II, 2093; Tetens, I, ix.

tions of our own Minds within, as the Objects of REFLECTION" were to Locke "the only Originals, from whence all our *Ideas* take their beginnings."[64]

This view of the mind's nature dominated European psychology until the second part of the eighteenth century. In 1765, however, Leibniz's answer to Locke, the *Nouveaux essais sur l'entendement,* was found and first published by Raspe. The *Nouveaux essais* immediately began to exert the strongest kind of counterinfluence on European intellectuals; indeed, the book's historical effect can hardly be overestimated.[65] "In my opinion," said Tetens proudly in a work of 1775, "our own Leibniz has seen far more deeply, acutely and correctly into the nature of the human understanding, its modes of thought, and in particular the transcendental knowledge of reason, than the more assiduously observing Locke. He has seen further than the otherwise clear-sighted Hume, than Reid, Condillac, Beattie, Search, and Home."[66] Such an endorsement implies an acceptance of the idea of inherent powers of mind, and thus for Coleridge's purposes a defense of the "I am" or irreducible sense of an autonomous self. For Leibniz had rejected the tabula rasa of the associationists as "a fiction,"[67] and had urged that "there are some ideas and principles that do not come to us

[64]Locke, pp. 104, 105.

[65]In fact, if one wishes to identify an event and a date as the origin of Romanticism, the publication of the *Nouveaux essais* in 1765 might be as good a candidate for this elusive honor as the outbreak of the French Revolution in 1789, the publication of *Lyrical Ballads* in 1798, or the appearance of Friedrich Schlegel's Fragment 116 in 1798. For not only did the *Nouveaux essais,* by its emphasis on "petites perceptions," open up a twilight world closed off by Descartes and undreamt of by Locke (*Leibniz,* V, 46–48), but the work called renewed attention to Leibniz's vision of "la matiere organique par tout" (V, 65), and to his conception of "puissance active" or "la Force"—of *"Forces agissantes primitives"* (V, 156). In his conception of "puissance active," both in matter and in the soul, Leibniz prepared the way both for the egotism and for the metaphorical, metaphysical, and physical dynamism that were hallmarks of Romanticism. In his conception of the organic he foreshadowed that emphasis on the organic view of nature that Whitehead has described as the essence of the Romantic reaction against eighteenth-century mechanism. And in his emphasis on "petites perceptions" he instituted the theory of the unconscious mind and of the importance of dreams—both of incalculable effect for Romanticism (see, e.g., Albert Béguin, *L'Ame romantique et le rêve* [Paris: Librairie José Corti, 1939]). G. H. Schubert's *Symbolik des Traumes* (Bamberg: C. F. Kung, 1814) which was read by Coleridge and influenced Freud (see, e.g., Jones, II, 312), arose out of ground fertilized by the *Nouveaux essais.* "The body," Leibniz said, "responds to all the soul's thought, rational or not, and dreams have also their marks in the brain as well as the thought of those who are awake" (*Leibniz,* V, 106).

[66] Tetens, *Über die allgemeine speculativische Philosophie,* p. 91.

[67]*Leibniz,* V, 99. This was not a new attitude on Leibniz's part. In 1686, some four years before the publication of Locke's *Essay Concerning Human Understanding,* he had declared himself against the tabula rasa. See above, chap. 2, n. 53.

from the senses, and that we find in ourselves without forming them, although the senses give us occasion to perceive them."[68] Moreover, by his conception of *vis activa* (active force) or *vis insita* (inherent force) as the nature of the monad, Leibniz paved the way for a rejection of the mind's passivity.[69] Cassirer notes, by way of inaugurating a discussion of Tetens: "when the mind becomes a mirror of reality [as it did in Leibniz's monad doctrine] it is and remains a living mirror of the universe, and it is not simply a sum total of mere images but a whole composed of formative forces. The basic task of psychology and epistemology will henceforth be to elucidate these forces in their specific structure and to understand their reciprocal relations. . . . The psychological formulation and defense of the spontaneity of the ego now prepare the ground for a new conception of knowledge and of art."[70] Of these late followers of Leibniz engaged in the psychological formulation and defense of the spontaneity of the ego, Tetens was, says Cassirer, "the most original and ingenious psychological analyst."[71]

Coleridge was as much aware of Leibniz as he was of Tetens. Indeed, in chapter 9 of the *Biographia Literaria*, the position of Locke is adduced in the language of Leibniz: "nihil in intellectu quod non prius in sensu"—"nothing in the mind that is not first in the senses." Coleridge also paraphrases Leibniz's amendment of the position: "praeter ipsum intellectum"—"except the mind itself."[72] The amendment provides as good a programmatic statement as any of Coleridge's arguments against the associationism of his youth. And it takes on added significance in light of the fact that

---

[68]*Leibniz*, V, 67. Cf. the statement of Proclus above, chap. 2, n. 53.

[69]The "puissance active" of the *Nouveaux essais* (see above, n. 65) was the "vis insita" of *De ipsa natura*, which "produces immanent actions, or what is the same thing, acts immanently" (*Leibniz*, IV, 510). Leibniz says in that treatise that his opinions "de vi insita" were "first published in the *Acta Eruditorum* of Leipzig in March, 1694, and further elaborated in my *Specimen dynamicum* in the same journal for April, 1695"—where the force was called *vis activa* (*Leibniz*, IV, 516). See below, n. 91.

[70]Cassirer, *Enlightenment*, pp. 124–25. Cf. *Leibniz*, VI, 616; IV, 485.

[71]Cassirer, *Enlightenment*, p. 125. Cf. the statement of Lewis White Beck that Tetens provided "an important recognition of the activity involved in knowing, which from now on in the history of philosophy is to be seen as an activity, not as a passive contemplation of pictures in the mind. No one in the eighteenth century between Leibniz and Kant so clearly saw the active aspects of knowing" (Beck, p. 418).

[72]*Biographia*, I, 141. Cf. Leibniz: "On m'opposera cet axiome receu parmy les Philosophes, *que rien n'est dans l'ame qui ne vienne des sens*. Mais il faut excepter l'ame même et ses affections. *Nihil est in intellectu, quod non fuerit in sensu*, excipe: *nisi ipse intellectus*. Or l'ame renferme l'estre, la substance, l'un, le même, la cause, la perception, la raisonnement, et quantité d'autres notions, que le sens ne sauroient donner" (*Leibniz*, V, 100–101).

the two massive volumes of Tetens represent a kind of enormously expanded gloss upon the position of Locke as criticized by Leibniz's addendum.

It is in the empirical examination of two related edifices of thought, science and poetry, that Tetens looks for his evidence for active powers of mind that stand outside the law of association, and to which he gives the general name *Denkkraft*.[73] He finds particularly vulnerable the associationist account of the mental activities revealed in poetry.

> Psychologists commonly explain poetic creation as a mere analysis and synthesis of ideas that are produced in sensation and drawn forth again. But does this really quite account for fictions? If so, then poetic creation is nothing more than a mere transposition of phantasms, from which no new simple ideas can arise in our consciousness. According to this supposition, every discrete sensuous appearance must, if analyzed into the component parts that can be differentiated by reflection, consist of nothing but pieces, which taken individually are pure imaginings or renewed ideas of sense.[74]

But, says Tetens, such is not the case; and he proceeds to examine a certain fiction used by poets, that of Pegasus. "The representation of Pegasus," he says,

> is an image of a winged horse. We have the image of a horse from sensation, and also the image of wings. Both are pure phantasms, sundered from other representations and bound together with one another here in the image of Pegasus. To that extent this is nothing but an effect of the fancy. But this is only an *analysis* and a *putting together again*.[75]

After further discussion, Tetens continues:

> It seems to me that there is more in the image than a mere putting together. The wings of Pegasus might have been a pure phantasm in the head of the first poet who produced this image; likewise the representation of the horse. But there is a place in the image, at the shoulders of the horse, somewhat more obscure than the others, where the wings are joined to the body; at that point the images of

---

[73]E.g., "Geometry, optics, astronomy—these works of the human mind, these irrefutable proofs of its greatness, are real and well-founded branches of knowledge. By what principles does human reason build such immense edifices? . . . It is in such enterprises that *Denkkraft* must be revealed in its greatest energy" (Tetens, I, 428–29). For the place of *Denkkraft* in Tetens's scheme see above, n. 43.

[74]Tetens, I, 116.

[75]Ibid., pp. 116–17. The winged horse is an image that appears elsewhere in philosophical discussion as to the nature of perception, e.g., in *Spinoza*, II, 132–34, and in James, *Principles*, II, 289.

the horse's shoulders and of the roots of the wings flow into one another. There is accordingly a spontaneous appearance, which disappears if the image of the horse and the image of the wings are again clearly separated from one another.[76]

By such form of empirical observation, which seems to prefigure the phi-phenomenon that lies at the basis of twentieth-century Gestalt psychology, Tetens concludes that *"Dichtkraft* can create no elements, no fundamental materials, can make only nothing out of nothing, and to that extent is no creative power. It can only separate, dissolve, join together, blend; but precisely thereby it can produce new images, which from the standpoint of our faculty of differentiation are discrete representations (I, 139). There is accordingly a "Selbstthätigkeit"—"a spontaneous activity"—in "the receptivity of the psyche," and on this "the ability to have secondary sensations depends" (I, 162). The "receptivity of our psyche" passes over into a "percipirende, reproducirende und dichtende Kraft"—"a perceiving, reproducing and co-adunating power" (I, 164).

Tetens's argument for "Selbstthätigkeit" in mental process, for "selbstbildende Dichtkraft," with such conceptions being derived in the course of an examination of association psychology, must have seemed to Coleridge like a fountain in the desert. He wrote in 1801, perhaps shortly before encountering the *Philosophische Versuche:* "Newton was a mere materialist—*Mind* in his system is always passive—a lazy Looker-on on an external World. If the mind be not *passive,* if it be indeed made in God's Image, & that too in the sublimest sense—the Image of the *Creator*—there is ground for suspicion, that any system built on the passiveness of the mind must be false, as a system." The phrase about the mind as "the Image of the *Creator*" seems to be a foreshadowing of the primary imagination as a "repetition in the finite mind" of the creative activity of "the infinite I AM." But the tone of the passage does not suggest that Coleridge at this moment had in hand the threefold elaboration of the mind's imaginative activity. The statement, however, occurred in the same month as his declaration that he had "overthrown the doctrine of Association, as taught by Hartley, and with it all the irreligious metaphysics of modern Infidels—especially, the doctrine of Necessity."[77] Apparently, then, some sort of intellectual conversion—which for Coleridge must have seemed to be based on cognitive demonstration—took place in March 1801,

[76]Tetens, I, 117–18.
[77]*Collected Letters,* II, 709, to Thomas Poole, 23 March 1801; p. 706, to Poole, 16 March 1801. See above, p. 89.

against association psychology and in favor of active powers of mind. Whether we suppose the reading of Tetens to have preceded and actually to have caused this change, or to have followed and confirmed it, it seems quite unarguable that those emphases of Tetens that I have described would be of central importance to Coleridge.[78]

They were still important when the *Biographia Literaria* came to be written, for there the problems are the same: to argue against association psychology and to affirm the spontaneous power of mind, although now in the specific form of imagination.[79] As Coleridge says in chapter 8 of that work, association theory neither "involves the explanation, nor precludes the necessity, of a mechanism and co-adequate forces in the percipient, which at the more than magic touch of the impulse from without is to create anew for itself the correspondent object."[80] Such an active principle was not elaborated in association psychology before Tetens.[81] As Coleridge

[78]It is clear at any rate that by that time Coleridge was aware of Leibniz's opposition to the tradition of Locke; e.g., see his letter to Josiah Wedgwood in February 1801. "Now Leibnitz not only opposed the Philosophy of Locke" (*Collected Letters*, II, 702). I rather feel, however, that Kant, as is traditionally the view, should be ascribed a larger part in the conversion—mainly because Coleridge's passage about overthrowing the doctrine of association also talks of extricating the "notions of Time, and Space." The reference could, of course, be to Leibniz, but Kant seems more likely. It is important to remember, however, that Coleridge was reading Leibniz at the same time and as intensely as he was Kant; and to syncretize the two would have been a characteristic procedure on his part. He writes in February 1801 that he turned "at times half reluctantly from Leibnitz or Kant even to read a smoking new newspaper / such a purus putus Metaphysicus am I become" (*Collected Letters*, II, 676). He had announced his intention to read Leibniz in June 1800 (I, 590), and was trying to see his works at the Durham library in July 1801 (II, 747).

[79]We may see this in a letter written during the actual composition of the *Biographia*. Speaking in 1815 of his "Autobiographia literaria, or Sketches of my literary Life & opinions as far as Poetry and *poetical* Criticism is concerned," Coleridge says that one of "the foundation Stones of the Constructive or Dynamic Philosophy in opposition to the merely mechanic" will be "a disquisition on the powers of association, with the History of the Opinions on this subject from Aristotle to Hartley, and on the generic difference between the faculties of Fancy and Imagination" (*Collected Letters*, IV, 578–79, to R. H. Brabant, 29 July 1815). In the interests of our understanding of the continuity of Coleridge's intellectual endeavor, however, it must be stressed that the *Biographia's* attempt to elucidate imaginative function elaborates, rather than rejects or replaces, a realization arrived at as early as 1796, by which "Fancy [i.e., imagination] is the power / That first unsensualises the dark mind . . . / Emancipates it from the grosser thrall / Of the present impulse" (Coleridge, *Poems*, I, 134). Also by 1796 (a date, incidentally, clearly in advance of his knowledge either of Tetens or of Kant) Coleridge had seen that the "Doctrine of necessity" is "rendered not dangerous by the Imagination" (*Notebooks*, I, 156). See further McFarland, *Coleridge*, pp. 157–58. Also see above, p. 89.

[80]*Biographia*, I, 137.

[81]Hartley's own view of imagination made no provision at all for *Dichtkraft* or for secondary imagination. "The Recurrence of Ideas," he says, "especially visible or audible ones, in a vivid manner but without a regard to the Order observed in past Facts, is ascribed to the Power of Imagination or Fancy" (Hartley, I, 383).

wryly says, "in Hartley's scheme, the soul is present only to be pinched or *stroked*, while the very squeals or purring are produced by an agency wholly independent and alien."[82] Tetens, in insisting that a third element, *Dichtkraft*, must be added to those accounted for by the law of association, provided exactly what Coleridge required.[83]

Therefore we must amend the theory, advanced by commentators such as D. G. James,[84] that sees Kant as the prototype for Coleridge's discrimination of the imaginative faculties. Whatever Kant's role, the correspondences between his descriptions of imagination and those of Coleridge are by no means so close as between those of Tetens and Coleridge.[85] There is, for instance, only a

[82]*Biographia*, I, 117. Hartley had said that *"Sensations"* were "those internal Feelings of the Mind, which arise from the Impressions made by external Objects upon the several Parts of our Bodies. . . . The ideas which resemble Sensations, are called *Ideas of Sensation:* All the rest may therefore be called *Intellectual Ideas.* It will appear in the Course of these Observations, that the *Ideas of Sensation* are the Elements of which all the rest are compounded" (Hartley, I, ii). Coleridge's objection to such a view was that it destroyed the meaning of human action and personality. "The assumption," he says, that "all acts of thought . . . are parts and products of this blind mechanism, instead of being distinct powers, whose function it is to controul, determine, and modify the phantasmal chaos of association," subordinates "final to efficient causes in the human being," and makes the "soul" a mere "ens logicum," something "worthless and ludicrous" (*Biographia*, I, 116–17).

[83]We can see very clearly the superimposition of "I am" controlled secondary imagination on associationist fancy in Coleridge's statement that "images, however beautiful, though faithfully copied from nature . . . do not of themselves characterize the poet. They become proofs of original genius only as far as they are modified by a predominant passion . . . or when they have the effect of reducing multitude to unity . . . or lastly, when a human and intellectual life is transferred to them from the poet's own spirit" (*Biographia*, II, 23). Compare Tetens's statements about Linnaeus and Milton adduced above (Tetens, I, 159). *Dichtkraft* intrudes into the law of association (see above and Tetens, I, 113), and this, for Coleridge, was what the activity of thought itself did. Crabb Robinson reports his conversation. "Thought . . . is a laborious breaking through the law of association" (*Miscellaneous Criticism*, p. 389). Again, in December, 1803: "The *streamy* Nature of Association, which Thinking = Reason, curbs & rudders" (*Notebooks*, I, 1770). Indeed, if we substitute Tetens's *Denkkraft*, or rational power of thought, for *Dichtkraft*, Coleridge's statements would agree identically with the opinion of Tetens. For the intrusion of *Dichtkraft* itself, cf. the question posed by Tetens: "For how many moments does the fancy operate in a vital man merely as fancy, according to the rule of association, without having the busy *Dichtkraft* mix itself in, and join together the series of images in a new way?" (Tetens, I, 140).

[84]James, *Scepticism*, pp. 18–24. E.g., p. 24, "Such we may believe was the essence of Kant's doctrine in the *Critique of Pure Reason*, and we may reasonably regard it as the source of Coleridge's reflections on the imagination." Cf. Baker, e.g., p. 29: "Kant administered the *coup-de-grace* to Hartley."

[85]Shawcross, however, goes too far when he says that "it is evident . . . that Coleridge's conception of the imagination was not fundamentally affected by his study of Kant" (Shawcross, I, xliii). For example, a statement in chapter 7 of the *Biographia* sounds thoroughly Kantian: "There are evidently two powers at work, which relatively to each other are active and passive; and this is not possible without an intermediate faculty, which is at once both active and passive. (In philosophical language, we must denominate this intermediate faculty in all its degrees and

twofold, not a threefold division of imaginative activity in the first *Critique;* and Kant's "productive imagination" does not emphasize dissolving, diffusing, and blending activities as do Coleridge's secondary imagination and Tetens's *Dichtkraft.* And in any case, Kant's own theories of imagination, as De Vleeschauwer demonstrates in his magisterial work on the transcendental deduction in Kant, were themselves derived from Tetens. "As to the theme of imagination," says De Vleeschauwer, "it is evident, although Kant disguises it somewhat by its integration in the transcendental methodology, that it derives from the psychological work of the eighteenth century. The birth, in effect, of the imagination from the internal sense comes directly from the psychology contemporary to Kant, and discloses increasingly the influence of Lockian empiricism." But, De Vleeschauwer points out, "the single memorable psychological event"[86] that occurred in Germany at this time was the publication of Tetens's *Philosophische Versuche,* and after exhaustive discussion he concludes as follows: "We shall terminate this chapter by demonstrating that Kant studied the *Philosophische Versuche* of Tetens. Anticipating this conclusion, the legitimacy of which is guaranteed by the correspondence of Kant, we believe that it is not going beyond the bounds of prudence so necessary in this kind of discussion to say that in all probability the introduction of imagination as a factor in the critical philosophy was due to the reading of Tetens."[87]

Coleridge's secondary imagination, therefore, looks past Kant's productive imagination to the *Dichtkraft* of Tetens. Authorized by the empirical observation of poetry rather than by a critic's notion of what poetry should be, both secondary imagination and *Dichtkraft* are themselves articulations of the metaphysical *vis activa* of

---

determinations, the IMAGINATION)" (*Biographia,* I, 124–25). See further McFarland, *Coleridge,* pp. 33–34, 306–10. Coleridge, impelled by his commitment to system and his urge to reconcile, customarily syncretized his sources. His major ideas exhibit a blending of his own thought with these syncretisms rather than an exclusive allegiance to a single source. For instance, though his insistence that the imagination "dissolves, diffuses, dissipates" (*Biographia,* I, 304) utilizes terms unique to Tetens (see above, n. 45), his statement that the imagination is a "synthetic" power (*Biographia,* II, 16) takes up a term emphasized not by Tetens but by Kant, e.g.: "Synthesis in general . . . is the mere result of the power of imagination, a blind but indispensable function of the soul, without which we should have no knowledge whatsoever"; "the pure synthesis of imagination"; "the reproductive synthesis of the imagination is to be counted among the transcendental acts of the mind"; "we must assume a pure transcendental synthesis of imagination as conditioning the very possibility of all experience" (*Kant,* IV, 64, 88, 79, 78).

[86]De Vleeschauwer, *Déduction transcendentale,* I, 290, 299.

[87]Ibid., p. 315. As Hamann wrote to Herder in May 1779: "Kant is at work on his Ethics of Pure Reason and always has Tetens lying before him" (*Hamann,* IV, 81).

Leibniz.[88] Thus in a note of 1804 Coleridge speaks of the "*Ego/* its metaphysical Sublimity—& intimate Synthesis with the principle of Co-adunation—without *it* every where all things were a waste—nothing, &c—."[89] Although the "principle of Co-adunation" here invoked is clearly the secondary imagination or *Dichtkraft,* the phrase about the ego's "metaphysical Sublimity" can refer neither to poetry nor to psychology, but only to metaphysics—that is, not to Tetens, but to Leibniz.

Indeed, one of the epigraphs to chapter 13 of the *Biographia Literaria*—a chapter, we may recall, bearing the subtitle "On the imagination, or esemplastic power"—is a Latin quotation from Leibniz's *Specimen dynamicum.*[90] It is, significantly, in this treatise that the conception of *vis activa* is most fully discussed. "Active force," says Leibniz there, is either "primitive or derivative"; the "primitive force" (which is what concerns us) is "nothing else than the first entelechy" or "the soul."[91] Coleridge's epigraph comes from a passage a few pages further on, and it stresses metaphysical rather than poetical principles. "In addition to considerations purely mathematical, and subject to the fancy, I have concluded that certain metaphysical principles must be admitted. . . . A certain higher, and so to speak, formal principle must be added to that of material mass."[92]

The epigraph, however, is not drawn wholly from *Specimen dynamicum.* Its first sentence is from the *De ipsa natura,* the treatise in which Leibniz discusses active force in the alternative phrasing of

[88]For Leibniz, "each monad is a living mirror, or a mirror endowed with an internal action [*action interne*] . . . it represents the universe according to its point of view"; it is "the nature of the monad to represent" (*Leibniz,* VI, 599, 617). Thus the representational activity or *vis representativa* is a form of the *vis activa* or primary substance. Cf. Beck, p. 282: "Leibniz . . . had emphasized the spontaneous creativity of consciousness in its representations, even in its perception of the world; the representative power (*vis representativa*), with the emphasis upon the power, has its most natural and characteristic function in the creation of images not given ready-made to the senses." For Coleridge's knowledge of the phrase *vis representativa* see *Biographia,* I, 133.

[89]*Notebooks,* II, 2057. Note the similarity of this statement to the passages at nn. 91 and 92 below.

[90]*Biographia,* I, 295.

[91]*Mathematische Schriften,* p. 236: "Duplex autem est *Vis Activa* . . . nempe ut *primitiva,* quae in omni substantia corporea per se inest . . . aut *derivativa.* . . . Et primitiva quidem (quae nihil aliud est quam ἐντελέχεια ἡ πρώτη) *animae* vel *formae substantiali* respondet." Cf. *Leibniz,* IV, 512. It seems possible and even perhaps probable that Coleridge's "primary" imagination owes its name to Leibniz's "primitive" active force, and equally so that "secondary" imagination reflects in its own name Locke's concession of a "secondary perception" that depends on "will" (see below, chap. 6).

[92]*Biographia,* I, 295; *Mathematische Schriften,* VI, 241–42. Coleridge, significantly, changes Leibniz's Latin word *imaginationi* to *phantasiae.*

vis insita, or inherent force. The sentence from this treatise refers to the Platonists as recognizing the necessity of formative powers as well as matter;[93] and elsewhere Leibniz speaks of Plato himself as supplying in his doctrine of *anamnesis*[94] a prototype of the doctrine of inherent mental force.[95]

So we may conclude that the lineage of the secondary imagination extends not only backward beyond Kant to Tetens, but also beyond Tetens to Leibniz, and finally beyond Leibniz to Plato. With antecedents of this kind, it is inevitable that Coleridge's threefold theory of imagination actually bears less on poetry than it does on those things that always mattered most to him—as they did to Leibniz and to Kant—that is, "the freedom of the will, the immortality of the soul, and the existence of God."[96]

And yet, even as one notes the special transmitting role of Tetens in the channeling of the current of secondary imagination back to the high reservoirs of Leibniz, Plato, and Christian concern, a corollary fact must be noted as well. Tetens was the most scientifically responsible of the eighteenth-century investigators of imagination; but there were others, even if without his demonstrative rigor, who were saying very much the same things.

Every decade, in truth, produced similar formulations. For instance, though Tetens's work appeared in 1777, a large part of what he was urging was adumbrated precisely ten years before, in 1767, and adumbrated also precisely ten years before that, in 1757. Thus in that year Edmund Burke wrote:

> Besides the ideas . . . which are presented by the sense; the mind of man possesses a sort of creative power of its own; either in representing at pleasure the images of things in the order and manner in which they were received by the senses, or in combining those

[93]*Leibniz*, IV, 509: "Surely if corporeal things contained nothing but matter, they could most truly be said to consist of a flux and to have nothing substantial, as the Platonists long ago recognized."
[94]*Phaedo* 72E–75E; *Meno* 81C–D.
[95]E.g., *Leibniz*, IV, 451–52; V, 42.
[96]*Kant*, III, 518. Cf. Coleridge: "God created man in his own image . . . gave us REASON . . . gave us CONSCIENCE—that law of conscience, which . . . unconditionally *commands* us attribute *reality*, and actual *existence*, to those ideas and to those only, without which the conscience itself would be baseless and contradictory, to the ideas of Soul, of Free-will, of Immortality, and of God!" (*Friend*, I, 112). It is, furthermore, significant that the first epigraph to chapter 13 of the *Biographia* is Milton's "O Adam, One Almighty is, from whom / All things proceed, and up to him return" (*Biographia*, I, 295). Again, see Coleridge's statement that "the free-will" is "our only absolute *self*" (I, 114), or the concluding words of the *Biographia* about preserving "the Soul steady and collected in its pure *Act* of inward Adoration to the great I AM, and to the filial WORD that re-affirmeth it from Eternity to Eternity" (II, 247–48). Cf., e.g., *Leibniz*, V, 65.

images in a new manner, and according to a different order. This power is called Imagination; and to this belongs whatever is called wit, fancy, invention, and the like. But it must be observed, that this power of the imagination is incapable of producing any thing absolutely new; it can only vary the disposition of those ideas which it has received from the senses.[97]

Except that Tetens conducts his investigation as a formal psychologist taking note of empirical data, there is little he says that is not at least in principle contained in Burke's statement. Burke understands that images derived from sensory experience are necessary to imagination; he also understands, quite in accord with Tetens's *Dichtkraft*, except that he does not elaborate the understanding, that "the mind of man possesses a sort of creative power of its own . . . in combining those images in a new manner and according to a different order."

The same factors are bubbling in William Duff's mind ten years later, in 1767. "Imagination is that faculty whereby the mind not only reflects on its own operations, but which assembles the various ideas conveyed to the understanding by the canal of sensation, and treasured up in the repository of the memory, compounding or disjoining them at pleasure; and which, by its plastic power of inventing new associations of ideas, and of combining them with infinite variety, is enabled to present a creation of its own, and to exhibit scenes and objects which never existed in nature."[98]

Such repetitions of analysis and formulation surely testify as much to the common urgencies of the topic when confronted by individual minds as to their authors' reading of one another. Granted the dominance of a psychology based on the association of ideas, inevitably the capacity of the mind to "present a creation of its own, and to exhibit scenes and objects which never existed in nature"—a capacity that anyone can verify from his own experience—would pave the way for conceptions that strained against the hegemony of the Lockean tradition. Tetens, in line with the paradoxes insisted on throughout this volume, was at one and the same time an original investigator and one who could claim actual priority on only one small if crucial point, and even that only as a matter of specific demonstration in scientific context.

[97]Burke, pp. 16–17.
[98]Duff, pp. 6–7.

• 5 •

The Poetic Working of Secondary Imagination

*A*lthough the doctrine of imagination is one that connects itself with the freedom of the will, the immortality of the soul, and the existence of God, it is also, in its most evident manifestation, the source of creativity in the arts, and a fortiori in poetry. No doubt the enormous value placed on creation has something to do with the sense of achievement deriving from any high craftsmanship, which in its turn, by a diminishing gradation descending back into the shadows of prehistory, has something to do with man as toolmaker becoming more than man as mere animal. To make something is the first step toward higher life.

This making can at some point branch from the instrumental and utilitarian to the instrumental and aesthetical, and in the higher arts to the purely aesthetical. Or rather in the higher arts the instrumentally utilitarian is transformed into the ideally functioning: the great poem raises the sense of human worth in the same line of values as does the invention of the plough or the weaving of cloth.

One cannot justify a view by which the making of a great poem is more important than the weaving of cloth or the making of a plough; it is equally certain, however, that though these latter are things of the cultural basis, the making of a poem seems to occupy a higher sphere. The poet is proudly proclaimed as maker by the very etymology of his name. *"What is a Poet?"* asks Jonson. "A *Poet* is that which by the *Greeks* is called . . . ὁ Ποιητής, a Maker, or a fainer: . . . From the word ποιεῖν, which signifies to make, or fayne." But this kind of identification, which Renaissance theorists repeatedly made, is linked to a still higher function. "Among the *Romanes*," says Sir Philip Sidney, "a Poet was called *Vates*, which is as much as a diviner, foreseer, or Prophet."[1]

[1]*Jonson*, VIII, 635; *Sidney*, III, 6.

With *poietes* shading into *vates*, the idea of making is raised to connection with divine things. Coleridge's primary imagination is accordingly "a repetition in the finite mind of the eternal act of creation in the infinite I AM." The secondary imagination is "an echo of the former, co-existing with the conscious will, yet still as identical with the primary in the *kind* of its agency, and differing only in *degree*, and in the *mode* of its operation."[2] The primary imagination, in other words, is that power of mind that gives us reality and holds it in place; the secondary, that power of mind that allows us to summon images whether a correspondent external datum is present or not. Although all of us constantly use the secondary imagination, it is in the creations of poets and other artists that its characteristics are unmistakably displayed.

The connection of the poet creating his poem to God creating the world is a Platonist thought of venerable antiquity, and divine things and poetic things are explicitly linked together in the *Ion*.[3] But the tradition was ever renewed, and its witness occurs in the most disparate places. Leibniz says: "The spirit not only has a perception of the works of God but is even capable of producing something that resembles them, though in miniature"; "In its own realm and in the small world in which it is allowed to act, the soul imitates what God performs in the great world." More than a century earlier, Sir Philip Sidney had accorded "right honour to the heavenly maker of that maker, who having made man to his owne likenes, set him beyond and over all the workes of that second nature, which in nothing he sheweth so much as in Poetry; when with the force of a divine breath, he bringeth things foorth surpassing her doings."[4]

Still earlier, Ficino (the "illustrious Florentine" to whom Coleridge pays tribute in the *Biographia Literaria* as a formative influence on his thinking),[5] had noted in his *Theologia Platonica* that

> what is quite wonderful, human arts produce by themselves whatever nature produces, as if we were not the slaves, but the rivals of nature. Thus, Zeuxis painted grapes in such a manner that the birds flew to them. Apelles painted a steed and a she-dog in such manner that in passing by, horses would neigh and dogs bark. . . .
>
> Thus man imitates all the works of the divine nature, and

---

[2]*Biographia*, I, 304.

[3]"Well, do you see that the spectator is the last of the rings I spoke of, which receive their force from one another by the virtue of the magnet? You, the rhapsodist and actor, are the middle ring, and the first one is the poet himself. But it is the deity who, through all the series, draws the spirit of men wherever he desires, transmitting the attractive force from one into another." (Plato, *Ion* 535E–536A).

[4]*Leibniz*, VI, 604, 605; *Sidney*, III, 8–9.

[5]*Biographia*, I, 144.

perfects, corrects and improves the works of the lower nature.
Therefore the power of man is almost similar to that of the divine
nature, for man acts in this way through himself. Through his own
mind and art he governs himself, without being bound by any limits
of corporeal nature; and he imitates all the works of the higher
nature.[6]

Coleridge of course knew Sidney and he had read widely in
Leibniz, especially in 1801; his copy of Ficino's *Platonica Theologia*,
in a "new impression" of 1525, is in the British Library, signed and
dated, "S. T. Coleridge . . . 9 Oct 1805." So all these formulations
were available in him, and these and other sources presumably
acted as subliminal accretions and almost imperceptible layers in
the building of the coral reef of his own doctrine of poetic
creativity. Sidney speaks of "Poetry" as best displaying the human
maker's "likeness" to the heavenly maker. Leibniz for his part
speaks not of "secondary imagination" but of "soul" as imitating
"what God performs in the great world." Ficino's asseveration,
"Denique homo omnia divinae naturae opera imitatur et naturae
inferioris opera perficit, corrigit et emendat," appears in a work
called not merely *Platonic Theology,* but in its full title *Platonic Theology Concerning the Immortality of the Soul.*[7]

Thus the structure of argumentation that in the thirteenth chapter of the *Biographia* represents the relationship of deity, primary
imagination, and secondary imagination reverberates with the conception of soul. Indeed, the idea of poet as maker being merely the
highest form in a continuum of man as toolmaker, weaver, and
cultivator, and thus of poetic creativity as being a chief witness to
man's very essence, is cannily recognized by Ficino.

> Our mind does not flatter our imagination . . . by different games in
> a kind of play; but sometimes, also, the thinking reason acts more
> seriously, and eager to bring forth its products, leaps forth and
> visibly shows the power of its genius in the manifold textures of
> wool and silk and in pictures, sculptures, and buildings. In produc-
> ing these things, our mind often does not take into consideration
> any physical comfort or pleasure of the senses, for sometimes it even
> endures discomfort and trouble from them of its own free will. It
> rather aims at an amplification of its eloquence and at a proof of its
> power.

[6]Ficino, Lib. XIII, Cap. 3, p. 219ᵛ. Again: "Diximus alias quemadmodum per
varias artes omnia dei opera aemulatur: atque ita instar dei efficit omnia"—"Elsewhere we have described how our soul through its various arts imitates all the
works of God: and thus effects all things, after the model of God" (Lib. XIV, Cap. 4,
p. 235).

[7]*Collected Letters,* I, 590; II, 676, 747; Ficino, *Platonica Theologia de Immortalitate
animorum* (Florentiae, 1482).

In these works of art we may notice how man handles all
materials of the world and in all manners, as if they were subjected
to him. I say, he handles elements, stones, metals, plants and
animals, and transforms them into many forms and figures, an
achievement of which the animals are incapable. . . . He treads on
the earth, sails on the water, ascends into the air by means of very
high towers, not to mention the wings of Daedalus or Icarus. . . .
Man not only makes use of the elements, but also adorns them, a
thing which no animal ever does. How wonderful is the cultivation
of the soil all over the earth, how marvelous the construction of
buildings, and cities, how skillful the control of the waterways!

Man is really the vicar of God, since he inhabits and cultivates all
elements and is present on earth without being absent from the
ether.[8]

In this kind of amplification we can see how smoothly the com-
pressed Coleridgean statement dovetails its function as a philosophical connective for his overriding theological needs with the
specific function of the creation of poetry.

If we seek in the poetry itself evidences of the secondary imagination at work, we can find them most intriguingly displayed. The
exotic poems, "Kubla Khan," "Christabel," and "The Ancient
Mariner" are of course all witnesses to the play of secondary imagination. They all create heterocosms, worlds parallel to but not
found in the brazen world of actuality; and Coleridge quite fittingly
described "The Ancient Mariner" as a work of "pure imagination."[9]

For our present purposes, however, it might be even more rewarding to examine the secondary imagination as it works in the
so-called conversation poems, and specifically in two of them, "Reflections on Having Left a Place of Retirement" and "This Lime-
Tree Bower My Prison." Ever since George McLean Harper extended the subtitle of "The Nightingale. A Conversation Poem" to
a whole class of Coleridge's poems, critics have found themselves
more and more fascinated by the structure of these efforts.[10] Albert
Gérard has elucidated this structure in terms of what he calls a
"systolic" rhythm that swings back and forth between the re-
strictedly local and the expansively general, between the poetically
subjective and the naturalistically objective.[11] M. H. Abrams has
carried the discussion still further and in fact finds in these poems

---

[8]Ficino, Lib. XIII, Cap. 3, pp. 219ᵛ–220.

[9]*Table Talk*, p. 87 (31 May 1830).

[10]George McLean Harper, "Coleridge's Conversation Poems," *Spirit of Delight*
(New York: Henry Holt & Co., 1928), pp. 3–27. The essay first appeared in 1925 in
Quarterly Review.

[11]Gérard, *Discordant Harp*, pp. 20–39.

the paradigm for a major characteristic of English Romantic poetic practice as such, which he calls "the greater Romantic lyric."[12] Other critics have found other fascinations. A recent commentator, for instance, has seen them as politically oriented statements: Coleridge's setting up of the personal and familial as haven against the socially extended disruptions of the French Revolution.[13]

The conversation poems, in short, seem by common agreement to be not only superior works of poetic art, but to be an extraordinarily rich ground for theoretical clarifications.

To those already in the public domain, therefore, I should like to add elucidations in terms of the play of secondary imagination. For Coleridge seems in these poems to be explicitly testing that faculty, somewhat the way a mechanic tunes a motor. He seems to be providing, not so much for an audience as for himself, what Ficino in the words cited above called "an amplification" of the mind's "eloquence" and "a proof of its power." One may say, parenthetically, that although Coleridge did not explicitly elaborate a "secondary" function for imagination until the thirteenth chapter of the *Biographia,* published in 1817, he was not inventing, but describing, an activity of mind that is permanently there. Accordingly, there is no more contradiction in speaking of the play of secondary imagination in poems written before the elaboration of the formula than there would be in talking of the growth of California redwoods in the centuries preceding Columbus.

In his "Reflections on Having Left a Place of Retirement," written as early as 1795, on the occasion of his relinquishing his cottage at Clevedon and moving to Bristol for closer proximity to his printer, Coleridge achieves in full measure the systolic rhythm. The poem alternates between the world of the country and that of the city, between nature as beautiful local spot and nature as extended vista, between the sacredness of the familial relationship and the sacredness of human society, between the present and the future, between the pastoral mode and the heroic mode. In this constant series of shiftings back and forth, the effecting agency, "the proof" of the mind's "power," is the imagination.

Coleridge begins the poem with a pastoral evocation of a single spot. "Low was our pretty Cot: our tallest Rose / Peep'd at the chamber-window." In this specifically localized awareness, Coleridge seems to be unmistakably augmenting the sense of "here."

---

[12]M. H. Abrams, "Structure and Style in the Greater Romantic Lyric," in *From Sensibility to Romanticism; Essays Presented to Frederick A. Pottle,* ed. Frederick W. Hilles and Harold Bloom (New York: Oxford University Press, 1965).

[13]Everest, pp. 527–60.

He continues, in meticulous detail, to weave the illusion of a palpable reality: we ourselves are in this place, almost as though we had taken a journey and arrived there.

> Low was our pretty Cot: our tallest Rose
> Peep'd at the chamber-window. We could hear
> At silent noon, and eve, and early morn,
> The Sea's faint murmur. In the open air
> Our Myrtles blossom'd; and across the porch
> Thick Jasmins twined: the little landscape round
> Was green and woody, and refresh'd the eye.
> It was a spot which you might aptly call
> The Valley of Seclusion! . . .

The naming—"The Valley of Seclusion"—acts to seal off the palpable sense of place. It and the details preceding it witness one of imagination's chief characteristics; for as Shakespeare says,

> . . . imagination bodies forth
> The forms of things unknown, the poet's pen
> Turns them to shapes, and gives to airy nothing
> A local habitation and a name.[14]

The pastoral selection of details, the rose peeping at the chamber window, silent noon, the sea's faint murmur, blossoming myrtles and twined jasmins, performs the pastoral function that Fontenelle in 1688, in his *Discours sur la nature de l'églogue,* called "Illusion," which "consists, in exposing to the Eye only the Tranquility of a Shepherd's Life, and in dissembling or concealing its meanness, as also in showing only its Innocence and hiding its miseries."[15] Pope followed Fontenelle by saying that "we must therefore use some illusion to render a Pastoral delightful; and this consists in exposing the best side only of a shepherd's life, and in concealing its miseries." Coleridge's lines conform to this kind of filtering and purification of reality, as they also do to Pope's specification that the pastoral should be a poem characterized by "simplicity, brevity, and delicacy."[16] The sealing off and pastoralization of the "here" combine to locate it as blessed spot, and Coleridge emphasizes the delimitation by introducing into this country paradise a denizen of the city ("A wealthy son of Commerce," "Bristowa's citizen") who, sauntering by,

---

[14]Coleridge, *Poems,* I, 106–8; *A Midsummer Night's Dream,* V.i.14–17.
[15]See p. 284 of Motteux's translation of Fontenelle's *Discours,* included in the English translation of Le Bossu's *Treatise of the Epick Poem* ([René Le Bossu], *Monsieur Bossu's Treatise of the Epick Poem* . . . [London: Printed for Tho. Bennet, 1695]), under the title *Of Pastorals.*
[16]*Pope,* I, 27, 25.

> . . . paus'd, and look'd
> With a pleas'd sadness, and gaz'd all around,
> Then eyed our Cottage, and gaz'd round again,
> And sigh'd, and said, it was a Blesséd Place.

"Bristowa's citizen" is of course not merely an activation of the age-old tension between the country and the city, but specifically a necessity of pastoral realization, where the "Tranquility of a Shepherd's Life" attracts only by contrast to the hurly-burly of city or court. The pastoral world is peopled not by actual shepherds but by urban or courtly sophisticates playing the role of shepherds. Paul Alpers has emphasized, speaking of *As You Like It:*

> But even when we recognize that the pastoral world of Arden is to be defined by its inhabitants, there is something odd about it: there are more courtiers in it than natives, and the courtiers define the tone and concerns of the play. Shakespeare thus makes explicit what has always been clear about pastoral—that it is a sophisticated form, that it is of the country but by and for the court or city. Hence the emphasis of the play is not on the represented shepherds but on the courtiers who represent themselves as shepherds—or to put it more precisely, as inhabitants of the forest of Arden.[17]

The poet next reaffirms the sense of blessing and of sealed-off place, with its privileged inhabitants.

> And we *were* bless'd. Oft with patient ear
> Long-listening to the viewless sky-lark's note
> (Viewless, or haply for a moment seen
> Gleaming on sunny wings) in whisper'd tones
> I've said to my Belovéd, 'Such, sweet Girl!
> The inobtrusive song of Happiness,
> Unearthly minstrelsy! then only heard
> When the Soul seeks to hear; when all is hush'd,
> And the Heart listens!'

There then intervenes a "but," and by this rhetorical device a whole new scene is substituted. The "but" is a single creating word, a logos (to use the Greek term that was a focal point for Coleridge's entire systematic preoccupation with philosophy and theology). It is as Godlike in its creative power as is Kubla Khan decreeing the pleasure dome. A new "here" is substituted for the "here" of the cottage.

> But the time, when first
> From that low Dell, steep up the stony Mount

17 Alpers, p. 457.

I climb'd with perilous toil and reach'd the top,
Oh! what a goodly scene! *Here* the bleak mount,
The bare bleak mountain speckled thin with sheep;
Grey clouds, that shadowing spot the sunny fields;
And river, now with bushy rocks o'er-brow'd,
Now winding bright and full, with naked banks;

What seems especially to indicate that Coleridge is in this poem involved in "an amplification" of the mind's "eloquence" and "a proof of its power," is that the initial "here," constructed and set apart with such meticulous virtuosity, Edenized, so to speak, is dismissed into nothing as easily as it has been constructed from nothing (the Christian God not only creates, but specifically creates out of nothing).[18] The new "here" that replaces it also is meticulously realized. If the power of imagination were not specifically on display, then either the first "here" would not be so palpably presented, or the second one would not be presented as "here"— that is, it could easily be referred to in some kind of brief narrative evocation as "there" or "once." Instead, it is totally constructed; it is made a world in itself: we *see* and involve ourselves in

The bare bleak mountain speckled thin with sheep;
Grey clouds, that shadowing spot the sunny fields.

Coleridge continues, the mode changing from the pastoral to the heroic, the sense of the intensely personal changing to the sense of the divine, both transformations additional proofs of the imagination's power.

And seats, and lawns, the Abbey and the wood,
And cots, and hamlets, and faint city-spire;
The Channel *there*, the Islands and white sails,
Dim coasts, and cloud-like hills, and shoreless Ocean—
It seem'd like Omnipresence! God, methought,
Had built him there a Temple: the whole World
Seem'd *imag'd* in its vast circumference:
No *wish* profan'd my overwhelmèd heart,
Blest hour! It was a luxury,—to be!

The philosophical specification "to be," which looks neither to past nor to future but only to an intensely realized present, accentuates the virtuosity with which the mountaintop world has been brought to reality.

Although the mountaintop is a construct of imagination, a true *creatio ex nihilo*, its palpable reality is cunningly reinforced by invo-

[18]See, e.g., Gerhard May, *Schöpfung aus dem Nichts; Die Entstehung der Lehre von der Creatio ex Nihilo* (Berlin: Walter de Gruyter, 1978).

cations of imagination's function that seem to lie outside its "here-ness." The seeming image suggested by the vista makes us accept the vista itself as reality: the "whole World / Seem'd *imag'd* in its vast circumference." Likewise, the reference to "The Channel *there,* the Islands and white sails, / Dim coasts, and cloud-like hills, and shoreless Ocean" augments the immovable permanence of the "here" from which the vista is seen. And yet the whole scene is imaginary, and the fullness of its reality is as momentary as that of the pastoral scene it has with such virtuosity annulled.

The *otium* of that initial pastoral scene is also transformed, as the mode changes from the pastoral to the heroic, by the "perilous toil" with which the poet climbs from "that low Dell, steep up the stony Mount." But then, the dell and the mount, cast into opposi-tions so various, coalesce in the common function of representing the delights of country against the encroachments of city.

> Ah! quiet Dell! dear Cot, and Mount sublime!
> I was constrain'd to quit you. Was it right,
> While my unnumber'd brethren toil'd and bled,
> That I should dream away the entrusted hours
> On rose-leaf beds,

The raising of the moral question, "Was it right?" lifts the poet from *otium,* from the "now," from the solitude of his personal life, to society, to toil, to the city.

> . . . he that works me good with unmov'd face,
> Does it but half: he chills me while he aids,
> My benefactor, not my brother man!
> Yet even this, this cold beneficence
> Praise, praise it, O my Soul! oft as thou scann'st
> The sluggard Pity's vision-weaving tribe!
> Who sigh for Wretchedness, yet shun the Wretched,
> Nursing in some delicious solitude
> Their slothful loves and dainty sympathies!
> I therefore go, and join head, heart, and hand,
> Active and firm, to fight the bloodless fight
> Of Science, Freedom, and the Truth in Christ.

Yet though the moral call evicts the poet from his "Place of Retirement," that "place"—"the Valley of Seclusion"—which has been created from nothing and then returned to nothing, is once more created (reversing the conditional question that was to rule in "Kubla Khan," "Could I revive within me? . . ."), to assert the hegemony of the poet's imagination.

Yet oft when after honourable toil
Rests the tir'd mind, and waking loves to dream,
My spirit shall revisit thee, dear Cot!
Thy Jasmin and thy window-peeping Rose,
And Myrtles fearless of the mild sea-air.
And I shall sigh fond wishes—sweet Abode!
Ah!—had none greater! And that all had such!
It might be so—but the time is not yet.
Speed it, O Father! Let thy Kingdom come!

The "dear Cot" is re-created by imagination and at the same time still a third re-creation is promised—the "Kingdom come" of the earthly paradise, when all can share in such pastoral bliss and therefore no moral call need evict the fortunate few.

Throughout the poem there has been an extraordinary *kinesis:* the present gives way to the future, the pastoral dell gives way to the mountain, the mountain gives way to the abode of the wretched, the city, which in its turn gives way to a re-creation of the dell. These constant changes, together with the vividness with which scenes are created only to be banished, not only show the secondary imagination at work, but as it were exult in the imagination's power. Ficino said that man the artistic maker "handles all materials of the world and in all manners, as if they were subjected to him . . . handles elements, stones, metals, plants and animals, and transforms them into many forms and figures."[19] Or as Coleridge himself said, the secondary imagination, "co-existing with the conscious will," "dissolves, diffuses, dissipates, in order to recreate." It echoes "the repetition in the finite mind of the eternal act of creation in the infinite I AM"; or as Ficino says, shows "Man" to be "the vicar of God."

That the poem's extraordinarily protean movement, which tests the power of the secondary imagination, is no mere accident can be demonstrated by considering a second poem, "This Lime-Tree Bower My Prison."[20] The "Retirement" poem and the "Bower" poem are even more closely related than previous conceptions of the genre of "conversation" poem have made clear. In fact, they are so similar that one is drawn to conclude that both are "proofs" of the mind's Godlike power as it wields the miraculous wand of imagination.

The "Bower" poem, like the "Retirement" poem, sets up a pas-

19See above, n. 8.
20Coleridge, *Poems*, I, 178–81.

toral place; like the "Retirement" poem it moves from dell to mountaintop; like the earlier poem it changes from the pastoral to the heroic as it memorably creates the vista seen from the mountain; like the earlier poem it sets up a tension between country and city; like the earlier poem it takes up the theme of solitude vis-à-vis the experience of a group. Most of all, like the earlier poem, it exults in the creation and the dissolution of realities rendered almost palpable by the poet's art.

The situation in "This Lime-Tree Bower My Prison" is that the poet must stay behind because of an injury to his foot, while some of his friends, especially one who is from the city, take a walk in nature. Here the exploration of the powers of the imagination achieves even greater virtuosity than it does in "Reflections on Having Left a Place of Retirement," for a dichotomy is set up between the scene inhabited by the solitary poet and the walk he imagines his friends as taking. The scene of the solitary poet (which is of course imagined) presents itself as real. From this presented reality a second extension of imagination takes place: the friends are visually accompanied on their walk although the poet cannot possibly be along to see. This second world, which is explicitly made to seem imaginary as related to the reality of the first world, which is in fact already imaginary, is playfully given as much detail of reality as is the first world. It is then banished by a return to the "reality" of the first world and the poem proceeds to a philosophical conclusion in the manner of the "Retirement" poem.

The "Bower" poem begins with a framing device, as Coleridge's poems so often and variously do.[21] Not measured verse, but prose explanation first meets us after the title, "The Lime-Tree Bower My Prison," following a secondary explanation, omitted later, that the poem is "addressed to Charles Lamb, of the India House, London." The prose explanation says: "In the June of 1797 some long-expected friends paid a visit to the author's cottage; and on the morning of their arrival, he met with an accident, which disabled him from walking during the whole time of their stay. One evening, when they had left him for a few hours, he composed the following lines in the garden-bower." Modern scholarship has increasingly tended to contest Coleridgean assertions about the speed with which his poems were written, or indeed about the congruence of the composition with the event supposedly prompting the poem.[22] No matter. The explanation, which seems to reside

[21]For discussion of the various ways such framing devices function in Coleridge's poetry, see Wheeler.
[22]See, e.g., Schneider, Fruman.

in the world of palpable fact, already moves toward the dissolvings and recreations of imagination.

After the explanation, which seems to set the poem in the matrix of palpable reality, the poet radically reinforces that matrix by an almost muttered invocation of the here-and-now.

> Well, they are gone, and here must I remain,
> This lime-tree bower my prison! . . .

Nothing is more palpable than a prison, and its invocation as "this" and "here" nails down, so to speak, the reality of the poet's scene and allows him to embark immediately on the "imaginary" participation in the friends' scene. The "imaginary" status of that world is guaranteed by the word "meanwhile," which keeps the poet firmly in his lime-tree bower despite the increasingly meticulous presence accorded the friends' progress.

> They, meanwhile,
> Friends, whom I never more may meet again,
> On springy heath, along the hill-top edge,
> Wander in gladness, and wind down, perchance,
> To that still roaring dell, of which I told;
> The roaring dell, o'erwooded, narrow, deep,
> And only speckled by the mid-day sun;
> Where its slim trunk the ash from rock to rock
> Flings arching like a bridge;—that branchless ash,
> Unsunn'd and damp, whose few poor yellow leaves
> Ne'er tremble in the gale, yet tremble still,
> Fann'd by the water-fall! and there my friends
> Behold the dark green file of long lank weeds,
> That all at once (a most fantastic sight!)
> Still nod and drip beneath the dripping edge
> Of the blue clay-stone.

The lines are remarkable. The virtuosity of the scene as pure work of imagination is signaled by the word "perchance," which, ostensibly indicating the tentative and unrealized, introduces, in masterful surprise, the creation of the most minute reality: "that branchless ash, / Unsunn'd and damp," "The roaring dell, o'erwooded, narrow, deep, / And only speckled by the midday sun." The triumph of this word painting is exultantly declared by the parenthetical expression, "a most fantastic sight"; for there had been nothing there to see at the time of the "perchance," but now the friends, and thus we ourselves, "behold." What we "behold" is "the dark green file of long lank weeds" that "nod and drip beneath the dripping edge / Of the blue clay-stone." And yet this carefully articulated presence is a deliberately flaunted imagining, one that not even in ordinary language can be called other than a "secondary" imagining.

Another aspect of the imagined reality "seconds" the pastoral mode of Theocritus, which at its most intense evokes precisely such intimate sense of space and delicacy of observation. A classic locus from the Seventh Idyll can serve as point of reference.

> Many an aspen, many an elm bowed and rustled overhead, and hard by, the hallowed water welled purling forth from a cave of the Nymphs, while the brown cricket chirped busily amid the shady leafage, and the tree-frog murmured aloof in the dense thornbrake. Lark and goldfinch sang and turtledove moaned, and about the spring the bees hummed and hovered to and fro. All nature smelt of the opulent summer-time, smelt of the season of fruit. Pears lay at our feet, apples on either side, rolling abundantly, and the young branches lay splayed upon the ground because of the weight of their damson plums.

Although many kinds of landscape are invoked in the Theocritan mode, it is this "dell" sense, as it were, that receives the richest lading of sensuous imagery. For a single additional example, Lacon, in the Fifth Idyll, says: "You'll sing better sitting under the wild olive and this coppice. There's cool water falling yonder, and here's grass and a greenbed, and the locusts at their prattling." Comatas answers with another "dell" evocation. "Thither will I never come. Here I have oaks and bed-straw, and bees humming bravely at the hives, here's two springs of cool water to thy one, and birds, not locusts, a-babbling upon the tree, and, for shade, thine's not half so good."[23]

But having established the Theocritan voice, Coleridge then deserts it for the heroic as, repeating the structural device of the "Retirement" poem, he emerges from the pastoral dell onto the heroic mountain, with a consequent change of mode. Here, too, the scene is wholly articulated, in witness to the power of imagination.

> Now, my friends emerge
> Beneath the wide wide Heaven—and view again
> The many-steepled tract magnificent
> Of hilly fields and meadows, and the sea,
> With some fair bark, perhaps, whose sails light up
> The slip of smooth clear blue betwixt two Isles
> Of purple shadow! Yes! they wander on
> In gladness all; but thou, methinks, most glad,

[23]Theocritus, pp. 105, 67.

> My gentle-hearted Charles! for thou hast pined
> And hunger'd after Nature, many a year,
> In the great City pent. . . .
>   . . . Ah! slowly sink
> Behind the western ridge, thou glorious Sun!
> Shine in the slant beams of the sinking orb,
> Ye purple heath-flowers! richlier burn, ye clouds!
> Live in the yellow light, ye distant groves!
> And kindle, thou blue Ocean! . . .

The apostrophe is remarkably intense; the lines virtually burn with gladness. Their tone is not amenable to the pastoral mode; but in a larger sense, the movement from the dell to the mountain, and from minutely evoked presence to an almost symphonic fanfare of salutation, does fit in with the larger possibilities of Theocritan complication. Charles Segal has pointed out that an "elusive . . . aspect of the bucolic world is closely associated with . . . sea and mountains. Played off against the shady trees, soft grasses, cool water, and the soothing sounds of bees, cicadas, or birds, sea and mountain help shape that inner rhythm of closed and open, finite and infinite, which is so fundamental a part of the inner dynamics of Theocritan bucolic."[24]

The apostrophe to sun, clouds, and ocean marks a climax, and a turning from the imagined experience of the group back to the solitary reality of the poet himself.

The apostrophe to sun, clouds, and ocean provides, as it were, a platform for the apprehension of deity, and this movement parallels the use of the mountain vista in the "Retirement" poem. Shakespeare says, in his famous discussion of "imagination," that "the poet's eye" characteristically "doth glance from heaven to earth, from earth to heaven."[25] Alexander Gerard, again, notes that "IMAGINATION" can "lead us from a perception that is present, to the view of many more, and carry us through extensive, distant, and untrodden fields of thought. It can dart in an instant, from earth to heaven, and from heaven to earth; it can run with the greatest ease and celerity, through the whole compass of nature, and even beyond its utmost limits."[26] Here, though, the theological realization, which of course in this instance as in the previous one is wholly consonant with the decorum of imagination as set forth by Ficino, Sidney, and Leibniz (and indeed almost demanded by that decorum), is more glancingly summoned than in the "Retirement" poem.

[24]Segal, pp. 222–23.
[25]*A Midsummer Night's Dream*, V.i.12–13.
[26]Gerard, *Essay*, p. 30.

> . . . So my friend
> Struck with deep joy may stand, as I have stood,
> Silent with swimming sense; yea, gazing round
> On the wide landscape, gaze till all doth seem
> Less gross than bodily; and of such hues
> As veil the Almighty Spirit, when yet he makes
> Spirits perceive his presence.

Perhaps the reaching to deity is more tentative here because the apostrophe to sun, clouds, and ocean must serve a further function in the development of the poem. The solitary reality of the poet himself has been suspended as "true" reality against the "imagined" reality since the outset of the poem. But where the otiose solitude of the poet was rebuked in the "Retirement" poem, here there is no moral call to evict him from it, and that solitude is instead beautifully linked to the experience of the group. Pastoral as such is a social form, and Romantic solitude can hardly be seen as compatible with its mode without some sort of special dispensation. That dispensation is here provided by Coleridge, in a "dell" creation that perhaps outdoes in finely discriminated presence even the first such creation in the poem.

> A delight
> Comes sudden on my heart, and I am glad
> As I myself were there! Nor in this bower,
> This little lime-tree bower, have I not mark'd
> Much that has sooth'd me. Pale beneath the blaze
> Hung the transparent foliage; and I watch'd
> Some broad and sunny leaf, and lov'd to see
> The shadow of the leaf and stem above
> Dappling its sunshine! And that walnut-tree
> Was richly tinged, and a deep radiance lay
> Full on the ancient ivy, which usurps
> Those fronting elms, and now, with blackest mass
> Makes their dark branches gleam a lighter hue
> Through the late twilight: and though now the bat
> Wheels silent by, and not a swallow twitters,
> Yet still the solitary humble-bee
> Sings in the bean-flower! . . .

The lines are exquisite. Their specific function is, by the extreme detail of their pastoral evocation of leaf and shade, to revalidate the Theocritan mode while they create a *seen* world: "to see / The shadow of the leaf and stem above / Dappling its sunshine." Perhaps most of all the invocation of "the humble-bee" points to Theocritus, for the humming of bees is one of the chief evocations of his most characteristic moments.

Yet the humblebee here is as "solitary" as the poet himself. In the passage from the Seventh Idyll quoted above, "the bees hummed to and fro" about the spring: in the Fifth Idyll there were "bees humming bravely at the hives"; here the solitary humblebee "Sings in the bean-flower." The delicacy of the single bee, symbolizing in the same way as its Theocritan plural, points the path for the solitary poet to rejoin a pastoral society, and the continuum of his solitariness with his friends' socialness is supplied by the common bond of nature's beauty.

> . . . Henceforth I shall know
> That Nature ne'er deserts the wise and pure;
> No plot so narrow, be but Nature there,
> No waste so vacant, but may well employ
> Each faculty of sense, and keep the heart
> Awake to Love and Beauty! and sometimes
> 'Tis well to be bereft of promis'd good,
> That we may lift the soul, and contemplate
> With lively joy the joys we cannot share.

As if to emphasize the new interchangeability of pastoral society and pastoral solitude, the poet concludes with a salute to his friend Charles Lamb, now himself placed in the beautifully attenuated matrix of pastoral solitude. That solitude is imaginatively coordinated with the evocation of twilight:

> My gentle-hearted Charles! when the last rook
> Beat its straight path along the dusky air
> Homewards, I blest it! deeming its black wing
> (Now a dim speck, now vanishing in light)
> Had cross'd the mighty Orb's dilated glory,
> While thou stood'st gazing; or, when all was still,
> Flew creeking o'er thy head, and had a charm
> For thee, my gentle-hearted Charles, to whom
> No sound is dissonant which tells of Life.

These final lines also conclude, with a flourish, as it were, the virtuosolike manipulations of secondary imagination; for the poet, having so carefully established the palpable presence of himself in the bower with the solitary bee singing in the bean-flower, once again "dissolves" that scene and "recreates" the scene of his friend, but this time with a change from late afternoon ("Ah! slowly sink / Behind the western ridge, thou glorious Sun!") to early twilight ("Had cross'd the mighty Orb's dilated glory"). A last arabesque of imagination is the presentation of Lamb, "gazing" and rapt: for the "real" Charles Lamb, as opposed to the imaginary re-creation here, was an urbanite largely immune to the charm of the country. As he wrote to Wordsworth in 1801:

> My attachments are all local, purely local—. I have no passion . . . to groves and vallies.—The rooms where I was born, the furniture which has been before my eyes all my life . . . old chairs, old tables, streets, squares . . . these are my mistresses—have I not enough, without your mountains? . . . Your sun & moon and skys and hills & lakes affect me no more . . . than as a gilded room with tapestry and tapers, where I might live with handsome visible objects. . . . So fading upon me from disuse, have been the Beauties of Nature, as they have been confinedly called; so ever fresh & green and warm are all the inventions of men and assemblies of men in this great city—.[27]

So much for the permutations of the secondary imagination in "This Lime-Tree Bower My Prison." If, as argued above, there is a perfect propriety in tracing the work of secondary imagination in Coleridgean poems written (the one in 1795, the other in 1797) before the formulation of the secondary imagination appeared in 1817 (although we can trace the function, if not the name, to earlier dates), there is also a propriety in seeing it at work in poems not written by Coleridge. Both proprieties arise from the fact that secondary imagination is a permanent element in poetic practice: Coleridge is its cartographer, not its fabricator. He discerns its mode of operation; he does not create its reality. Indeed, those aspects of secondary imagination necessary to poetic creation are open to anyone's ratiocination and have always been more or less in the intellectual public domain. For instance, Zachary Mayne in 1728 takes specific note of the same imaginative functions that Coleridge subsumes under secondary imagination.

> For without having any regard to the Appearances of Things at the time of their being perceived by our *Senses*, we can, by our *Imagination*, alter and vary them, as many ways as we please. We can, for instance, *Imagine* a Body to be much greater or less; or any Quality or Power, more or less forcible and intense, as we have a Mind. We can, by our *Imagination*, vary the Shape or Figure of a Thing an infinite number of Ways; transpose its Parts; and change its Situation and Distance, with respect to other Things; and make different Applications of Agents to Patients, from any we have ever seen or observed, or that perhaps are any where to be found.[28]

These are the imaginative functions that make possible the writing of poetry or the creation of other forms of art.

[27]Lamb, I, 267–68.
[28]Mayne, pp. 71–72.

Accordingly, a third illustration, this more brief than the two just brought forward, may be summoned from another poet. That poet is in this context most appropriately Keats, for both the "Bower" poem and the "Retirement" poem point to Keats; or rather, Keats points to them.

In particular, the "Bower" poem foreshadows Keats's "To Autumn" and, by that same token, Stevens's "Sunday Morning." Helen Vendler says of the relation of "To Autumn" and Stevens's great poem:

> The entire absence of immersed attention to the details of the natural scene is nowhere more striking than in Stevens' divergence from his Romantic forebears, even when he is echoing them. The famous and beautiful ending of *Sunday Morning* derives, as everyone has noticed, from Keats's more famous and more beautiful final description of autumn:

> While barred clouds bloom the soft-dying day,
>   And touch the stubble-plains with rosy hue,
> Then in a wailful choir the small gnats mourn
>   Among the river sallows, borne aloft
>   Or sinking as the light wind lives or dies;
> And full-grown lambs loud bleat from hilly bourn;
>   Hedge-crickets sing; and now with treble soft
> The red-breast whistles from a garden-croft;
>   And gathering swallows twitter in the skies.

In Stevens, this becomes:

> Deer walk upon our mountains, and the quail
> Whistle about us their spontaneous cries;
> Sweet berries ripen in the wilderness;
> And, in the isolation of the sky,
> At evening, casual flocks of pigeons make
> Ambiguous undulations as they sink
> Downward to darkness, on extended wings.

Vendler then continues with a contrast of the two passages that emphasizes in Keat's practice the sort of detailed "presence" that characterizes the two Coleridgean poems.

> Both passages seem to be generalized scenes, but in Keats the implication of a present event (this is happening *now*, not this is what happens on autumn days), perceptible in the use of "while" in lieu of the more usual "when," is made unequivocal as the poem focuses, with real pathos, in the mind of a single observer with a vantage point in space to which the sounds are referred: the red-breast whistles not in, but from, the garden croft; the lambs bleat from the hilly bourn. Keats's observer is also located at a single and

particular moment in time—"And *now* with treble soft / The red-breast whistles."[29]

Such palpable sense of "here" and "now," as I have argued with respect to Coleridge's poems just rehearsed, is a prime indication of the poet's power as he wields the sceptre of secondary imagination. And if this characteristic looks back to the Coleridge poems, a more specific feature reveals "This Lime-Tree Bower my Prison" as the Bloomean "strong precursor" of Keats's "To Autumn." For if Stevens's "casual flocks of pigeons" are an unmistakable misprision of Keats's "gathering swallows," the "gathering swallows" that "twitter in the skies" are even more unmistakably a misprision of Coleridge's "now the bat / Wheels silent by, and not a swallow twitters" of the "Bower" poem.[30] The verb *twitters* is perhaps the most magnificent single word in the Keatsian stanza, its inspired diminuendo, and its placement as final verb, combining to hold in place the lovely twilight stillness of the autumnal scene. In the "Bower" poem, too, *twitters* emphasizes the "late twilight" of Coleridge's Theocritan pastoralizing of his solitude and thus is almost as important a word in its poem as it is in that of Keats.

Indeed, Keats is virtually haunted by Coleridgean poetry in "To Autumn's" magnificent conclusion.[31] For the swallows that twitter and so reverberate against Coleridge's swallow that does not twitter are preceded in Keats's penultimate line by "The red-breast" that "whistles from a garden-croft." The redbreast is again a misprision of Coleridge, and in fact of an unforgettable image in one of the most beautiful passages in all his poetry.

> Therefore all seasons shall be sweet to thee,
> Whether the summer clothe the general earth
> With greenness, or the redbreast sit and sing
> Betwixt the tufts of snow on the bare branch
> Of mossy apple-tree, while the nigh thatch
> Smokes in the sun-thaw; whether the eave-drops fall
> Heard only in the trances of the blast,
> Or if the secret ministry of frost
> Shall hang them up in silent icicles,
> Quietly shining to the quiet Moon.[32]

---

[29]Vendler, pp. 47–49.

[30]And Coleridge's "Now the bat / Wheels silent by" in its turn suggests misprision of the famous bat of Collins's "Ode to Evening": "Now air is hush'd, save where the weak-ey'd bat, / With short shrill shriek flits by on leathern wing" (ll. 9–10). The shriek of Collins's bat, silenced by Coleridge, especially suggests the Bloomean struggle with the precursor.

[31]Keats, *Poems*, p. 476.

[32]Coleridge, *Poems*, I, 242.

The "redbreast" here, in "Frost at Midnight," is a winter redbreast that sits and sings "Betwixt the tufts of snow on the bare branch / Of mossy apple-tree," while the "red-breast" in Keats's poem is an autumn redbreast that "whistles from a garden-croft." Their warblings in each case, however, occur in stanzas of exquisite nuance and stillness, a stillness accentuated by their own immemorial songs.

And yet it is not "To Autumn" that most dramatically illustrates the kind of Coleridgean testing of secondary imagination that we have seen in his two early poems. Rather it is in "Ode to a Nightingale" that we see this same exultant flourishing of imagination's creative wand.[33] That poem too has Coleridge as precursor, but in this case the "Retirement" poem rather than the "Bower" poem. In "Ode to a Nightingale," Keats's "viewless wings of Poesy" on which he will fly to rejoin the nightingale are clearly a misprision of Coleridge's "Retirement" poem, with its "viewless sky-lark's note / (Viewless, or haply for a moment seen / Gleaming on sunny wings)." In Coleridge's poem, the juxtaposition of "viewless" with "wings," as well as the emphasis supplied by the repetition of "viewless," authenticates that poem as Bloomean "strong precursor" for Keats's usage.

Keats's poem, indeed, is almost orgiastic in its marshaling of the resources of the secondary imagination, and here too it can look to the "Retirement" poem as strong precursor. We know how deeply Keats was committed to the Romantic apotheosis of imagination. In fact, one of his most notable statements of homage to that function is a *ne plus ultra* of that apotheosis: "I am certain of nothing but of the holiness of the Heart's affections and the truth of Imagination."[34] The overarching theme of this book, that imagination and its correlate term, originality, took upon themselves the aura and meaning earlier committed to the conception of soul, is nowhere more vividly illustrated than in this statement. The "Heart's affections" is virtually a synonym for one definition of soul, and "holiness" drives toward the religious grounding of that conception. But "Heart's affections" is placed in double harness with imagination's truth, and the two represent in effect a dividing, a new economy as it were, of soul's powers.

Keats considered "Imagination the Rudder" of "Poetry" (I, 170). In "Ode to a Nightingale," we sense his hand on that rudder, performing intricate maneuvres in confidence of the seaworthiness of his craft and the skill of its helmsman. The second stanza of the

[33] Keats, *Poems*, 369–72.
[34] Keats, *Letters*, I, 184.

poem is a marvel. Utilizing one of the most oft repeated situations of human life, that in which a recourse to liquor is supposed to lift burdens from the drinker, the stanza deliberately invites comparison with the universal colloquialism of every taproom: "I need a drink." But that phrase is stunningly transcended by Keats's imaginative expansion,[35] which raises the vulgarism to the status of paradisal world:

> O, for a draught of vintage! that hath been
>   Cool'd a long age in the deep-delved earth,
> Tasting of Flora and the country green,
>   Dance, and Provençal song, and sunburnt mirth!
> O for a beaker full of the warm South,
>   Full of the true, the blushful Hippocrene,
>   With beaded bubbles winking at the brim,
>   And purple-stained mouth;
> That I might drink, and leave the world unseen,
>   And with thee fade away into the forest dim

The creative function of imagination, that in which the poet's God-like ability is witnessed by the presentation of a reality where no reality had been, can hardly receive a stronger witness than in these lines. A disembodied wish here becomes a geographical evocation:

> Tasting of Flora and the country green,
>   Dance, and Provençal song, and sunburnt mirth!
> O for a beaker full of the warm South.

The drink itself receives the most sensuous of embodiments: "With beaded bubbles winking at the brim."

But Keats does not content himself with this astonishing creation of a texture of life and experience. Like Coleridge, he flourishes the power of imagination by annulling this world as soon as he created it, and moving to another world, created, if such be possible, with even more palpable and sensuous conviction of reality. Having evoked the geography of wine, he insouciantly dismisses it and replaces the escape it provides with that offered by the poetic imagination.

> Away! away! for I will fly to thee,
>   Not charioted by Bacchus and his pards,
>   But on the viewless wings of Poesy,

---

[35]For philosophical underpinning and justification of the *in vino veritas* motif, see Ortega's remarkable meditation on three paintings in the Prado called "Three Bacchanalian Pictures," in Ortega, *Velazquez*, pp. 14–20.

At this point, the poet is faced with a delicious problem: if the "viewless wings of Poesy" are preferred to the chariot of "Bacchus and his pards," how can the new heterocosm they invoke be created so as to transcend the one just rejected? The problem calls on all the resources of the secondary imagination, for as we have just seen, the "draught of vintage" stanza is at one and the same moment quintessential Keats, a triumph of imagination, and a constructed world of universal appeal. As if to demonstrate the almost limitless powers of imagination, Keats does transcend this wonder, however, and he does so by recourse to the heterocosmic richness of pastoral. He then adds a virtuoso twist, a kind of poetic entrechat, by deliberately taking away the feasibility of seeing the world he creates. At the end of the "draught of vintage" stanza he has prepared the conditions of this new world by reference to "the forest dim"; when in stanza 4 he chooses "the viewless wings of Poesy," he emphasizes that "tender is the night" and that "here there is no light." So the pastoral creation that follows (and I am aware of nothing like this except for some lines in *A Midsummer Night's Dream*) is a pastoral of night.

> I cannot see what flowers are at my feet,
>   Nor what soft incense hangs upon the boughs,
> But, in embalmed darkness, guess each sweet
>   Wherewith the seasonable month endows
> The grass, the thicket, and the fruit-tree wild;
>   White hawthorn, and the pastoral eglantine;
>   Fast fading violets cover'd up in leaves;
>   And mid-May's eldest child,
>   The coming musk-rose, full of dewy wine,
>   The murmurous haunt of flies on summer eves.

The sensuousness of the passage is almost unbelievable; yet it is provided by lines that are not only a secondary extension of the secondary imagination that composes the poem—a visit to a place that is deliberately declared to be attainable only by the viewless wings of poesy—but it is, marvelously, even a tertiary extension of imagination. John Keats the poet sits at his table. That is primary imagination.[36] He creates a poem in which he dwells as poet with

---

[36]As will become apparent in the succeeding chapter, the word *imagination* always tends to have a dual reference. It performs two functions, one designative, the other symbolic. The former is what the word describes, the latter is what it looks toward. In terms of what it describes or designates, primary imagination is simply reality as we know it: at any time our perception of reality necessarily is constituted as a complex of images, and it can occur in no other way. In this designative sense, Keats writing at his table, as a portion of reality, is a constitution of primary imagination. But primary imagination also has a symbolic function: it points upward

aching heart. That is secondary imagination. Then he dissolves a world he has expanded by secondary imagination, and creates a secondary world reached by viewless wings from within the poem already in existence. That is a secondary extension of secondary imagination. Then, wondrously, he drains the faculty of vision from this secondary extension, and by the word *guess* cantilevers beyond this world still a third state of existence, presented in detail of such opulence as to amaze the senses. "Such tricks hath strong imagination." Is there anything to surpass this in the whole range of poetry?

And yet even after this Keats continues, prodigiously, with his alternation of creation and annullment. There follows on the night-time pastoral of stanza 5 the matchless brief presentation in stanza 7, so palpable that our own hearts ache, of "Ruth, when, sick for home, / She stood in tears amid the alien corn." (One is tempted to digress for an entire page on *alien* as modifier of *corn*). And this is immediately followed in its turn by a glimpse, yet a glimpse of such plangency as to constitute almost the essence of Romantic longing, of "magic casements, opening on the foam / Of perilous seas, in faery lands forlorn."

But Keats in creating and annulling such presence is merely doing, however memorably, what poetry as the product of imagination always seeks to do, or at least should seek to do. In a notebook collocation written sometime between 1808 and 1811, Coleridge muses on the imaginative function and in doing so

---

toward deity. In this symbolic sense, Jonathan Wordsworth well says that "Coleridge's definition of the primary imagination" is "the greatest of all Romantic border statements" (Wordsworth, *William Wordsworth*, p. 83). Shawcross had said that "primary imagination is the organ of common perception, the faculty by which we have experience of an actual world of phenomena" (Shawcross, I, 272), and Richards had said that "Primary Imagination is normal perception that produces the usual world of the senses . . . the world of motor-buses, beef-steaks, and acquaintances, the framework of things and events within which we maintain our everyday existence, the world of the routine satisfaction of our minimum exigencies" (Richards, p. 58). Arguing against these definitions, Wordsworth asks, "Why should a man describe 'the world of the routine satisfaction of our minimum exigencies' as the result of 'a repetition in the finite mind of the eternal act of creation in the infinite I AM?' It seems a little extravagant" (Wordsworth, *William Wordsworth*, p. 84). He thus rejects "the traditional view of the primary imagination as relatively unimportant" and argues that it does not "take into account the linking of the three definitions: it seems logical to suppose that in choosing to end with fancy Coleridge meant to proceed from most to least important" (pp. 85–86). Exactly. But where Jonathan Wordsworth goes astray is in thinking that the maintaining of everyday existence is unimportant; primary imagination serves precisely as Berkeley's *esse est percipi* does (Berkeley's formula is assuredly one of Coleridge's prime sources): it proffers us our world. For the possible influence on Coleridge's primary imagination of Boehme's idea that God creates the world by imagining it, see McFarland, *Coleridge*, pp. 330–31.

stresses the poet's capacity to make a "present" reality. He speaks of "Fancy, or the aggregative Power . . . the bringing together Images dissimilar in the main by some one point or more of Likeness." He speaks of "Imagination" as the "power of modifying one image or feeling by the precedent or following ones," and of "one of its effects" as "that of combining many circumstances into one moment of thought to produce that ultimate end of human Thought, and human Feeling, Unity and thereby the reduction of the Spirit to its Principle & Fountain, who alone is truly *one*." Between these two fundamental observations (the latter of which dramatically focuses the theological utility of the imagination), Coleridge has made one equally fundamental that pertains to poetry in general. The "power of & energy of" a great poet, he says, is "to make every thing present by a Series of Images—This an absolute Essential of Poetry." In the preceding entry, he has broached the topic by referring to "Instances of the poetic Power of making every thing present to the Imagination."[37]

This "making every thing present to the Imagination," making "every thing present by a series of Images," has been the very substance of the two exquisite poems of Coleridge analyzed above, and of the two mighty poems of Keats also invoked. A final instance may serve to confirm that such making present is in truth an "absolute Essential of Poetry" as well as the most characteristic witness to the imaginative function. In this regard, to the consideration of "To Autumn" and "Ode to a Nightingale" may be joined a consideration of "The Eve of St. Agnes."[38]

This poem, like the other two, follows fittingly in any discussion of Coleridge's poetic theory and practice, for like the other two it is an unmistakable misprision of a Coleridgean predecessor. "Christabel" is not only the strong precursor of "The Eve of St. Agnes" (a role it shares with "Romeo and Juliet") but is so insistently so that one is led to suspect that Keats had Coleridge's poem open before him as he wrote. Yet this radical dependence was the matrix of a matchlessly original poem by Keats: the relation of the two poems, in truth, is a choice illustration of the originality paradox.

The predecessor poem is everywhere in Keats's mind. "The owl," who "for all his feathers was a'cold" of Keats's second line, has flown in from the group in the second line of "Christabel." "And the owls have awakened the crowing cock." The "toothless mastiff bitch" of Coleridge's poem becomes "The wakeful bloodhound" of Keats's. "The middle of night by the castle clock" that

---

[37]*Notebooks*, III, 3247, 3246.
[38]Keats, *Poems*, pp. 299–318.

begins "Christabel" is transformed into the "honey'd middle of the night," when "Young virgins might have visions of delight, / And soft adorings from their loves receive" that locates the significance of St. Agnes's Eve. The "chain-droop'd lamp" of "The Eve of St. Agnes" echoes the "lamp with twofold silver chain" of "Christabel"; the "carven imag'ries" of Keats's poem resonate against the "Carved with figures strange and sweet" of Coleridge's. Above all, there is the common denominator of cold and night: "St. Agnes' Eve—Ah, bitter chill it was!"; and Coleridge establishes at the beginning of his own poem that "The night is chilly, but not dark."

There are other echoes.[39] Yet Keats's poem, as a poem, is itself not an echo but a misprision of "Christabel." The cadence of verse and texture of imagery are entirely different in Keats, as the closedness and condensation of his poem is in utter contrast to the uncompleted openness of Coleridge's, which looks forward to lengthy continuance.

What Keats does, to supreme degree, is to create the world of his poem. Nowhere in his practice, nor in the practice of other poets, is there a more unremittingly detailed attainment of presence. We feel the cold: "The hare limp'd trembling through the frozen grass." We hear the sound: "The music, yearning like a God in pain"; "The silver, snarling trumpets 'gan to chide." We even, as it were, touch the textures invoked: "And still she slept an azure-lidded sleep / In blanched linen, smooth, and lavender'd."

All these sensory presentations are modulated, repeatedly, from flaming brilliance to whispering diminuendo:

> At length burst in the argent revelry,
> With plume, tiara, and all rich array

but against that:

> The kettle-drum, and far-heard clarionet,
> Affray his ears, though but in dying tone:—
> The hall door shuts again, and all the noise is gone.

The modulations of sound, indeed, are one of the special imaginative glories of the poem.

> By one, and one, the bolts full easy slide:—
> The chains lie silent on the footworn stones:—
> The key turns, and the door upon its hinges groans.

---

[39] And echoes of Shakespeare, of Scott, of Wieland, and others as well, all of which have been duly pointed out by various commentators, especially R. K. Gordon, E. C. Pettet, and Ernest de Selincourt.

And yet in that very evocation, there is the palpable "footworn stones" from another realm of sensory perception.

The poem exults in the fullness of its imaginative power. As in the virtuoso expansion involved in the "O for a draught of vintage" stanza in "Ode to a Nightingale," so in this poem Keats takes the bare and commonplace perception, "there was a window," and triumphantly elaborates it into the richest of all embodiments of the sensuousness generated by the Spenserian stanza as a form.

> A casement high and triple-arch'd there was,
> All garlanded with carven imag'ries
> Of fruits, and flowers, and bunches of knot-grass,
> And diamonded with panes of quaint device,
> Innumerable of stains and splendid dyes,
> As are the tiger-moth's deep-damask'd wings,
> And in the midst, 'mong thousand heraldries,
> And twilight saints, and dim emblazonings,
> A shielded scutcheon blush'd with blood of queens and kings.

The stanza is an exercise in "presence" almost tactile in its immediacy. It is capped with a flourish by the stunning onomatopoetic lushness of the Alexandrine, which is centered on a verb, *blush'd*, that is at one and the same time a quintessence of sensory nuance and, as Christopher Ricks has demonstrated, an index to the Keatsian ethos.

But in this poem too, still paralleling the fugal progression of "Ode to a Nightingale," Keats goes even farther in display of what imagination can do. I have argued elsewhere that the final stanza of "Ode to a Nightingale" is a mistake;[40] be that as it may, the final stanza of "The Eve of St. Agnes" is a spectacular triumph and vindication of the Godlike power of the imagination.

> And they are gone: ay, ages long ago
> These lovers fled away into the storm.
> That night the Baron dreamt of many a woe,
> And all his warrior-guests, with shade and form
> Of witch, and demon, and large coffin-worm,
> Were long be-nightmar'd. Angela the old
> Died palsy-twitch'd, with meagre face deform;
> The Beadsman, after thousand aves told,
> For aye unsought for slept among his ashes cold.

The brilliant achievement of the poem as a whole has been the creation of a world, in all its tactile, auditory, and visual splendor. This world deliberately replaces the "real" world and constitutes

---

40See McFarland, *Romanticism*, pp. 234–35.

its own place and time. Real time ceases and real place is annulled. But now, with the last stanza, another place supervenes and another time begins. The other place, however, is indefinite: "they are gone . . . fled away into the storm." They are gone, however, not into another delimited space but *out of* the poem's delimited space—that is, they are "gone" from "here" into the infinite. And the time indication that begins the new series likewise marks the displacement from "here"; the "there" it invokes is also indefinite—it is a "goneness," not an arrival. That is to say, the fact that they are gone, "ay, ages long ago," stops the lovers' time by the device of starting mundane time within the world of the poem. The lovers, in short, have gone "ages long ago" not into another chronology but into eternity.

The infinite and the eternal can be indicated only negatively, and this the poem does by its almost miraculous device of transforming its own original world, which was from the outset as time-free as the Grecian urn, into the mundane and corruptible world of "reality." The lovers, eternally the same, are gone "ages long ago"; but the mundane clock begins to tick in the evacuated and suddenly mortal world they leave behind: "Angela the old / Died palsy-twitch'd, with meagre face deform." Coldness has been the matrix of the poem's excitement and has been the validating contrary to the heat of passion.

> Beyond a mortal man impassion'd far
> At these voluptuous accents, he arose,
> Ethereal, flush'd, and like a throbbing star

But now coldness becomes the absolute of the evacuated world and the symbol of death. The word *cold* that is the poem's last word confirms but also transforms the "bitter chill" of the first line: "The Beadsman, after thousand aves told, / For aye unsought for slept among his ashes cold." The invocation of false eternity as an endless progression of time—"For aye unsought for"—is the validating contrary of the true eternity of the lovers' intensity. "Aeternitas non est successio sine fine sed nunc stans," runs the scholastic definition—"Eternity is not succession without end, but a standing now."

There is a temptation to linger over such a wondrous poem, but the purpose of this chapter has been to elucidate the secondary imagination at work rather than to develop formal criticism of poems as such. Although "The Eve of St. Agnes," like the "Ode to a Nightingale" and "To Autumn," is virtuoso embodiment of that imagination in its characteristic modes of operation, it, along with the two poems by Coleridge, represents only a kind of special demonstration of the poet's Godlike power. For all poems are products of secondary imagination.[41] All poems, that is, that aspire to the condition of soul-fact. Yet secondary imagination is more than the faculty of poetry; it is, still more largely, the indispensable vehicle of our humanity—of "our large discourse, looking before and after."

Secondary imagination is not confined to the creation of poetry. It is, on the contrary, the agency of all our thought whatever that summons images to mind when correspondent objects are not present. As such, it moves along a continuum from our most humble preoccupations of daily existence to our most exalted conceptions of divinity. It holds our lives together, and focuses their meanings. It combines many circumstances of thought and feeling, as Coleridge said, "to produce that ultimate end of human Thought, and human Feeling, Unity and thereby the reduction of the Spirit to its Principle & Fountain, who alone is truly *one*."[42]

---

[41]The statement may seem to contravene Coleridge's own distinction between imagination and fancy. But he made different formulations in different circumstances; the distinction of imagination and fancy is not a critical tool, or not properly so, but rather an attempt to free the interests of soul from the yoke of association psychology. In actual critical practice, what may be claimed as a poem constructed by fancy is better described as simply a bad poem. This tack, indeed, is precisely what Coleridge himself adopts when Wordsworth wants to denigrate Gray's sonnet on the death of Richard West as riddled by poetic diction as opposed to the language of common life. Coleridge counters that the problem is rather that it is simply a bad poem, e.g.: "The second line, 'And reddening Phoebus lifts his golden fire,' has indeed almost as many faults as words. But then it is a bad line, not because the language is distinct from that of prose; but because it conveys incongruous images, because it confounds the cause and the effect, the real *thing* with the personified *representative* of the thing; in short, because it differs from the language of GOOD SENSE!" (*Biographia* II, 75). Such, mutatis mutandis, can be our own attitude to any attempt to distinguish imaginative poetry from a poetry of fancy.

[42]See above, n. 37.

• 6 •

The Higher Function of Imagination

*T*he conception of imagination as having lower and higher functions was an essential of Coleridge's position, as indeed the differing emphases of the preceding two chapters confirm: imagination as a philosophical connective exists alongside imagination as a poetic instrumentality. If in this pairing there might be a reluctance to set one above or below the other, in other instances a graded hierarchy is essential to Coleridge's procedure. "*Imagination*, as Coleridge uses it," notes I. A. Richards in his pioneering *Coleridge on Imagination*, "is, of course, very often a term implying higher values than *Fancy* (critics who point this out with an air of discovery or complaint should re-read him). . . . Coleridge does not separate his psychology from his theory of value."[1]

Coleridge's most characteristic philosophical tack, and at the same time the one most rewarding in terms of increased subtlety, was what he called "desynonymizing."[2] He insists that "all Languages perfect themselves by a gradual process of desynonymizing words originally equivalent."[3] Accordingly, what was usually called "reason" was sundered by Coleridge into the paired terms *reason* and *understanding*, with their commonly accepted synonymity split into distinct functions, conceived as higher and lower. Thus too for other pairings such as *idea* and *concept*, *genius* and *talent*, *imitation* and *copy*.[4] The process was utilized a fortiori

[1]Richards, p. 96.

[2]"The whole process of human intellect is gradually to desynonymize terms" (*Philosophical Lectures*, p. 173); "in all societies there exists an instinct of growth, a certain collective, unconscious good sense working progressively to desynonymize those words originally of the same meaning" (*Biographia*, I, 82).

[3]*Notebooks*, III, 4397.

[4]For discussion of Coleridge's commitment to "desynonymization" with respect to *imitation* and *copy* see Marks, pp. 42–50.

for *imagination,* which was desynonymized into *imagination* and *fancy,* and then further desynonymized into *primary imagination, secondary imagination,* and *fancy.* In all these discriminations one term was accorded a higher function than the other. Derrida, in fact, has argued that in any nominal polarity or binary division, one term inevitably possesses a hidden superiority: *up* is privileged above *down, light* above *dark*—or to use his own examples "normal/abnormal . . . serious/nonserious."[5]

Coleridge at one point insists that imagination and fancy are not higher and lower terms of the same function but in fact are wholly separate faculties: "Repeated meditations led me first to suspect . . . that fancy and imagination were two distinct and widely different faculties, instead of being, according to the general belief, either two names with one meaning, or at furthest, the lower and higher degree of one and the same power."[6] Though one might entertain a certain skepticism as to whether the imaginative process is split into two separate faculties, and even, as will subsequently appear, whether indeed it is a "faculty" at all, one is willing to allow Coleridge his insistence. He was much concerned to extricate the mind's autonomy from the entanglements of association psychology, and by sacrificing fancy as an offering to that psychology, and insisting that imagination arises in a different ontological realm, he was able to dramatize his position—even though, in another place with other concerns at the fore, he says, following Bacon, that "the office of philosophical *disquisition* consists in just *distinction;* while it is the priviledge of the philosopher to preserve himself constantly aware, that distinction is not division" (II, 11).

In any event, by insisting on an absolute split between fancy and imagination, Coleridge dramatizes the higher function of the latter, which is then differentiated into still higher gradation by the distinction between secondary imagination and primary imagination. Though these two forms are "identical" in the *"kind"* of their agency, and differ "only in *degree,*" the secondary is an "echo" of the primary, which in its turn is "a repetition in the finite mind of the eternal act of creation in the infinite I AM" (I, 304). The added gradations change what was originally a polar opposition into an ascending ladder.

[5]Derrida, p. 236. "All metaphysicians from Plato to Rousseau, Descartes to Husserl, have proceeded in this way, conceiving good to be before evil, the positive before the negative, the pure before the impure. . . . . And this is not just one metaphysical gesture among others, it is *the* metaphysical exigency, that which has been most constant, most profound and most potent."
[6]*Biographia,* I, 82.

That ladder rises to Godhead itself, to "the infinite I AM." The thrust is inexorably upward, toward the most honorific conceptions the mind can entertain. It is this upward movement, even more than the attempt to discriminate its exact mode of operation, that typifies the Romantic concern with imagination. Wordsworth, indeed, sometimes does not try to discriminate at all but simply elevates the function in the most emotional words at his command. He speaks of

> . . . Imagination, which, in truth,
> Is but another name for absolute power
> And clearest insight, amplitude of mind,
> And Reason in her most exalted mood.[7]

From tracing the "progress" of imagination allied to "spiritual Love,"

> . . . have we drawn
> Faith in life endless, the sustaining thought
> Of human Being, Eternity, and God (XIV, 203–5)[8]

Thus imagination is persistently hailed as functioning in the same spiritual realm as does the idea of soul. The poet, "described in *ideal* perfection," Coleridge says, "brings the whole soul of man into activity," but the poet does so specifically "by that synthetic and magical power, to which we have exclusively appropriated the name of imagination." When in Wordsworth "Imagination—here the Power so called / Through sad incompetence of human speech / That awful Power rose from the mind's abyss," it overwhelmed all awareness except this: "to my conscious soul I now can say— / 'I recognize thy glory.' "[9] In such and similar examples, where imagination, subsiding from its glimpse of Godhead, hovers in tantalizing proximity to soul, we see that it begins not only to participate in but actually to take over the aura of soul.

Romantic imagination, in short, not only moves in the sphere of soul, but it reciprocates and draws to itself the very meaning of soul.

In a way it might seem that such a transfer was potentially enclosed in the two topics from the beginning. Aristotle, whose discussion of imagination was the most influential of those origi-

---

[7]*Prelude*, XIV, 189–92 (p. 521).

[8]In this context, Goethe's Werther indicates not only metaphorically but literally the new status of imagination: "Was die Einbildungskraft für ein göttliches Geschenk ist," he exclaims—what a divine gift is the imagination (*Gedenkausgabe*, IV, 461).

[9]*Biographia*, II, 15–16; *Prelude*, VI, 592–94, 598–99 (p. 239).

nating in antiquity, incorporates that discussion as a factor in his treatise on the soul, customarily referred to as *De Anima,* and indicates that the subject is important but unclear. When in the historical progress of thought the topic of soul as such began to seem threadbare and the postulate of soul only precariously tenable, if tenable at all, it would seem only natural for the less revealed and less well understood part of the complex to seem fresher and less vulnerable than the larger term. Imagination, as Kant significantly defined—or rather obscured—its function, exercises a "hidden art [*verborgene Kunst*] in the depths of the human soul," and its real mode of activity nature is "hardly likely ever to allow us to discover and to have open to our gaze."[10]

The question then becomes not so much, How is it possible that imagination could transfer to itself the aura and hoped for value of soul? but rather, Why was it so urgent for it to do so? The historical phenomenon that engages our attention is the enormous acceleration, beginning in the late seventeenth and early eighteenth centuries, of the sense of imagination's importance. We may boldly present an answer in its largest outline: imagination became so important because soul had been so important and because soul could no longer carry its burden of significance. That significance was an assurance that there was meaning in life. No soul, no meaning. But even if soul wilted under the onslaught of science and skepticism, so long as there was imagination as secondary validator then at least there remained the possibility of meaning.

This largest truth is simple, as large truths tend to be. In its historical ramification, it is exquisitely complex. To save the significance of soul was not of course only the concern of those who honored imagination; indeed, one can see the entire course of European thought from the seventeenth century onward (and certainly the process started earlier) as alternating between attacks on soul and obsessive attempts to save the significance of soul or to adjust to the loss of that significance. For a single example from the late Victorian and Edwardian era, one may point to the rise of interest in psychic phenomena and occult philosophy, the retraversing, in the words of Richard Ellmann about Yeats's preoccupations, of the "back alleys" of Western culture.[11] From Madame Blavatsky to Baron von Hügel (one thinks of Eliphas Lévi in France) this kind of upsurge was an attempt to save the significance of soul. As such, it is far more important than its nominal status as temporary fashion in the history of ideas would suggest.

[10]*Kant*, III, 136.
[11]Ellmann, p. 294.

Indeed, so eminently respectable an academic philosopher as Sidgwick developed an interest in such phenomena, for precisely the
reason that they promised to fill the emptiness left by the philosophical demise of soul.

> For two periods, from 1882–5 and 1888–93, Sidgwick was President
> of the Society for Psychical Research, which led to his interest in
> what were considered fraudulent experiments, and to an acquain-
> tance, unusual for a Cambridge don, with the theosophist, Madame
> Blavatsky. Nevertheless, as there was a fad for para-psychology in
> Cambridge and London at the time, neither the one nor the other
> much damaged his philosophical reputation. . . . Members of the
> SPR sought in its activities liberation from Victorian materialism,
> most in the hope that the conclusions of its research work would
> restore to them the consolation of religion denied by Victorian
> science; but others (like William James) merely seeking empirical
> knowledge without the metaphysical underpinnings of theology and
> earlier philosophy. Some (like Oliver Lodge, at first) regarded it as a
> scientific challenge to explain the phenomena that concerned the SPR
> by ordinary physical laws. The most poignant case, however, was
> that of the SPR's first president, Henry Sidgwick, whose interest in
> para-psychological phenomena might be seen as the aftermath of the
> religious crisis that led to the resignation of his fellowship. Unable to
> ground his belief in personal immortality by philosophical argument,
> Sidgwick devoted much of his time to the SPR in search of empirical
> evidence for the existence of the soul. The search was, of course, an
> admission of philosophical defeat.[12]

If Sidgwick sought in vain to feed a philosophical hunger from
the dubious granary of psychical research, earlier philosophers had
better possibilities available to them. Probably no mind of absolutely first rank since the Renaissance so assiduously and variously
maintained the claims of soul as did Leibniz. "Thus the point
noted by the ancient Platonists is very true and very worthy of
consideration, that the existence of mental things and particularly
of this 'I' that thinks and that is called spirit or soul, is incomparably more assured than the existence of external things; and that
thus it would not at all be impossible, speaking with metaphysical
rigor, that basically there are only mental substances, and that
external things are only appearances." Much too sophisticated
himself to espouse this doctrine in bald terms, Leibniz nevertheless
devoted all his mighty intellect to the defense of those conceptions
of a priori human domain that had historically been focused by the
conception of soul. As Cassirer says by way of synopsis: "The

[12]Levy, pp. 77–78, 85.

decisive step that separates Leibniz's philosophy from all other attempts at mediation, lies therefore in the knowledge that no question can be posed to the material world except as a content of thought. Henceforth all being (*Sein*) exhausts itself in unity of consciousness (*Bewusstseinseinheit*) and content of consciousness (*Bewusstseinsinhalt*)."[13]

Leibniz's own tactic in the defense of soul was to set up his monad doctrine, that is, to convert everything to a myriad of infinitesimal souls—for that is what the monads are. Of the varied sources his enormous learning made available to him, one surmises that this one from the *De Anima* itself might well have had some role in the provenance of the distinction between the unconscious mind (perception) and the conscious mind (apperception) that made the monad doctrine feasible: "Anaxagoras . . . on many occasions . . . speaks of mind as responsible for what is right and correct, but at others he says that this is the soul: for mind he regards as existing in all living things, great and small, noble and base; but mind in the sense of intelligence does not appear to belong to all living things alike, nor even to all men."[14]

In any event, both Leibniz's monads and Sidgwick's psychical research are ways of defending soul that do not enlist the doctrine of imagination. The special utility of imagination in that defense, however, is that its witness is constantly renewed and cannot be relegated to the scientifically obsolete (as with the monad doctrine) or to the philosophically disreputable (as with psychical research). Aristotle says that the topic of imagination is shrouded in obscurity (περὶ δὲ φαντασίας ἄδηλον) (414^{b}15–20). Kant says that imagination is a blind but indispensable function of the soul ("eine blinde, obgleich unentbehrliche Function der Seele"). Fichte says that it is an almost always misunderstood faculty that alone makes life and consciousness possible ("Dieses fast immer verkannte Vermögen . . . ist dasjenige, was allein Leben und Bewusstseyn . . . möglich macht").[15] None of them says, however, or wants to say,

---

[13]*Leibniz*, VI, 502–3; Cassirer, *Leibniz*, p. 371. Cf. the Nobel Prize-winning mathematical physicist Eugene Wigner in our own day: "The principal argument against materialism is not that . . . it is incompatible with quantum theory. The principal argument is that thought processes and consciousness are the primary concepts, that our knowledge of the external world is the content of our consciousness and that the consciousness, therefore, cannot be denied. On the contrary, logically, the external world could be denied—though it is not very practical to do so" (*Symmetries and Reflections: Scientific Essays of Eugene P. Wigner*, ed. Walter J. Moore and Michael Scriven [Bloomington, Ind.: Indiana University Press, 1967], pp. 176–77).
[14]Aristotle, *De Anima*, 404^{b}1–10.
[15]*Kant*, III, 91; *Fichte*, I, 399.

that imagination is not important, or that it does not exist, or that it is left behind in further advances of knowledge.

Imagination's vitality is therefore perennial, and its concept can be used philosophically as well as literarily. Fichte, for instance, carries Leibniz's asseveration that "this 'I' that thinks and that is called spirit or soul, is incomparably more assured than the existence of external things" to a point so extreme that his philosophy, even within his own lifetime, came to be regarded as a curiosity.[16] One recalls Heine's frolicsome suggestion that Fichte would even have to disbelieve in his wife's existence, and Mrs. Fichte would not like that.[17] But historically, Fichte's thought is of great interest as a "reaction formation," so to speak, to the increasing beleaguerment of the concept of soul. To see the "I" as the font of all reality whatever is so palpable a denial of reality as to suggest that the true situation seemed the threatening reverse of what Fichte maintains.

Of special interest to our purposes here is that Fichte's apotheosis of the "I" is bonded to an apotheosis of imagination.[18]

Seeking the "absolutely first, quite unconditioned fundamental proposition of all human knowledge,"[19] Fichte had found it in the so-called logical law of identity, that is, that anything is what it is, or $A = A$. Better still, if A, then A. This, he said, is "completely certain and agreed upon" (I, 286). Following insistences in Leibniz, he understood that the logical law of contradiction, that is, that if A is A it cannot be not-A, is merely the law of identity in another form.[20] But this sameness is at the same time a diversity. Not-A, being not-A, must be a new entity, or B.

---

[16]Thus Crabb Robinson reported enthusiastically in 1801 that Clemens Brentano, in response to a query as to whether he was a Kantian or a Fichtian, said: "Why ffichte (who is much the greatest Man Sir) out-Kants' Kant" (*Germany*, p. 66). But by 1814 Robinson laconically notes a statement made to him by Wilhelm Schlegel: "Fichte, he said, was aware before his death that he had survived his fame" (*Diary*, I, 454). Consider, however, the opinion of a twentieth-century commentator that "the importance of Fichte has hardly ever been fully appreciated . . . Fichte is the first to provide an exact system of axioms, and a system of universal concepts the form and content of which are derived from the axioms by analytical methods. . . . Fichte not only completes the system of Kant, but also adds profundity to it" (Fischer, p. 288).

[17]*Heine*, VIII, i, 93. Fichte, unlike most philosophers, was happily married. For Mrs. Fichte see Ilse Kammerlander, *Johanna Fichte; Ein Frauenschicksal der deutschen Klassik* (Stuttgart: Kohlhammer, 1969).

[18]See, e.g., Fernando Inciarte, *Transzendentale Einbildungskraft; zu Fichtes Frühphilosophie in Zusammenhang des transzendentalen Idealismus* (Bonn: H. Bouvier & Co:, 1970); Pasquale Salvucci, *Dialettica e immaginazione in Fichte* (Urbino: Argalìa, 1963).

[19]*Fichte*, I, 285.

[20]Cf. T. D. Weldon: "Leibniz maintains that in every true proposition *praedicatum inest subjecto*, the predicate is contained in the subject, and that consequently all valid inference is explicitly analytical in character and involves simply the discovery

These logical realizations can occur in only one place: in a human consciousness. Substituting this consciousness (Descartes's "cogito" and Kant's "I think," which "must be able to accompany all my representations"), for the "fundamental proposition" A = A, Fichte, by manipulation of the diversity in sameness of the laws of identity and contradiction, finds that "all reality is posited in the ego" (I, 327) but also that "the ego posits itself as determined through the non-Ego" (I, 322). In a tireless working out of the concepts of thesis, antithesis, and synthesis (it is he, and not, as popularly misconceived, Hegel, who emphasizes these terms), of "reciprocal determination" ("Wechselbestimmung"), and of "subject" and "object," Fichte provides a logical framework to account for all reality.[21]

Of crucial importance in this dynamic of interrelationships is the conception of imagination (*Einbildungskraft*).[22] Imagination is "the most wonderful of the faculties of the positing ego" (I, 398). It hovers between and unites the antithetical divisions of the positing ego: "die Einbildungskraft ist ein Vermögen, das zwischen Bestimmung und Nicht-Bestimmung, zwischen Endlichem und Unendlichem . . . schwebt"—"imagination is a faculty that is suspended between determination and nondetermination, between finite and infinite" (I, 410). "Die Aufgabe war die, die Entgegengesetzten, Ich und Nicht-Ich, zu vereinigen. Durch die Einbildungskraft, welche widersprechendes vereinigt, können sie vollkommen vereinigt werden"—"The task was this, to unite the opposed entities, I and not-I. Through the imagination, which unites contradictory elements, they can be completely united (I, 411).

---

of what is actually contained in the original subject. On these principles it follows that the supreme principle of all valid thinking is the principle of identity, and it should be found that the whole universe can be deduced analytically from the notion of substance" (Weldon, p. 27). The law of contradiction was promulgated by Aristotle as a refutation of Heraclitus's doctrine of the coalescence of opposites (Aristotle, *Metaphysics*, 1005ᵇ15–25; 1011ᵇ15–25); it is therefore a philosophical irony that Fichte's manipulation of this, "the most certain of all principles," as Aristotle calls it, should lead to a reconstitution of that very doctrine of opposites.

[21]E.g.: "Neither is the subjective to be annulled by the objective, however, nor the objective by the subjective, just as in the argument above the 'I' in general was not to be cancelled by the 'not-I,' and vice versa. Rather both subsist alongside each other. They must accordingly be synthetically united, which occurs through the third function in which they are both the same, through determinableness (*Bestimmbarkeit*). Both—not the subject and object in themselves, but the subjective and objective posited through thesis and antithesis—are reciprocally determinable through one another, and merely in so far as they are can they be conceived together, and be fixed and maintained through the synthesizing active power of the 'I' (the imagination)" (*Fichte*, I, 400).

[22]Imagination is the "tätige Vermögen des Ich" by which the subjective and objective are "fixiert and festgehalten" in synthesis (*Fichte*, I, 400).

In such functions, imagination takes on an elevated importance. On the "activity of the imagination," says Fichte, "the possibility of our consciousness, our life, our being for ourselves, that is, our being as I, is founded" (I, 420). It is "accordingly taught in my philosophy that all reality—meaning reality for us, as could not otherwise be meant in a system of transcendental philosophy—is brought forth solely through the imagination" (I, 420). As the most important function of "das Ich," which in turn is ultimate reality, imagination has in this apprehension almost wholly accreted to itself the Platonic ontology of soul.

We should err, however, if we assume that some sudden transfer of status historically took place between soul and imagination as emblems of a priori human domain. Quite the contrary. The two terms, with their respective valences, exist side by side for many scores of years leading up to and through the Romantic period (in an attenuated sense they still do), and thinkers frequently oscillate between them. Soul was a term that could not be abandoned readily, though more and more it was yoked in a kind of harness with other conceptions. As a commentator points out, Kant in his "disagreement with rational psychology could use soul, *cogito* and 'I think' synonymously."[23]

We may see in some detail Kant's ambivalence about soul and other terms in some fascinating sections of the *Critique of Pure Reason*. It is Kant's "productive" imagination that Fichte elevates to propagator of all reality.[24] In Kant himself, however, imagination, though an important mental function, is less laden with significance. Rather it is what Kant, following Leibniz, calls "the principle of apperception" that is "the highest principle in the whole sphere of human knowledge."[25] Pure apperception, says Kant, is "das stehende und bleibende Ich"—"the abiding and unchanging 'I'" (IV, 91).

It is interesting that this formula, which seems a "strong precursor" for Fichte's "Ich," and is also a receptacle for all the interests of "soul," occurs on the same page of the first edition of the *Critique of Pure Reason* in which Kant names the productive imagination. We can see, too, that this locus is central for Fichte's later elaboration of the function of imagination in terms of his antithetical interests, for Kant says that

[23]Janke, p. 146.
[24]E.g., "Das in ihm tätige Vermögen ist schon oben produktive Einbildungskraft genannt worden" (*Fichte*, I, 419). Cf. Kant: "Die Einbildungskraft ist also auch ein Vermögen einer Synthesis *a priori*, weswegen wir ihr den Namen der produktiven Einbildungskraft geben" (*Kant*, IV, 91).
[25]*Kant*, III, 110.

all consciousness as truly belongs to an all-comprehensive pure apperception, as all sensible intuition, as representation, does to a pure inner intuition, namely to time. It is this apperception that must be added to pure imagination in order to render its function intellectual. For since the synthesis of imagination connects the manifold only as it *appears* in intuition, as, for instance, in the shape of a triangle, it is, though exercised *a priori*, always in itself sensible. And while concepts, which belong to the understanding, are brought into play through relation of the manifold to the unity of apperception, it is only by means of the imagination that they can be brought into relation to sensible intuition. (IV, 91).

A few pages earlier, Kant has even more directly presented the ground of Fichte's bonding of imagination to the sense of "I".

The transcendental unity of apperception thus relates to the pure synthesis of imagination, as an *a priori* condition of the possibility of all combination of the manifold in one knowledge. But only the *productive* synthesis of the imagination can take place *a priori*; the reproductive rests upon empirical conditions. Thus the principle of the necessary unity of pure (productive) synthesis of imagination, prior to apperception, is the ground of the possibility of all knowledge, especially of experience. . . . Since this unity of apperception underlies the possibility of all knowledge, the transcendental unity of the synthesis of imagination is the pure form of all possible knowledge; and by means of it all objects of possible experience must be represented *a priori*. (IV, 88)

This last sentence of Kant's, with its statement that imagination provides "the pure form of all possible knowledge" and is necessary for the representation of "all objects of possible experience," is clearly the ground of Fichte's view that "all reality" is "brought forth solely through the imagination." Both thoughts also provide precursorship for Coleridge's primary imagination. Indeed, Coleridge's specification that the primary imagination is the "prime agent of all human perception" is directly anticipated by Kant's contention that "no psychologist has yet realized that imagination is a necessary ingredient of perception itself" (IV, 89n). In the light of the paradoxes surrounding originality pointed to in the earlier chapters of this book, we may be entitled to say that none of these thinkers has much originality if by that term we mean exclusive priority; for Fichte derives his doctrine of imagination wholly from Kant, Kant, as noted in an earlier chapter, most of his from Tetens, and Coleridge most of his from Fichte, Kant, and Tetens. In this context, Coleridge's exhortation, "Once & all read Tetens, Kant,

Fichte, &c—& there you will trace or if you are on the hunt, track me," takes on added precision.[26]

On the other hand, all three thinkers, Coleridge, Fichte, and Kant, have deep originality if by that term we mean Mill's insistence that originality is another name for thought itself: "whoever thinks at all, thinks to that extent, originally."[27]

In any event, Kant's disposition of imagination places it in closest proximity to the conception of soul. He says in summary, "A pure imagination, which conditions all *a priori* knowledge, is thus one of the fundamental faculties of the human soul [*ein Grundver-mögen der menschlichen Seele*]."[28] The contiguity of "reine Ein-bildungskraft" and "menschliche Seele" in such a formula invites, even demands, metonymic substitution. And yet even with this, Kant has not invested the whole hoard of a priori human domain in imagination. He has "laid off," to use the colloquialism of racetrack bettors—for the wager is so very momentous, is indeed the Pascalian *pari* itself—a still larger part of it into apperception.[29]

The complex transaction is occasioned and necessitated by the fact that Kant is the immediate successor of the skepticism of Hume and the French *philosophes*. By its agency, Kant is able to subject the term *soul* itself to the harshest attacks of Enlightenment rationalism. We think here of a commentator's telling observation that "Kant has been without question the most influential modern philosopher" and that "it is doubtless true that his vast influence comes from the very fact that he is sympathetic to the fundamental contentions of everybody."[30] It is as though Kant, having transferred the precious cargo from the galleon of "soul" to the sturdy holds of "apperception" and "imagination," can then send the galleon on its way to be intercepted by Hume, the *philosophes*, and other skeptical privateers.

The interception occurs in an area of the *Critique* called "The Paralogisms of Pure Reason." A "paralogism," Kant explains, "is a syllogism that is fallacious in form, be its content what it may."[31] In that section of his critique called "Transcendental Dialectic," which is the second division of the "Transcendental Doctrine of

[26]*Notebooks*, II, 2375.
[27]*Mill*, I, 332.
[28]*Kant*, IV, 91.
[29]E.g., "There are three original sources (capacities or faculties of the soul) that contain the conditions of the possibility of all experience and cannot themselves be derived from any other faculty of the mind, namely *sense, imagination*, and *appercep-tion*" (*Kant*, IV, 74).
[30]Randall, pp. 106, 110.
[31]*Kant*, IV, 215.

Elements," Kant is concerned with what he calls "illusion" ("Schein"). He is concerned not with "empirical illusion" (such as an optical illusion), but with *"transcendental illusion,"* which generates "actual principles that incite us to tear down all those boundary fences [i.e. those set up by the categories of understanding] and to seize possession of an entirely new domain" (IV, 190). He warns that "transcendental illusion does not cease even after it has been detected and its invalidity clearly revealed by transcendental criticism (e.g. the illusion in the proposition: the world must have a beginning in time)."

> The cause of this is that there are fundamental rules and maxims for the employment of our reason . . . and that these have all the appearance of being objective principles. We therefore take the subjective necessity of a connection of our concepts, which is to the advantage of the understanding, for an objective necessity in the determination of things in themselves. This is an *illusion* that can no more be prevented . . . than the astronomer can prevent the moon from appearing larger at its rising, although he is not deceived by this illusion.
>
> The transcendental dialectic will therefore content itself with exposing the illusion of transcendent judgments. . . . That the illusion should, like logical illusion, actually disappear and cease to be an illusion, is something that transcendental dialectic can never be in a position to achieve. For we have to do here with a *natural* and inevitable illusion. . . . There exists, then, a natural and unavoidable dialectic of pure reason—not one in which a bungler might entangle himself through lack of knowledge . . . but one inseparable from human reason. (IV, 190–91)

It should be apparent from such formulation that the "illusion" with which Kant deals in the "Transcendental Dialectic" is multivalenced: "logical" illusion is merely wrong; "transcendental" illusion is empirically unverifiable but not logically wrong, or, if logically wrong, reconstitutes itself immediately, like smoke that has been waved away from a fire.

In this arena, where certain ideas are "illusion" but are at the same time "inseparable from human reason," Kant lays on the dissecting table the theological predicates of "soul." The "paralogisms" of pure reason that he analyzes occupy chapter 1 of the second book of the "Transcendental Dialectic" and are four in number. All four are set up in the form of syllogisms, and I cite the first syllogism in full, although I shall not do so for the other three.

> That, the representation of which is the *absolute subject* of our judgments and cannot therefore be employed as determination of another thing, is *substance.*

> I as a thinking being, am the *absolute subject* of all my possible
> judgments, and this representation of myself cannot be employed as
> predicate of any other thing.
> Therefore I, as thinking being (soul), am *substance*. (IV, 220)

There then follows—here as well as in the other three syllogisms—
a "criticism" that occupies several paragraphs.

> I can say of any and every thing that it is substance, in the sense
> that I distinguish it from mere predicates and determinations of
> things. Now in all our thought the 'I' is the subject, in which
> thoughts inhere only as determinations; and this 'I' cannot be
> employed as the determination of another thing. Everyone must,
> therefore, necessarily regard himself as substance. . . .
> But what use am I to make of this concept of a substance? That I,
> as a thinking being, *persist* for myself, and do not in any natural
> manner either *arise* or *perish*, can by no means be deduced from it.
> Yet there is no other use to which I can put the concept of the
> substantiality of my thinking subject, and apart from such use I
> could very well dispense with it. (IV, 220)

This cuts very near the bone. Its sharp attack on the theological
predicates of "soul," however, is intertwined with a palpable ambivalence. One might think that soul should, on the basis of the
last statement quoted above, be abandoned. This, however, Kant
does not do; he reaffirms the untenability of the Christian predicates as objects of reason but does not jettison soul, even though so
much of its urgency has already been transferred to apperception
and imagination.

> Consciousness is, indeed, that which alone makes all representations
> to be thoughts, and in it, therefore, as the transcendental subject, all
> our perceptions must be found; but beyond the logical meaning of
> the 'I,' we have no knowledge of the subject in itself, which as
> substratum underlies this 'I,' as it does all thoughts. The proposi-
> tion, *'The soul is substance,'* may, however, quite well be allowed to
> stand, if only it be recognized that this concept does not carry us a
> single step further, and so cannot yield us any of the usual deduc-
> tions of the pseudo-rational doctrine of the soul, as, for instance, the
> everlasting duration of the human soul in all changes and even in
> death. (IV, 221)

The same ambivalence pertains to the other three paralogisms:
sharp and decisive criticism of the predicates of soul is curiously
enough not accompanied by the thereby implied rejection of that
entity. For instance, in the second paralogism, which reaches the
syllogistic conclusion that the soul is "simple" rather than com-
posite, Kant rejects the aid of the Cartesian *cogito*.

Nor is simplicity of myself (as soul) really *inferred* from the proposition, "I think'; it is already involved in every thought. The proposition, 'I am simple' must be regarded as referred to as an immediate expression of apperception, just as what is referred to as the Cartesian inference, *cogito, ergo sum,* is really a tautology, since the *cogito* (*sum cogitans*) asserts my existence immediately. '*I am simple*' means nothing more than that this representation, 'I,' does not contain in itself the least manifoldness and that it is absolute (although merely logical) unity.

Thus the renowned psychological proof is founded merely on the indivisible unity of a representation, which governs only the verb in its relation to a person. It is obvious that in attaching 'I' to our thoughts we designate the subject of inherence only transcendentally, without noting in it any quality whatever. (IV, 224)

Though this would seem conclusive as a rejection, in the same section ambivalence reappears. "Thinking beings, *as such,* can never be found by us among outer appearances, and their thoughts, consciousness, desires, etc., cannot be outwardly intuited. All these belong to inner sense. This argument does, in fact, seem to be so natural and so popular that even the commonest understanding appears to have always relied upon it, and thus already, from the earliest times, to have regarded souls as quite different entities from their bodies" (IV, 225).

The two remaining paralogisms are those of "personality" (i.e., that the soul is a "person") and "ideality" (that outer relations are merely ideal). But the real situation with regard to the latter, as Kant summarizes it, is that

all controversy in regard to the nature of the thinking being and its connection with the corporeal world is merely a result of filling the gap where knowledge is wholly lacking to us with paralogisms of reason, treating our thoughts as things and hypostatising them. . . . Nothing but the sobriety of a critique, at once strict and just, can free us from this dogmatic delusion, which through the lure of an imagined felicity keeps so many in bondage to theories and systems. Such a critique confines all our speculative claims rigidly to the field of possible experience; and it does this . . . by an effective determining of these limits in accordance with established principles, inscribing its *nihil ulterius* on those Pillars of Hercules, which nature herself has erected in order that the voyage of our reason may be extended no further than the continuous coastline of experience itself reaches. (IV, 246–47)

In a long concluding discussion after all four paralogisms, Kant asserts they are four because "apperception" is thereby "carried through all the classes of the categories," namely, subsistence,

reality, unity, and existence. He has, he says, shown "the systematic interconnection of all these dialectical assertions of a pseudora-
tional doctrine of the soul in an order determined by pure reason"
(IV, 251). The "transcendental and yet natural illusion of the paralogisms of pure reason" (IV, 247) can, in the systematic ordering
that runs parallel with the table of the categories, thus be rendered
as the propositions that "the soul" knows in itself—

1. *the unconditioned unity of relation*, i.e., that it itself is not inherent
   in something else but *self-subsistent*.
2. *the unconditioned unity of quality*, i.e., that it is not a real whole
   but *simple*.
3. *the unconditioned unity in the plurality in time*, i.e., that it is not
   numerically different at different times but *one* and *the very same
   subject*.
4. *the unconditioned unity of existence in space*, i.e., that it is not the
   consciousness of many things outside it, but the consciousness *of
   the existence of itself* only, and of other things merely as its
   representations*. (IV, 251–52)

Curiously enough, the extended syllogistic analysis of the four
paralogisms, all of which as referred to were in the first edition of
the *Critique of Pure Reason*, was replaced, in the second edition a
half-dozen years later, by a briefer and less analytic version, devoted considerably to a refutation of arguments about the permanence of the soul in Mendelssohn's *Phaedo*. A commentator describes the difference between Kant's first and second versions.

> The treatment of the four *Paralogisms* which in the first edition
> occupied thirty-three pages is reduced to five. The problems of the
> mutual interaction of mind and body, of its prenatal character and of
> its immortality, the discussion of which in the first edition required
> some ten pages, are now disposed of in a single paragraph (B426–7).
> The remaining twenty-two pages of the new chapter are almost
> entirely devoted to more or less polemical discussion of criticisms
> which had been passed upon the first edition. These had been in
> great part directed against Kant's doctrine of apperception and of
> inner sense, and so could fittingly be dealt with in connection with
> the problems of rational psychology.[32]

As to why Kant chose to alter and shorten his discussion, the
most obvious answer would be that he thought the changes would
be improvements. The same commentator notes: "In [re]formul-
ating the several arguments of the four *Paralogisms*, Kant develops
and places in the forefront a statement which receives only passing

[32]Kemp Smith, pp. 466–67.

mention in A352–3. 362, 366–7, 381–2, namely, that the truths contained in the judgments of rational psychology find expression in merely identical (*i.e.*, analytic) propositions. This enables Kant to formulate both the *Paralogisms* and his criticisms thereof in much briefer and more pointed fashion" (p. 467). Well and good. And yet the radical nature of the changes suggests that this might not be the whole answer. One commentator cuts the Gordian knot by saying that "it would be a waste of time to worry ourselves about particular points of Kant's exposition, since the theory of mind he seeks to refute is completely out of date, so that no present-day philosopher will be prepared to attach much importance to it."[33] Such may be the case with regard to present-day philosophers, but it begs the question at issue.

A more credible additional answer might be to point to Kant's caution about possible adverse reaction from state authority, for the second version is less direct in its assault on the theological predicates of soul than is the first. Edward Caird noted that "while he deeply sympathised in the aspirations of his time after greater social and political freedom, his temper inclined him to avoid anything like rebellion against constituted authority: and the most dubious act of which he was guilty was that, in submission to an order from the government of the pietistic successor of the great Frederic, he promised during that king's reign to be absolutely silent on theological subjects."[34] And yet if caution were the predominant consideration, it would have seemed more prudent to jettison the discussion entirely than merely to recast it.

What we seek is a deeper concatenation of purpose underlying the particularities of the two versions of the paralogisms. As license for such a search, we might avail ourselves of Paul de Man's conception of authorial blindness as a condition of insight, or we might employ the parallel deconstructionist theory of Derrida and thus tease out the thread of illogicality in the whole enterprise. Again, we might choose, as I shall here, to seek for that deeper authorial intention described by Leavis:

> The critic will be especially wary how he uses extraneous knowledge about the writer's intentions. Intentions are nothing in art except as realized, and the tests of realization will remain what they were. They are applied in the operation of the critic's sensibility; they are a matter of sense, derived from his literary experience, of what the living thing feels like—of the difference between that which has been willed and put there, or represents no profound integration,

[33]Cassirer, *Kant*, p. 252.
[34]Caird, I, 62.

and that which grows from a deep centre of life. These tests may very well reveal that the deep animating intention (if that is the right word) is something very different from the intention the author would declare.[35]

The "intention the author would declare," under which the revisions of the paralogisms were undertaken, might well be accounted for by the considerations described above by Norman Kemp Smith and Edward Caird. The "deep animating intention," however, the one "growing from a deep centre of life," is, I suggest, for Kant something else. My own sense of "what the living thing feels like" is that Kant, despite the transfer of soul's value to apperception and imagination, still cut too deeply against the bone in the first version of the paralogisms. The second version, in rejecting Mendelssohn's view of soul more rigorously than the predicates of soul as such, somewhat blunts the attack and thus leaves soul in a certain state of ambivalence. To that ambivalence there are clues enough, not only in Kant's statements within the paralogisms, adduced above, but also in the very character of the section as it appears in the first edition. As Kemp Smith says,

> The patchwork character of the *Critique*, the artificial nature of the connections between its various parts, is nowhere more evident than in this section on the *Paralogisms*. According to the definition given of transcendental illusion, we naturally expect Kant's argument to show that the *Paralogisms* rest upon a failure to distinguish between appearance and reality. . . . But Kant's manner of expounding the *Paralogisms* shows that this chapter must originally have been written independently of any intention to develop such teaching as that of the sections to which, in the *Critique*, they are made to lead up.[36]

The "patchwork character" to which Kemp Smith refers was a thesis broached by Hans Vaihinger in 1902 to the effect that Kant's *Critique* is replete with contradictions that result from his hasty piecing together, in a mosaic manner, of materials that he had not always modified or worked through.[37] Kant himself told Mendelssohn in 1783 that although the *Critique* "is the product of at least twelve years of reflection, I completed it hastily, in about four or five months." The lengthy period of gestation is readily verifiable. For instance, Kant had written Markus Herz as early as 1772

---

[35]Leavis, *Pursuit*, p. 225.

[36]Kemp Smith, p. 457.

[37]E.g.: "Aufmerksames und scharfes Studium der Deduktion A lehrt auf Schritt und Tritt, dass wir es in ihr nicht mit einer einheitlichen Darstellung zu thun haben. Kant kann dieselbe unmöglich in einem Zuge niedergeschrieben haben" (Vaihinger, p. 23).

(the *Critique* did not appear until 1781) that he was "in a position to bring out a 'Critique of Pure Reason' (*Critick der reinen Vernunft*)" and that the first part should be published "within about three months."[38]

Though Kemp Smith wholeheartedly accepts the "patchwork" theory, H. J. Paton, a commentator of hardly less authority, emphatically does not. Paton's trenchant opinions require to be cited at some length here, for they allow for the deep inner ambivalence I urge, rather than for the external conceptions of Vaihinger.

Paton provides detailed refutation of Vaihinger's position—indeed he does so in more than one publication[39]—and also of the somewhat parallel theory of Erich Adickes, but one must content oneself here with the merest summary of his standpoint. Adickes, notes Paton, "has propounded the theory that Kant's procedure was to insert passages into an original nucleus. . . . I believe his general view to be unproved, although not unreasonable, and his account of the details to be hazardous and even fanciful. Nevertheless although he is prepared to speak of the *Kritik* as a mosaic, it would be a mistake to attribute to him the patchwork theory in its extreme form. For that we must go to Vaihinger."[40] Speaking of Vaihinger's discernment of four strata in the transcendental deduction of the categories, Paton writes:

> With amazing self-confidence he proceeds to divide up these main strata into substrata, which he affects to put in a temporal order regarded as at least probable. Finally he examines, on the same principles, some of Kant's loose jottings (at that time almost entirely undated), and succeeds, as is only to be expected, in discovering passages which he can fit into his four strata. This he regards as a confirmation of his argument.
>
> To my mind the whole discussion is a monument of wasted ingenuity, rendered the more pathetic by the learning and clarity of the exposition. (I, 39–40)

Paton's own opinion is that "the inequalities in Kant's thought have been grotesquely exaggerated," although he is willing to admit that "Kant's mind, like that of other philosophers, worked on

---

[38]*Kant*, X, 345, 132.

[39]See also H. J. Paton, "Is the Transcendental Deduction a Patchwork?", *Proceedings of the Aristotelian Society*, n.s., 30 (1930), 143–78. At the end of this assault, in which he says he has "felt obliged to criticise Prof. Vaihinger with severity," Paton however adds unexpectedly: "although the greatest of Kantian scholars is in need of no testimonial from me," and in spite of "what I regard as his fundamental errors, I have learned more of the Transcendental Deduction from his brief pamphlet than from all the commentaries I have ever seen" (p. 178).

[40]Paton, I, 38.

different levels; that he thought out some problems more fully than others; and that he was capable of solving one problem without at first realising all its implications in relation to other problems" (I, 40). But to concede that is not to accept the patchwork theory.

> What I wish to protest against is the doctrine that Kant took isolated and contradictory notes, dating from different periods, and joined them together in a purely external manner. If there are any who think that this description exaggerates the doctrine of Vaihinger, I can only ask them to re-read what he has written in his monograph on the Transcendental Deduction.
>
> I venture to hold both that the general theory of Vaihinger is incredible and that its detailed application is demonstrably false. The finding of contradictions in Kant had become with him almost an obsession. This is seen to some extent even in his *Commentary*, which derives its immense value from his erudition and power of analysis rather than from his capacity to enter into another man's mind. (I, 40–41)

Paton argues that the acceptance or rejection of the patchwork theory is not merely a difference of opinion among scholars, but rather has decisive consequences for our understanding of Kant's meaning.

> This question cannot be regarded as a biographical problem of no importance, since it has serious consequences both for teaching and for exposition.
>
> The youthful mind is too intelligent to suppose that a work composed in this casual way is worth the immense labour which is necessary to understand it. . . . If the patchwork theory is true, the study of the *Kritik* ought to be removed from the philosophical curricula of the universities.
>
> For exposition the consequences seem to me even more serious. . . . To my mind it makes further criticism impossible.
>
> The essence of criticism, and the only way in which we can penetrate more deeply into the mind of an author, is to check our interpretation of one passage in the light of another, until gradually the whole becomes clear. If our interpretation is contradicted by other passages, we are compelled to reconsider it, and so we may come nearer the truth. On the patchwork theory there is no such compulsion, and the way is open for purely subjective impressions. Indeed, if an interpretation is contradicted by what Kant says elsewhere, the commentator merely notes a further confirmation of the patchwork theory; and the number of contradictions which he can find is limited only by the extent of his capacity for misunderstanding Kant. (I, 42–43)

If we accept Paton's animadversions, as I am urging that we do, then we shall not be wholly satisfied with Kemp Smith's argument that the paralogisms as represented in the first edition of the *Critique* simply witness "the artificial nature of the connections between its various parts" (with the implication that they are thereby quite properly replaced by the blander version of the second edition). On the contrary, one must heed Schopenhauer's admonition, in his "Kritik der Kantischen Philosophie". "Let no one imagine he knows the *Critique of Pure Reason,* and has a clear conception of Kant's teaching, if he has read only the second or one of the subsequent editions. This is absolutely impossible; for he has read only a mutilated, spoiled, and to a certain extent ungenuine text. It is my duty to state this here emphatically, as a warning to everyone." This caveat follows an anecdote where Schopenhauer says he originally read only the second edition, and "accused Kant of contradicting himself," but "when I later read Kant's principal work in the first edition, which had already become scarce, I saw, to my great joy, all those contradictions disappear."[41]

Be that as it may, one would seem justified, on Leavis's principles and on deconstructionist ones as well, in concluding (a) that the discrepancy in form and emphasis between the first and second versions of the paralogisms witnesses inner turmoil on the part of Kant, and that (b) the seemingly freestanding or "patchwork" character of the first version witnesses a long-continued existence of that turmoil. His intention, even in its most subliminal force, was itself ambivalent.

Indeed, Kemp Smith himself, despite his adherence to the patchwork theory, frequently suggests the existence of such turmoil. Speaking of apperception, he says at one point:

> To the last this initial excess of emphasis upon the unity of apperception remained characteristic of Kant's Critical teaching; and though in the later statements of his theory, its powers and prerogatives were very greatly diminished, it still continued to play a somewhat exaggerated role. The early spiritualistic views were embodied in a terminology which he continued to employ; and unless the altered meaning of his terms is recognised and allowed for, misunderstanding is bound to result. The terms, having been forged under the influence of the older views, are but ill adapted to the newer teaching which they are employed to formulate.
>
> There was also a second influence. When Kant was constrained in the light of his new and unexpected results, to recognise his older views as lacking in theoretical justification, he still held to them in his own personal thinking. For there is ample evidence that they continued to represent his *Privatmeinungen.*[42]

[41]Schopenhauer, II, 515–16, 514–15.
[42]Kemp Smith, p. 261.

The word *Privatmeinungen* might well be translated by Polanyi's phrase, "personal knowledge," which, at least in Polanyi's view, runs deeper than formal scientific principle. Another Kantian commentator says, after quoting a long passage from the revised version of the paralogisms, that he adduces the quotation lest we "get a very wrong impression of Kant's attitude in the *Paralogisms*, and because it is the passage in this *Critique* which goes furthest towards setting his proof of immortality on moral grounds. It is not that Kant doubted survival, and indeed immortality, but that he doubted the alleged theoretical proofs of it and the claim to comprehend its necessity." This is about as deep-lying an ambivalence as one could encounter; and the same commentator concisely sums up the oscillation between personal knowledge and rational logic. "Kant thus rejects the *a priori* proof of immortality which was the main object of rational psychology, but he was nevertheless a strong believer in immortality on moral grounds."[43] Kemp Smith, too, observes near the end of his comments on the second version of the paralogisms that

> Kant's retention of the Idea of the self is chiefly of interest as revealing the strength and tenacity of his spiritualist leanings. We may judge of the disinterestedness and courage of his thinking by the contrary character of his pre-conceptions. For even when they have been shown to be theoretically indemonstrable, they continue to retain by honorific title the dignity from which they have been deposed. The full force of the objections is none the less recognised.
> "The simplicity of substance . . . is not presupposed as the real ground of the properties of the soul. For these may rest on altogether different grounds of which we can know nothing." That, however, is only Kant's unbiassed estimate of the theoretical evidence; it is not an expression of his own personal belief.[44]

How all this ambivalence might go so deep in Kant's attitude, the unconscious tropism as well as the consciously elaborated position, depends on the question as to how far theological predicates, culminating in the postulate of immortality, are necessary to maintain the assurance of soul. Immortality is certainly the most obvious guarantee of soul; it is not, however, for all thinkers the essence of soul, but rather a kind of outrigger that keeps soul from capsizing into the abyss of meaninglessness. Soul itself is an idea that rests upon an intuition of unity and meaning in the self—a kind of numinous feeling. Of course, many and even most would feel that without immortality soul is an illusion. Tennyson says:

[43]Ewing, pp. 206, 204–5.
[44]Kemp Smith, pp. 476–77.

My own dim life should teach me this,
   That life shall live forevermore,
   Else earth is darkness at the core,
And dust and ashes all that is.

But not everyone feels this. For a single example, a commentator has recently argued that English mistranslations of Freud's German have obscured the fact that Freud was concerned with ministering to the soul. "His greatest concern was with man's innermost being, to which he most frequently referred through the use of a metaphor—man's soul—because the word 'soul' evokes so many emotional connotations. It is the greatest shortcoming of the current English versions of his works that they give no hint of this." The same commentator, however, notes that "nowhere in his writings does Freud give us a precise definition of the term 'soul.' I suspect that he chose the term *because* of its inexactitude, its emotional resonance." The commentator goes on to insist: "I should point out, however, that when Freud speaks of the soul he is talking not about a religious phenomenon but about a psychological concept. . . . Freud's atheism is well known—he went out of his way to assert it. There is nothing supernatural about his idea of the soul, and it has nothing to do with immortality; if anything endures after us, it is other people's memories of us—and what we create. By 'soul' or 'psyche' Freud means that which is most valuable in man while he is still alive."[45]

While Kant's pietistic heritage allows no equation of his own attitude with Freud's atheism, Freud's insistence on soul without the outrigger of immortality directs us to certain questions. Is it actually immortality that we long for? Might it not rather be intensity of life with psychological freedom from the fear of annihilation? Swift's Struldbrugs, no less than Tennyson's Tithonus, are reminders that immortality, if by that term no more is meant than unending extension of our human lot, is not very appealing. For many of us, and perhaps even most, the progressive realization of our inadequacies and debilities would demand—clamor for—a different matrix of existence and a different "I" were unending extension in prospect. Some changes would certainly have to be made, some radical changes. Only with a restoration of the heightened intensities of early experience, the rapture of first love, the protective illusions of childhood, would even modest extensions—say three hundred years—be enticing.

In any event, Kant's own interest in immortality was as an out-

---

[45]*In Memoriam*, section 34, ll. 1–4; Bettelheim, pp. xi, 77.

rigger that guaranteed meaning, not as an infinite extension of life as we know it. As a commentator has recently pointed out: "what he is interested in is always whether man is necessarily immortal and not whether as a matter of fact man will live forever. . . . The lectures of the 1760s . . . claim an afterlife is 'very likely' because (i) 'the status of the world, without (enduring) rational beings is noth-ingness,' and otherwise (ii) 'rational beings who die would be as if they had never been.' "[46]

Whatever the variations in his marshaling of rational arguments, Kant did believe in immortality, even if eventually only as a demand of practical rather than pure reason. The numinous and unitary aspect of "soul" he had, as we have noted earlier, "laid off" into imagination and apperception. *Apperception* was the more technical term and looked backward to Kant's great German forebear; *imagination* was the more emotionally charged term and looked forward to the new intensities of Romanticism. Kemp Smith observes:

> On one point is Kant clear and definite, namely, that it is to productive imagination that the *generation* of unified experience is primarily due. In it something of the fruitful and inexhaustible character of noumenal reality is traceable. Doubtless one chief reason for his choice of the title imagination is the creative character which in popular thought has always been regarded as its essential feature. As Kant, speaking of schematism, which is a process executed by the imagination, states in A 141: "This schematism . . . is an *art* (*Kunst*) concealed in the depths of the human soul." This description may perhaps be interpreted in the light of Kant's account of the creative character of artistic genius in the *Critique of Judgment*, for there also imagination figures as the truly originative or creative faculty of the human spirit[47]

Kant's close linkage of imaginative function and "the depths of the human soul" was the situation that obtained in the intellectual climate of his time. For instance, alongside Kant's statement of 1781 adduced above by Kemp Smith, we may consider the independent statement of James Beattie in 1783, which locates imagination and soul in closest proximity. "The human soul is essentially active; and none of our faculties are more restless, than this of Imagination, which operates in sleep, as well as when we are awake."[48]

---

[46]Ameriks, pp. 177–78.
[47]Kemp Smith, p. 265.
[48]Beattie, p. 78. Actually, imagination and soul had always stood in closest proximity. Thus Proclus, in classical antiquity: "Therefore, just as nature stands above

Nonetheless, if imagination was proximate to soul, it was also proximate to apperception. For Kant, imagination and transcendental unity of apperception worked in tandem. "The transcendental unity of apperception thus relates to the pure synthesis of imagination, as an *a priori* condition of the possibility of all combination of the manifold in one knowledge. But only the *productive* synthesis of the imagination can take place *a priori*; the reproductive rests upon empirical conditions. Thus the principle of the necessary unity of pure (productive) synthesis of imagination, prior to apperception, is the ground of the possibility of all knowledge, especially of experience." Again, "the synthesis of the manifold through pure imagination, the unity of all representations in relation to original apperception, precede all empirical knowledge." In these formulations, the Platonic apprehension that "soul is the eldest of all things, and rules over bodies" is fully honored.[49]

But Kant had logically restricted the scope of transcendental unity of apperception in a way that dissipated its numinous aura almost as decisively as did the paralogisms the logical predicates of soul. In "the representation 'I am,' nothing manifold is given." "In the synthetic original unity of apperception, I am conscious of myself, not as I appear to myself, nor as I am in myself, but only that I am." What Kant calls *"transcendental apperception"* is "pure original unchangeable consciousness," but only when laminated together does either apperception or imagination mean anything. "All consciousness . . . belongs to an all-comprehensive pure apperception. . . . It is this apperception which must be added to pure imagination, in order to render its function intellectual." The "I'" of pure apperception is a mere identity. "That the 'I,' the 'I' that thinks, can be regarded always as *subject,* and as something which does not belong to thought as a mere predicate, must be granted. It is an apodeictic and indeed *identical* proposition; but it does not mean that I, as *object,* am for myself a *self-subsistent* being or *substance.*"[50]

Thus it seems reasonable to infer that the attenuating of predicates from the "abiding and unchanging 'I'" of pure apperception, added to the logical clipping of theological predicates in the discussion of soul contained in the original version of the paralogisms,

---

the visible figures, so the soul, exercising her capacity to know, projects on the imagination, as on a mirror, the ideas of the figures; and the imagination, receiving in pictorial form these impressions of the ideas within the soul, by their means affords the soul an opportunity to turn inward from the pictures and attend to herself" (Proclus, p. 113).

[49]*Kant,* IV, 88, 94; Plato, *Laws,* 967D.

[50]*Kant,* III, 112, 123; IV, 81, 91; III, 267.

made the situation too extreme for Kant's "deeper intention"—
what Nietzsche recognizes as his "subterranean Christianity of
values." The version of the paralogisms in the second edition is
briefer and less emphatic, and though it still maintains that "we
must renounce the hope of comprehending, from the merely theoretical knowledge of ourselves, the necessary continuance of our
existence," it also, and I think crucially, asserts, "Yet nothing is
thereby lost as regards the right, nay, the necessity, of postulating
a future life in accordance with the principles of the practical employment of reason, which is closely bound up with its speculative
employment."[51] This proviso substantially restores the theological
predications of soul so severely mauled in the first version.

If the dynamics of Kant's attitude toward soul, imagination and
apperception fluctuate constantly, with transfers and coun-
tertransfers of mental investment, such an effect is to be regarded
as a taxonomically elaborated testament to a universal truth about
the relation of the ideas of imagination and soul. Strictly speaking,
the thought that there is a "faculty" of "imagination" is as much a
mere assumption—a fiction, if one wishes—as the thought that
there is such an entity as "soul." All that can in precision be said is
that the human brain has the capacity of summoning images, just
as it has the capacity of remembering or reasoning. What we call
"imagination" must in rigor be defined only as Spinoza defined it:
"Imaginatio est idea, qua Mens rem aliquam ut praesentem con-
templatur"—"imagination is the idea by which the mind contem-
plates a thing as present."[52] That is the philosopher's definition.[53]
Another version is supplied by Kant: "*Einbildungskraft* ist das Vermögen, einen Gegenstand auch ohne dessen Gegenwart in der
Anschauung vorzustellen"—"imagination is the faculty of representing in intuition an object that is not itself present."[54]

Nevertheless, because the ideas of imagination and of soul share
proximity, they function somewhat as binary stars that draw off
one another's substance. Hence it is that "imagination" takes on a
double reference, one corresponding to its strict definition of the
summoning of images, and the other investing itself with the indefinite but honorific aura of soul.

It is astonishing how inevitable this double functioning has his-

---

[51]*Nietzsche*, III, 562; *Kant*, III, 277, 276.
[52]*Spinoza*, II, 301.
[53]Cf. Mayne, in 1728: "That Faculty which presents to the Mind's view the Images or Ideas of external sensible Objects, or by which the Mind perceives them, is what we call the *Imagination*." (Mayne, pp. 69–70).
[54]*Kant*, III, 119–20.

torically seemed to be. As a single illustration virtually at random, consider two of John Stuart Mill's paragraphs describing the mind of Bentham.

> Bentham's contempt, then, of all other schools of thinkers; his determination to create a philosophy wholly out of the materials furnished by his own mind, and by minds like his own; was his first disqualification as a philosopher. His second, was the incompleteness of his own mind as a representative of universal human nature. In many of the most natural and strongest feelings of human nature he had no sympathy; from many of its graver experiences he was altogether cut off; and the faculty by which one mind understands a mind different from itself, and throws itself into the feelings of that other mind, was denied him by his deficiency of Imagination.
>
> With Imagination in the popular sense, command of imagery and metaphorical expression, Bentham was, to a certain degree, endowed. . . . The imagination which he had not, was that to which the name is generally appropriated by the best writers of the present day; that which enables us, by a voluntary effort, to conceive the absent as if it were present, the imaginary as if it were real, and to clothe it in the feelings which, if it were indeed real, it would bring along with it. This is the power by which one human being enters into the mind and circumstances of another.[55]

For Mill's imagination of the second kind, the word *soul* could be substituted with little loss of meaning; it would make little difference whether he said Bentham exhibited deficiency of imagination or deficiency of soul.

Indeed, Mill's last specification, that imagination "is the power by which one human being enters into the mind and circumstances of another" moves the faculty into a realm, that of human morality, that might otherwise seem the exclusive domain of soul. Mill was here writing in 1840, and he may have been echoing Shelley's *Defence of Poetry,* which though written in 1821, was not published until that year. "A man, to be greatly good," said Shelley, "must imagine intensely and comprehensively; he must put himself in the place of another and of many others; the pains and pleasures of his species must become his own. The great instrument of moral good is the imagination; and poetry administers to the effect by

---

[55]*Mill,* X, 91–92. Mill goes on to say that this second kind of imagination "constitutes the poet, in so far as he does anything but melodiously utter his own actual feelings. It constitutes the dramatist entirely. It is one of the constituents of the historian. . . . Without it nobody knows even his own nature, further than circumstances have actually tried it and called it out; nor the nature of his fellow creatures, beyond such generalizations as he may have been enabled to make from his observation of their outward conduct."

acting upon the cause. . . . Poetry strengthens that faculty which is the organ of the moral nature of man, in the same manner as exercise strengthens a limb."[56] But the "faculty which is the organ of the moral nature of man" is surely "soul." A challenge to locate the reference of the statement, if it were presented to any ordinary person without specific context, would almost certainly elicit that word, even though in his own context Shelley has used instead *imagination*.

That the word *imagination*, because of the gravitational pull of soul, came customarily to mean not one, but two things, with one accorded a higher function than the other, is a truth illustrated by but not confined to Mill's usage. We need think only of Coleridge's imagination and fancy, or of Kant's productive and reproductive imagination, or of Tetens's *Phantasie* and *Dichtkraft*. The splitting is endemic. In his recent survey of theories of imagination in the eighteenth and nineteenth centuries, James Engell points out examples of splitting in such forerunners of Tetens and Kant as Wolff, Platner, and Sulzer, with the observation that "from 1770 on, the tendency to separate *Phantasie, Einbildungskraft*, and *Dichtungskraft*, or their equivalents, is a common practice in German thought."[57]

What was constantly pulling on the root term was the idea of soul. To keep this salient fact firmly in mind, a more extensive illustration is fitting. Wordsworth, in the "Essay, Supplementary to the Preface" of the 1815 edition of his poems, pushes the imaginative function relentlessly close to an explicit identification with theological ultimates. "In a higher poetry," he says, "an enlightened Critic chiefly looks for a reflection of the wisdom of the heart and the grandeur of the imagination," and then, a few lines farther down, he says that "Poetry is most just to its own divine origin when it administers the comforts and breathes the spirit of religion."[58] He subsequently begins to talk about "faith," about "the elevation of [man's] nature," about "the affinity between religion and poetry; between religion—making up the deficiencies of reason by faith; and poetry—passionate for the instruction of reason; between religion—whose element is infinitude . . . and poetry—ethereal and transcendent, yet incapable to sustain her existence without sensuous incarnation" (III, 65).

All this is set in motion by insistences in the preface to the same edition, where Wordsworth explains the ordering of his poems.

[56]*Shelley*, VII, 118.
[57]Engell, pp. 94–95, 101, 105–6.
[58]*Prose*, III, 64.

"Imagination, in the sense of the word as giving title to a class of the following Poems, has no reference to images that are merely a faithful copy, existing in the mind, of absent external objects; but is a word of higher import, denoting operations of the mind upon those objects" (III, 30–31). He speaks of "the conferring, the abstracting, and the modifying powers of the Imagination," and he says that "the Imagination also shapes and *creates;* and how? By innumerable processes; and in none does it more delight than in that of consolidating numbers into unity, and dissolving and separating unity into number,—alternations proceeding from, and governed by, a sublime consciousness of the soul in her own mighty and almost divine powers" (III, 33). Intriguingly, the equation of imagination and soul is shortly afterward overbalanced, not in favor of the latter, as one might have expected in an earlier period, but in favor of the former. The process parallels Kant's transfer of soul's aura to apperception and imagination; Wordsworth writes: "But the Imagination is conscious of an indestructible dominion;— the Soul may fall away from it, not being able to sustain its grandeur; but, if once felt and acknowledged, by no act of any other faculty of the mind can it be relaxed, impaired, or diminished.— Fancy is given to quicken and to beguile the temporal part of our nature, Imagination to incite and to support the eternal" (III, 36–37).

One can scarcely expect to find more ultimate testimony to the transference of the predicates of soul to those of imagination. *Imagination* here strains radically against its ordinary language synonym, *fancy*, and the agency here is undisguisedly the call of soul. But even in less elevated testimony and in less explicit situations, we find historically a gravitational straining against the root definition of imagination that constantly tends to split the function. Thus a modern scholar notes that the Arabic commentator Al Fārābi saw imagination as having a lower and higher function (and he does so, interestingly enough, in a complex that adumbrates Coleridge's in its involvement of reason and symbol along with imagination).

> Most remarkable is the theory of imagination adopted by Al-Fārābi; its Greek author had probably taken as his basis Aristotle's view of φαντασία modified by the Stoics but, under Neoplatonic influence, given it a new direction. . . . As the divine mind rules the universe, so reason should govern and control the life of man. No human faculty higher than reason can be conceived. . . . φαντασία, "imagination" or "representation," is intermediate between perception and reason; it not only provides reason with material derived from sense-perception but is also at the service of the rational faculty in other

ways . . . cf., e.g., what the Neoplatonist Plutarch, following Iamblichus, has to say about the double aspect of φαντασία and in particular its higher form. . . . Now, imagination is, according to Al-Fārābi, also capable of an activity of its own, which is no longer dependent on the material supplied by the senses and preserved in the memory, and does not consist in combining or separating this material. . . . Through this creative φαντασία a kind of access to metaphysical truth with the help of images is open, this being a still higher activity . . . which manifests itself in translating metaphysical truth into symbols.[59]

Another and possibly still more striking adumbration of Coleridge's view of imagination can be found in William Duff, who, writing in 1767, differentiates "creative Imagination, the distinguishing characteristic of true Genius" from "a quickness and readiness of fancy in assembling such ideas as lie latent in the mind, till the combining power of association, with the assistance of the retentive faculty, calls them forth." We note that Duff's fancy is governed both by "the retentive faculty" and "the combining power of association"; we recall that Coleridge's fancy is "a mode of Memory emancipated from the order of time and space" and "must receive all its materials ready made from the law of association." Shortly further on, Duff contrasts "the efforts of a RAMBLING and SPORTIVE Fancy" to "the copious effusions of a plastic Imagination."[60]

Duff of course stands in the mainstream of eighteenth-century theorizing about the role of imagination. But his kind of splitting into lower and higher function occurs also with thinkers not ordinarily in the forefront in reprises of imagination's history. For instance, a recent commentator on Montaigne finds occasion to note that "there are two kinds of imagination, or two functions of the imagination, according to Montaigne."[61] Again, a commen-

---

[59]Walzer, pp. 142–46.

[60]Duff, pp. 48–49, 52.

[61]Hallie, p. 76. Hallie distinguishes the "Poetic" imagination from the "assertive imagination." The former is benign, but the latter, which paradoxically "does not often involve metaphor" but is rather "a literal, not a literary language," seeks to persuade rather than delight, and is accordingly malign. "This imagination, which he sometimes calls '*fantasie*,' which confuses the name with the thing named, is for Montaigne the main perpetrator of the trouble that besets mankind" (pp. 74–77). Montaigne's division is generically similar to that of Zachary Mayne, who distinguishes "lively" imagination, which is the agency for poetry, from "vehement" imagination, which "destroys Wit, makes Men stupid, and quite robs them of their *Understanding*. For Madness, or a mopish Melancholy, is always proportionate in its Degree, to the Power, or Intenseness and Impetuosity of the *Imagination*" (Mayne, pp. 76–77). The tradition by which imagination is accorded a baneful function is almost as well entrenched historically as that by which it is conceived honorifically;

tator on Keats notes that Abraham Tucker—whose *Light of Nature* figured in the backgrounds of both Keats and Hazlitt—distinguished between imagination and understanding, with the former more honorific than the latter.

> Tucker was led . . . to draw a distinction between the faculties of imagination and understanding . . . one that in some ways looked forward to Coleridge's more famous discrimination. Imagination is that whole store of impressions and sensations of which the mind has cognizance, together with all the images and associations connecting them. It is synonymous, in other words, with the total contents of the mind and its faculties as they have developed through time and as they exist in their capacity fully to respond to new experience. An act of understanding, on the other hand, is the deliberate use of our faculties for some particular end or purpose.[62]

From such peripheral and only partly relevant examples from the still pools and inlets of the topic, we may turn to another one from its mainstream. Kant, in the *Kritik der Urtheilskraft*, hails the poetic power of imagination in terms that echo Ficino and Sidney and closely parallel Coleridge's distinction between secondary imagination and fancy.

> The imagination (as a productive faculty of cognition) is a powerful agent for creating, as it were, a second nature out of the material supplied to it by actual nature It affords us entertainment where experience proves too commonplace; and we even use it to remodel experience, always following, no doubt, laws that are based on analogy, but still also following principles which have a higher seat in reason. . . . By this means we get a sense of our freedom from the

---

its most influential early form was set by Plato's strictures against *eikasia* (*Republic* 509D–E ff., 534A). Especially from Descartes through Dr. Johnson one encounters repeated denunciations of imagination as irresponsible and harmful, in that it distorts reality. Spinoza, for instance, in *De intellectus emendatione*, repeatedly denigrates imagination in comparison with understanding, e.g.: "we have distinguished between a true idea and other perceptions, and shown that ideas fictitious, false, and the rest, originate in the imagination"; "we may also see how easily men may fall into grave errors through not distinguishing accurately between the imagination and the understanding" (*Spinoza*, II, 32, 32–33). But all that changed with Romanticism.

[62]Sperry, p. 24. See further Engell, pp. 162–65, 174. Tucker's (or Search's, to use the pseudonym he preferred) setting of imagination above understanding reversed the procedure of Mayne a half-century earlier and signalized the displacement of the so-called Age of Reason by Romanticism. Mayne had specifically made understanding superior to imagination, e.g.: "the Faculties of *Perceiving*, which *Brutes* have, as well as *Men*, namely *Sense* and the *Imagination*, are not *Intellectual*. . . . And consequently, it is *Reason* and *Understanding* alone, which constitutes the true and real Difference between *Mankind*, and those Creatures of an inferiour Rank and Order, called *Brutes*, to denote their being destitute of *Understanding*" (Mayne, "To the Reader").

law of association (which attaches to the empirical employment of
the imagination), with the result that the material can be borrowed
by us from nature in accordance with that law, but be worked up by
us into something else—namely, that which surpasses nature.[63]

But this splitting of imaginative function into creative productivity
and empirical employment immediately follows a remarkable invocation of the word *soul* in an aesthetic context.

> Of certain products which are expected . . . to stand on the
> footing of fine art, we say they are *soul*less (*ohne Geist*); . . . A poem
> may be very pretty and elegant, but is soulless. A narrative has
> precision and method, but is soulless. . . . Conversation frequently is
> not devoid of entertainment, but yet soulless. Even of a woman we
> may well say, she is pretty, affable, and refined, but soulless. Now
> what do we here mean by 'soul'?
>
> 'Soul' (*Geist*) in an aesthetical sense, signifies the animating princi-
> ple in the mind. But that whereby this principle animates the psychic
> soul (*Seele*)—the material which it employs for that purpose—is that
> which sets the mental powers . . . into a play which is self-maintain-
> ing and which strengthens those powers for such activity.
>
> Now my proposition is that this principle is nothing else than the
> faculty of presenting *aesthetic ideas*. But, by an aesthetic idea I mean
> that representation of the imagination which induces much thought,
> yet without the possibility of any definite thought, i.e. *concept* being
> adequate to it. (V, 313–14)

And from this fence-running discussion about the linguistics of
soul Kant then proceeds into the passage quoted above, about the
imagination creating a second nature.

Kant was here writing in a work that appeared in 1790, nineteen
years after the appearance of his first *Kritik*. His discussion stands
in the headwaters of the high Romantic current, and to it we may
add ones from the upstream and the downstream of that current.
They bracket a half-century period in a way that makes them almost seem like sluice gates for that section of time. In 1783 James
Beattie, cited above for his contemporaneity with but independence of Kant's first *Kritik*, wrote that "according to the common
use of words, Imagination and Fancy are not perfectly synonymous. They are, indeed, names for the same faculty; but the former seems to be applied to the more solemn, and the latter to the
more trivial, exertions of it. A witty author is a man of lively Fancy;
but a sublime poet is said to possess a vast Imagination. However,
as these words are often, and by the best writers, used indis-

[63]*Kant*, V, 314.

criminately, I shall not further distinguish them."[64] The passage is especially interesting because it witnesses the general state of intellectual usage that had obtained by that time. The philosopher's definitions of Spinoza and Kant adduced previously were by this time overlaid with ideas of honorific function that necessitated splitting. As Beattie goes on to say:

> Some authors define Imagination, "The simple apprehension of corporeal objects when absent." But the common use of language would warrant a more comprehensive definition. . . . In the language of modern philosophy, the word *Imagination* seems to denote; first, the power of apprehending or conceiving ideas, simply as they are in themselves, without any view to their reality: and secondly, the power of combining into new forms, or assemblages, those thoughts, ideas, or notions, which we have derived from experience, or from information.
> These two powers, though distinguishable, are not essentially different. (pp. 73–74)

Although Beattie does not here invest imagination with its theological aura, it is not uninteresting to observe that in close proximity to this discussion he finds occasion to speak of the immortality of the soul. "Let us however entertain a right idea of human nature; remembering, that it was made in the image of God, and that it is destined for immortality" (p. 71). And near the end of the treatise he says that "nothing can give keener anguish, or overwhelm the mind with a deeper gloom, than to be perplexed with doubts concerning that futurity which is the foundation of [a man's] dearest hopes" (p. 202). "Lastly, let those, who wish to preserve their imagination in a chearful and healthy state, cultivate piety, and guard against superstition; by forming right notions of God's adorable being and providence" (p. 205).

Thus Beattie, the opponent of Hume, in 1783. In 1830 Hegel, in a discussion of "reproductive imagination" as "active intelligence" responsible for "the production of images out of the unique innerness of the ego" ("das Hervorgehen der Bilder aus der eigenen Innerlichkeit des Ich"), splits the imaginative function into an ascending scale of three.

> Imagination has three forms into which it unfolds itself. It is, generally speaking, the determinant of the images.
> At first, however, it does no more than determine the images as entering into existence. As such, it is merely reproductive imagination. This has the character of a merely formal activity.

---

[64]Beattie, p. 72.

But, secondly, imagination not merely recalls the images existent
in it but connects them with one another and in this way raises them
to *general* ideas or representations. Accordingly, at this stage, imagination appears as the activity of associating images.

The third stage in this sphere is that in which intelligence posits
its *general* representations as identical with the *particular* of the
images so that the representations are given *imagistic* existence. The
sensuous existence has the double form of *symbol* and *sign,* so that
this third stage comprises the *symbolizing* and *signmaking imagination*
(*Phantasie*), which forms the transition to *memory* [*Gedächtnis*].[65]

Here, too, we see a streaming from the rudimentary philosopher's
definition to more honorific functions characterized by numinous
aura.

Hegel's relating of imagination to "symbol" points us to a comprehensive truth. Because the hope conveyed by the idea of soul
was so intense and at the same time so essential, its precious
burden tended, as we saw in the instance of Kant, to be split into
several linguistic bearers rather than into a single alternative word;
and this was a characteristic for Romanticism in general. There is
no contradiction when James Engell says that "the concept of the
imagination is the quintessence of Romanticism" and when Oskar
Walzel says that "the concept of organism is the key to the Romantic view of the world."[66] The two terms, so different in designation, are identical in numinous function. Nor are symbol and organism the only co-operating numinous terms. As noted at the end of
the third chapter, Alexander Gerard triangulated the words "imagination," "invention" or originality, and "genius," each by the
other two. To all these terms, moreover, at least one more can be
added: "sublimity" or the sublime.

They are all charged with the numinous of soul, and they are all
equivalent in import though not in designation.[67] In most instances they are summoned at some emotional apex where the
substitution of another of their number would serve to sustain the
meaning of the passage. Often they are used in coordination. For
instance, Wordsworth collocates "genius," "originality," and
"soul". "If every great poet . . . in the highest exercise of his genius . . . has to call forth and to communicate *power*, this service, in
a still greater degree, falls upon an original writer. . . . Of genius

[65]*Hegel,* X, 264.
[66]Engell, p. 4; Walzel, p. 15.
[67]How tantalizingly indefinite but pervasive was this numinous and aura is suggested by the words of a commentator about the currency of imagination in the
eighteenth century. "The common belief is that, by means of imagination, a super-
nal influence, capable of elevating and transforming the soul, flows into the mind"
(Tuveson, p. 133).

the only proof is, the act of doing well what is worthy to be done, and what was never done before. . . . Genius is the introduction of a new element into the intellectual universe. . . . What is all this but an advance, or a conquest, made by the soul of the poet?" In the succeeding paragraph he brings "sublimity" into the collocation. "And for the sublime,—if we consider what are the cares that occupy the passing day, and how remote is the practice and the course of life from the sources of sublimity, in the soul of Man, can it be wondered that there is little existing preparation for a poet charged with a new mission to extend its kingdom, and to augment and spread its enjoyments?" And then in the next paragraph he further adds imagination. "But in everything which is to send the soul into herself, to be admonished of her weakness, or to be made conscious of her power;—wherever life and nature are described as operated upon by the creative or abstracting virtue of the imagination . . . *there*, the poet must reconcile himself for a season to few and scattered hearers."[68]

It might be instructive to consider in more detail the historical dimensions of some of these Wordsworthian reciprocities. The leading emphasis, in this collocation, on genius and originality harvests a deep tradition in eighteenth-century theory. Kant in 1790 defined "genius" as "(1) a *talent* for producing that for which no definite rule can be given: and not clever aptitude for what can be learned according to some rule; consequently *originality* must be its primary property." He makes two additional points. "(2) Since there may also be original nonsense, its products must at the same time be models, i.e. be *exemplary*; and, consequently, though not themselves derived from imitation, they must serve that purpose for others, i.e. as a standard or rule of estimating. (3) It cannot indicate scientifically how it brings about its product, but rather gives the rule as *nature*. Hence, where an author owes a product to his genius, he does not himself know how the *ideas* for it have entered his head."[69]

Kant, too, was harvesting prior discussion. The term *genius*, though occasionally encountered earlier than the eighteenth century (Leibniz, for instances, refers to the "genius" of Pascal), did not become common coin until that century, largely through the popularizing efforts of Addison and through Pope's writings on Homer and Shakespeare.[70] Indeed, Homer and Shakespeare were

[68]*Prose*, III, 82, 83.
[69]*Kant*, V, 307–8.
[70]Indeed, by 1711 Addison could indicate the currency of the term by observing that "there is no Character more frequently given to a Writer, than that of being a Genius" (Addison, I, 482).

the empirical referents of the term as it bulldozed its way through
the established neoclassical boundaries of imitation, decorum, and
order.[71] ("Everyone," says Kant, "is agreed on the complete opposition between genius and the *spirit of imitation*.")[72]

By the midpoint of the eighteenth century, *genius* played like the
Northern Lights across the theoretical sky. A listing of some Eng-
lish titles may serve to suggest its intellectual omnipresence:
Leonard Howard, "The British Genius revived by success: A
Poem" (1753); Thomas Gray, *The Liberty of Genius* (1754, un-
finished); William Sharpe, *A Dissertation upon Genius* (1755); John
Gilbert Cooper, *The Genius of Britain* (1756); John Langhorne, "Ge-
nius & Valour" (1765); John Jennings, "An Ode to Genius" (1767);
William Duff, *An Essay on Original Genius* (1767); Richard Jago,
Labour & Genius, or The Mill Stream and the Cascade (1768); Robert
Wood, *An Essay on the Original Genius and Writings of Homer* (1769);
William Duff, *Critical Observations on the Writings of the Most Cele-
brated Original Geniuses in Poetry* (1770); James Beattie, "The Min-
strel, or the Progress of Genius" (1771); Courtney Melmoth, *The
Tears of Genius* (1774); Alexander Gerard, *An Essay on Genius* (1774);
Elizabeth Gilding, *The Breathings of Genius* (1776).

The titles alone tend to confirm Kant's later judgment that originality is the primary characteristic of genius, and an important
corollary is the idea that genius is both innate and incommensurable, and therefore in no need of learning. Wordsworth's counsel to
"quit your books," to

> Close up those barren leaves;
> Come forth, and bring with you a heart
> That watches and receives,

was intensively preconditioned by writings of the eighteenth-century theorists of genius. "The truth is," said Duff in 1767,

> a Poet of original Genius has very little occasion for the weak aid of
> Literature: he is self-taught. He comes into the world as it were

---

[71]Thus Addison says that "among great Genius's, those few draw the Admiration
of all the World upon them . . . who by the mere Strength of natural Parts, and
without any Assistance of Art or Learning, have produced Works that were the
Delight of their own Times and the Wonder of Posterity. . . . *Homer* has innumerable Flights that *Virgil* was not able to reach. . . . Our Countryman *Shakespear* was a
remarkable Instance of this first kind of great Genius" (Addison, I, 482–83). Again,
John Dennis, in his "Essay on the Genius and Writings of Shakespear," published
in 1712, says that "*Shakespear* was one of the greatest Genius's that the World e'er
saw for the Tragick Stage" (Dennis, II, 4.) In his work of 1770 called *Critical Observations on the Writings of the Most Celebrated Original Geniuses in Poetry*, William Duff
devoted sixty-three pages to Homer and seventy-one pages to Shakespeare.
[72]Kant, V, 308.

completely accomplished. Nature supplies the materials of his compositions; his senses are the under-workmen, while Imagination, like
a masterly Architect, superintends and directs the whole. Or, to
speak more properly, Imagination both supplies the materials, and
executes the work, since it calls into being "things that are not," and
creates and peoples worlds of its own. It may be easily conceived
therefore, that an original Poetic Genius, possessing such innate
treasure (if we may be allowed an unphilosophical expression) has
no use for that which is derived from books, since he may be
encumbered, but cannot be inriched by it; for though the chief merit
of ordinary Writers may consist in arranging and presenting us with
the thoughts of others, that of an original Writer will always consist
in presenting us with such thoughts as are his own.[73]

Duff's phrase, *innate treasure*, suggests an underlying but pervasive *telos* in the rise of concern with genius: the conception of
genius tended to rescue the conception of soul from the assaults of
Locke's tradition, which in denying innate ideas asserted the
hegemony of the material and external. Such, as I noted in my
discussion of Tetens in chapter 4, was the function of imaginative
theories; such, too, was the function of theories of genius.

One of the treatises on genius, to be sure, remains loyal to Locke
and the association of ideas. William Sharpe's *Dissertation Upon
Genius* (1755) declares for the conception of mind as tabula rasa
(and unlike Locke, Sharpe uses the phrase *tabula rasa* repeatedly).
As the subtitle of his treatise argues, he attempts to show that
"Degrees of Superiority in the human Genius are not, fundamentally, the Result of Nature, but the Effect of Acquisition." Sharpe
says at the outset that "while the Author was perusing the Doctrine of 'All our Ideas from Sensation, none, originally, from Reflexion,' and these appearing more and more confirm'd to him in
the subsequent course of his reading and recollection . . . he ap-
prehended it the duty of his leisure to commit his observations
upon that head, and the tendency of them to the support of the
doctrine here asserted, to writing." In the course of his argument,
which is subtle and perspicacious, Sharpe quotes another author
with approval. "'The imagination is a common store-house and
receptacle of all those images, which are transmitted through the
senses; and till this is furnished in some degree, the soul, while it is
in the body, is a still unactive principle (yet a principle) and then
only begins to operate, and first exert itself, when it is supplied by
sensation with materials to work upon.'" What is of interest here
for our present purposes is that the discussion of genius seems to

73Duff, pp. 281–82.

lead inevitably to an invocation of imagination and that in turn to an invocation of soul, even if soul is here depressed and deactivated. Sharpe himself confirms this deactivation when he says later that "a bright Genius does not owe to pure nature her activity" and goes on to ask, "What nature? Not that of the soul; which is, as has been already proved, originally a blank capacity, void of every actual medium in the world." To Sharpe, "the intellect is without form and void, till the senses have admitted to it the necessary materials of all its exercise."[74] The underlying situation is thus somewhat like that in organ transplants, where the body's immune defences must be suppressed for the alien organ to function. Here, in order to argue for strict associationist origins for genius, Sharpe must suppress the innate, which is *par excellence* a suppression of soul.

Sharpe, in truth, argues the case for genius by acquisition rather than by nature about as well as it can be argued (he urges that Shakespeare was actually quite learned, that Milton had stored up data before he went blind, and, foreshadowing Jaeger, that *paideia*, or the education of youth, was essential to ancient culture). Indeed, he goes somewhat beyond Locke himself, who had made certain concessions that were later to open the door for imagination and its collocation of numinous terms. Though not sympathetic to imagination ("Is there any thing so extravagant, as the Imaginations of Men's Brains? . . . *Of what use is all this* fine *Knowledge of Men's own Imaginations,* to a Man that enquires after the reality of Things?"), Locke nevertheless had noted that in the "faculty of repeating and joining together its *Ideas,* the Mind has great power in varying and multiplying the Objects of its Thoughts"; that *"the Mind often exercises an active Power in the making* these several *Combinations.* For it being once furnished with simple *Ideas,* it can put them together in several Compositions, and so make a variety of complex *Ideas,* without examining whether they exist so together in Nature"; that "to be able to bring into view *Ideas* out of sight, at one's own choice, and to compare which of them one thinks fit, this is an *Active Power"*; that in "secondary Perception . . . or viewing again the *Ideas,* that are lodg'd *in the Memory, the Mind is oftentimes more than barely passive,* the appearance of those dormant Pictures, depending sometimes on the Will."[75] Such concessions actually constitute a chink in the associationist armor for imagination as innate power to enter (and we will recall that Coleridge's

[74]Sharpe, pp. 2, 9, 55, 57, 23.
[75]Locke, pp. 562–63, 164, 288, 286, 152.

secondary imagination, like this "secondary Perception" conceded by Locke, rides in on that same "Will" that works against the mind's passivity: secondary imagination coexists "with the conscious will").

Though "genius" had enormous prestige in the eighteenth and early nineteenth centuries, it has found its numinous increasingly eroded in our own day; it now tends to be a word used mostly by awestruck schoolboys, and when invoked by the sophisticated it now often has overtones of irony. Such loss of numinous also characterizes the remaining term in Wordsworth's collocation, which is "sublimity" or the "sublime."

In the Romantic era and its prologue, to be sure, the "sublime" had as much prestige as did "genius." In fact, so important from a historical perspective was the sublime as a battering ram for the emerging Romantic sensibility that one commentator, Francis Gallaway, in *Reason, Rule, and Revolt in English Classicism* (1940), insists that "the cult of sublimity with its exaltation of . . . feeling in the presence of powerful and terrible phenomena was the greatest single force in the disintegration of the classical outlook" (p. 333). And the "sublime" and "genius" were vividly adjacent terms. "The sublime, in particular," notes Duff, "is the proper walk of a great Genius, in which it delights to range, and in which alone it can display its powers to advantage, or put forth its strength."[76]

But sublimity, which was a topic of surpassing urgency for eighteenth and early nineteenth century intellectuals, has as we say lost much of its currency in the present era. Furthermore, it has been the subject of several respected modern historical studies.[77] We need therefore not dwell on its role in the collocation, other than to remind ourselves that it too was a vehicle of transference for the intensities of soul. "It is the disposition of a soul (*Geistesstimmung*) evoked by a particular representation," stressed Kant in 1790, "and not the object, that is to be called sublime."[78] Again, Duff in 1767, speaking of the tropism of genius for the sublime, says,

[76]Duff, p. 150.
[77]See, e.g., Samuel H. Monk, *The Sublime: A Study of Critical Theories in XVIII-Century England* (Ann Arbor: University of Michigan Press, 1960); Walter John Hipple, Jr., *The Beautiful, The Sublime, and The Picturesque in Eighteenth-Century British Aesthetic Theory* (Carbondale: Southern Illinois University Press, 1957); Thomas Weiskel, *The Romantic Sublime: Studies in The Structure and Psychology of Transcendence* (Baltimore: The Johns Hopkins University Press, 1976); Albert O. Wlecke, *Wordsworth and the Sublime* (Berkeley and Los Angeles: University of California Press, 1973).
[78]*Kant*, V, 250.

As such a Genius always attempts to grasp the most stupendous objects, it is much more delighted with surveying the rude magnificence of nature, than the elegant decorations of art; since the latter produce only an agreeable sensation of pleasure; but the former throws the soul into a divine transport of admiration and amazement, which occupies and fills the mind, and at the same time inspires that solemn dread, that religious awe, which naturally results from the contemplation of the vast and wonderful. By dwelling on such subjects, the soul is elevated to a sense of its own dignity and greatness.[79]

The evocation of the sublime was, in brief, simply a fanning of the increasingly inert embers of soul.

Another term, *symbol*, which though not in the Wordsworthian collocation was, as we saw, directly attached to imaginative function by Hegel—and we may consider the import of a modern title on Coleridge called *The Symbolic Imagination*—relates directly to the sublime; indeed, I have elsewhere termed the sublime "a negative symbol."[80] Like the sublime, *symbol* for our purposes here requires only brief reference.

It has been frequently pointed out, especially in recent years, that an actual critical process recognizes only allegory in its analyses, and that accordingly in the distinction between symbol and allegory so much favored by Romantic writers, the higher status accorded symbol would appear to be something of a mystification. In terms of what we have been saying about the numinous transfer of the predicates of soul, however, the seeming contradiction disappears. The whole point of symbol is not to open itself to critical analysis but precisely to defy such analysis: symbol strives to maintain, not dissipate, the aura of soul. "True symbolism," as Goethe says, is a "living and momentary revelation of the impenetrable [*des Unerforschlichen*]." Symbolism, says Kant again, transfers "our reflection upon an object of intuition to quite a new concept, and one with which perhaps no intuition can ever directly correspond. . . . All our knowledge of God is purely symbolic."[81] As Friedrich Creuzer noted in 1810, in the third chapter of the first book of the first part of his *Symbolik und Mythologie der alten Völker, besonders der Griechen*, "If it is true, as the ancients understood, that the nature of symbol is precisely the dark and twilit, how can symbol deny its nature and be clear?" (§34). Allegory, he says is

---

[79]Duff, pp. 150–52.
[80]J. Robert Barth, *The Symbolic Imagination; Coleridge and the Romantic Tradition* (Princeton, N.J.: Princeton University Press, 1977); McFarland, *Romanticism*, p. 30.
[81]*Gedenkausgabe*, IX, 532; Kant, V, 352–53.

like "the luxuriantly spreading branches of a climbing plant," but "symbol is more like the half-closed bud, which locks in its calynx, undeveloped, the highest beauty" (§35).

The term especially invokes two co-ordinate numinous terms, "the infinite" and "the eternal," both of which are central to Romanticism. One recalls Hulme's trenchant observations:

> You might say if you wished that the whole of the romantic attitude seems to crystallise in verse round metaphors of flight. Hugo is always flying, flying over abysses, flying up into the eternal gases. The word infinite in every other line. . . .
>
> I object even to the best of the romantics. . . . They cannot see that accurate description is a legitimate object of verse. Verse to them always means a bringing in of some of the emotions that are grouped round the word infinite.[82]

The word infinite, and its alternative, eternal, both indicate the numinous, and both come to special focus in the conception of symbol. "In the Symbol," says Carlyle, ". . . there is ever, more or less distinctly and directly, some embodiment and revelation of the Infinite." A "Symbol," concurs Coleridge, is characterized "above all by the translucence of the Eternal through and in the Temporal."

Another formulation by Carlyle more directly presents the import of these formulas: "a Symbol is ever . . . some dimmer or clearer revelation of the Godlike." And Kant likewise reveals more explicitly the function of the "infinite" in the numinous collocation, in this instance joining it to "imagination" and soul": "though the imagination, no doubt, finds nothing beyond the sensible world on which it can lay hold, still this thrusting aside of the sensible barriers gives it a feeling of being unbounded; and that removal is thus a presentation of the infinite. As such it can never be anything more than a negative presentation—but still it expands the soul."[83]

So much for symbol. We may content ourselves with these brief remarks on symbol and on the sublime, not only because both topics have received substantial historical and theoretical treatment in recent years, but also because to pursue them further would be to wander too far from our path. The subject of organism, however, though recognized as important in the Romantic complex, has, except for the well-known treatment in *The Mirror and the Lamp*, by M. H. Abrams, not been very satisfactorily investigated. Moreover, it relates directly to the topics of imagination and originality.

[82]Hulme, pp. 120, 126–27; *Carlyle*, I, 175; *Lay Sermons*, p. 30.
[83]*Carlyle*, I, 177; *Kant*, V, 274.

It relates, however, not by what it is, but by what it was summoned as a defense against.

If a proper history of the rise of theories of organism is ever written, or at least one that penetrates to the reasons for the enormous charge of significance given to the conception of organism from the fifteenth century on, reaching a crescendo in the nineteenth century, it will at the same time be a history of the rise of mechanism. Stated quite simply, it was the increasing likelihood that human life was in some way either a machine, something like a machine, or something controlled by a machine, that charged the opposing conception of organism with its enormous dynamic force.[84] One of the most recurrent themes of popular literature in our own day is the fear that a computer will gain dominance over human life—and countless scripts for television and motion pictures treat the possibility with a delicious *frisson* of fictional terror. (In the immensely popular motion picture *Star Wars*, apprehension about the machine's threat to the human is effectively "denied" by endowing the two robots with more "human" attributes—fear, vanity, ineptitude, loyalty—than the humans themselves). A recent volume that won the Pulitzer Prize bears the pregnant title, *The Soul of a New Machine,* and the oxymoronic rubric releases its tension into a story that details how a certain group of electrical engineers designed and built a business computer. Everywhere there is the sense of the machine's encroachment, from Charlie Chaplin's classic *Modern Times* to the confession of the American scholar F. O. Matthiessen—who eventually committed suicide—that he feared himself "an energetic accurate little machine" rather than a "personality."[85]

Matthiessen's confession clearly sets machine against soul; as the opposition has worked itself out historically, however, the theoretical conception of the machine has found its most explicit counterstatement not in evocations of soul, a term worn so thin by the

[84]The sense of the encroachment of the machine was ubiquitous. Compare, for instance, the ironic reverie of Nietzsche. "The task is to make man as useful as possible and to approximate him, as far as possible to an infallible machine: to this end he must be equipped with the virtues of the machine. . . . The first stumbling block is the boredom, the monotony, that all mechanical activity brings with it. To learn to endure this . . . has hitherto been the task of all higher schooling. To learn something that is of no concern to us, and to find one's 'duty' precisely in this 'objective' activity; . . . that is the invaluable task and achievement of higher schooling. This is why the philologist has hitherto been the educator *as such*: because his activity provides the model of sublime monotony in action; under his banner the young man learns to 'grind' [*ochsen*]: first prerequisite for future efficiency in the fulfillment of mechanical duties (as civil servant, husband, office slave, newspaper reader, and soldier)" (*Nietzsche*, III, 630).

[85]Levin, *Memories*, p. 226.

eighteenth century that it could no longer be used very successful-
ly in cognitive argument, but in the new and exciting conception of
organism. That conception began to assume importance among
Italian thinkers of the Renaissance;[86] and it rapidly grew in importance in the eighteenth century, under the aegis of investigators
like Leibniz and Bonnet and Buffon.[87] The consuming interest of
seventeenth-century thinkers like Huyghens—and the Royal Society as a body—in the mechanics of clockworks gave way to a
gathering concern for Leeuwenhoek's microscopic protozoa,
organic vitalities that he called "animalcula" or living atoms.[88]

By Romantic times, the conception of organism had assumed
commanding, even definitive importance. Whitehead, indeed, in a
notable discussion, describes the shift from preoccupation with
models of mechanism to preoccupation with models of organism
as the essence of the Romantic reaction against the neoclassic period.[89] The application of Romantic fascination with organism to
aesthetics produced the doctrine of organic form, of which there
are few better formulations than that of Coleridge. "Remember
that there is a difference between form as proceeding, and shape as
superinduced;—the latter is either the death or the imprisonment
of the thing;—the former is its self-witnessing and self-effected
sphere of agency."[90]

What is not emphasized in this wording, however, is the underlying truth that organism was valued as the human answer to the
machine. The truth is more clearly demarcated in Coleridge's
warning against "confounding mechanical regularity with organic
form."[91] And he appropriates almost verbatim a fresh new formula
by "a continental critic," Wilhelm Schlegel.

> The form is mechanic when on any given material we impress a
> predetermined form, not necessarily arising out of the properties of
> the material, as when to a mass of wet clay we give whatever shape

[86]As Cassirer points out, "the nature philosophy of the Renaissance created the
material that Leibniz made the foundation of his concept and theory of organism"
(*Erkenntnisproblem*, I, 195). But for the transfer of an "idea . . . from Greek medi-
cine" to "Stoic philosophy," and from there "through the philosophy of Neo-
platonism down to Leibniz," see Jaeger, *Early Christianity*, pp. 22–23.

[87]In 1749, for instance, Buffon had propagated a theory of the *"molécule organique"*
as the building block of the universe (Wilson, p. 562).

[88]*Philosophical Transactions* 12 (1677), 821.

[89]Whitehead, pp. 105–33. The "nature-poetry of the romantic revival was a protest on behalf of the organic view of nature" (pp. 132–33).

[90]Shawcross, II, 262. For a predecessor formulation, compare Edward Young in
1759; the passage is of special interest in that it explicitly connects organism with
originality. "An *Original* may be said to be of a *vegetable* nature; it rises spon-
taneously from the vital root of Genius; it *grows*, it is not *made*" (Young, p. 12).

[91]Raysor, I, 198.

we wish it to retain when hardened. The organic form, on the other hand, is innate; it shapes as it develops itself from within, and the fullness of its development is one and the same with the perfection of its outward form. Such is the life, such the form. Nature, the prime genial artist, inexhaustible in diverse powers, is equally inexhaustible in forms. Each exterior is the physiognomy of the being within, its true image reflected and thrown out from the concave mirror. (I, 198)

Coleridge's opposition to mechanism is not confined to these formulations. On the contrary, the "mechanic philosophy" was the main adversary of his life's endeavor.

The leading differences between mechanic and vital philosophy may all be drawn from one point: namely, that the former demanding for every mode and act of existence real or possible *visibility*, knows only of distance and nearness, composition (or rather juxtaposition) and decomposition, in short the relations of unproductive particles to each other; so that in every instance the result is the exact sum of the component quantities, as in arithmetical addition. This is the philosophy of death, and only of a dead nature can it hold good. In life, much more in spirit, and in a living and spiritual philosophy, the two component counter-powers actually interpenetrate each other, and generate a higher third, including both the former.[92]

This passage is from an appendix to Coleridge's first *Lay Sermon*, called *The Statesman's Manual*. A fitting counterpart is another passage from the text of that treatise; in this formulation current social documents are aligned against the Bible (the subtitle of *The Statesman's Manual* was *The Bible the Best Guide to Political Skill and Foresight*), and the mechanic philosophy is aligned against imagination.

The histories and political economy of the present and preceding century partake in the general contagion of its mechanic philosophy, and are the *product* of an unenlivened generalizing Understanding. In the Scriptures they are the living *educts* of the Imagination, of that reconciling and mediatory power, which incorporating the Reason in Images of the Sense, and organizing (as it were) the flux of the Senses by the permanence and self-circling energies of the Reason, gives birth to a system of symbols, harmonious in themselves, and consubstantial with the truths, of which they are the *conductors*. (pp. 28–29)

Here, as in the view of Hegel, imagination reinforces its numinous by summoning the similar aura of symbol.

If in these formulations antagonism to the machine lies near the

[92]*Lay Sermons*, p. 89.

surface, in a far greater number, both in Coleridge and in other figures, it floats just under the terms of discourse. It is, indeed, astonishing in how many different ways nineteenth-century statement summons the opposition of soul and machine. Sometimes the statement is explicit. "And now the Genius of Mechanism smothers him worse than any Nightmare did," says Carlyle of nineteenth-century man, "till the Soul is nigh choked out of him, and only a kind of Digestive, Mechanic life remains. In Earth and in Heaven he can see nothing but Mechanism; has fear for nothing else, hope in nothing else." Sometimes, as in the following passage by Shelley, a kind of rhetoric pitting the human—in this instance the imaginative—against the mechanical suffuses a statement even though no specific contrast in those terms takes place: "But whilst the sceptic destroys gross superstitions, let him spare to deface, as some of the French writers have defaced, the eternal truths charactered upon the imaginations of men. Whilst the mechanist abridges, and the political economist combines, labour, let them beware that their speculations, for want of correspondence with those first principles which belong to the imagination, do not tend, as they have in modern England, to exasperate at once the extremes of luxury and want.[93]

As here the mechanical and the imaginative are named, although the topic of the passage does not explicitly align their opposition, in other kinds of statement that opposition is set up, but the names are muted. A fine example is afforded by Mary Shelley's *Frankenstein*, a novel that derives its central horror from the substitution of the externally put together for the internally vital—superinduced shape for proceeding form—even though the mechanical is not in flat terms set against the organic. But the opposition is nevertheless unmistakable. Mrs. Shelley says of her initial vision of the situation: "I saw—with shut eyes, but acute mental vision—I saw the pale student of unhallowed arts kneeling beside the thing he had put together. I saw the hideous phantasm of a man stretched out, and then, on the working of some powerful engine, show signs of life, and stir with an uneasy, half vital motion. Frightful must it be; for supremely frightful would be the effect of any human endeavour to mock the stupendous mechanism of the Creator of the world."[94]

As Frankenstein's dead creature mechanically usurps the function of living organism, so in Carlyle's distinguished essay *Characteristics*, the mechanical is cast as the chief enemy of the vitally

[93]*Carlyle*, I, 176; *Shelley*, VII, 132.
[94]*Frankenstein*, p. 11.

religious. "To begin with our highest Spiritual function, with Religion, we might ask, Whither has Religion now fled?" and in the course of his answer Carlyle says: "Religion, like all else, is conscious of itself, listens to itself; it becomes less and less creative, vital; more and more mechanical. Considered as a whole, the Christian Religion of late ages has been continually dissipating itself into Metaphysics; and threatens now to disappear."[95] Late in the same essay he says that

> Metaphysical Speculation, if a necessary evil, is the forerunner of much good. The fever of Scepticism must needs burn itself out, and burn out thereby the Impurities that caused it; then again will there be clearness, health. The principle of life, which now struggles painfully, in the outer, thin and barren domain of the Conscious or Mechanical, may then withdraw into its inner sanctuaries, its abysses of mystery and miracle; withdraw deeper than ever into that domain of the Unconscious, by nature infinite and inexhaustible; and creatively work there. From that mystic region, and from that alone, all wonders, all Poesies, and Religions, and Social Systems have proceeded: the like wonders, and greater and higher, lie slumbering there; and, brooded on by the spirit of the waters, will evolve themselves, and rise like exhalations from the Deep. (XXVIII, 40)

In this perspective, the "Conscious or Mechanical" is the opponent of the "Unconscious," which surrounds itself with the aura of soul.

From another perspective, Newman, in *The Idea of a University*, suggests that there "are two methods of Education; the end of the one is to be philosophical, of the other to be mechanical." He goes on later to summon indirectly the interests of "soul" against those of the mechanical. "This then is how I should solve the fallacy, for so I must call it, by which Locke and his disciples would frighten us from cultivating the intellect, under the notion that no education is useful which does not teach us some temporal calling, or some mechanical art, or some physical secret. I say that a cultivated intellect, because it is a good in itself, brings with it a power and a grace to every work and occupation which it undertakes."[96]

Newman's presentation of the opposition may seem somewhat oblique here, but the attributes of intellect and cultivation, of the humanistic arts in general, are more overtly identified as attributes of soul by Pater's prose. Speaking of "the transcript of the sense of fact" as distinguished from "fact," Pater says: "Literary art, that is, like all art which is any way imitative or reproductive of fact—

[95]*Carlyle*, XXVIII, 22–23.
[96]Newman, pp. 99, 147–48.

form, or colour, or incident—is the representation of such fact as connected with soul. . . . It will be good literary art not because it is brilliant or sober, or rich, or impulsive, or severe, but just in proportion as its representation of that sense, that soul-fact, is true, verse being only one department of such literature, and imaginative prose, it may be thought, being the special art of the modern world."[97]

The opposition of the definitively human—the "soul-fact"—and the mechanical receives another of its Protean formulations in Arnold's *Culture and Anarchy.* "When I began to speak of culture," Arnold recapitulates,

> I insisted on our bondage to machinery, on our proneness to value machinery as an end in itself. . . . For a long time, as I have said, the strong feudal habits of subordination and deference continued to tell upon the working class. The modern spirit has now almost entirely dissolved those habits, and the anarchical tendency of our worship of freedom in and for itself, of our superstitious faith, as I say, in machinery, is becoming very manifest. More and more, because of this our blind faith in machinery, because of our want of light to enable us to look beyond machinery to the end for which machinery is valuable, this and that man, and this and that body of men, all over the country, are beginning to assert and put in practice an Englishman's right to do what he likes; his right to march where he likes, meet where he likes, enter where he likes, hoot as he likes, threaten as he likes, smash as he likes. All this, I say, tends to anarchy.[98]

Underneath the Arnoldian nuances, the opposition is clear: culture is the standard-bearer of soul, anarchy the standard-bearer of the machine.[99]

These varied examples, and countless others like them, all stem from the realms of the humanities. In those of the sciences the struggle is more starkly revealed. As Donald Fleming, an historian

[97] Pater, pp. 6–7.
[98] Arnold, *Culture,* pp. 117, 118–19.
[99] If we accept Arnold's formula "sweetness and light" as standing for soul, the opposition becomes explicit. "The pursuit of perfection, then, is the pursuit of sweetness and light. He who works for sweetness and light, works to make reason and the will of God prevail. He who works for machinery, he who works for hatred, works only for confusion. Culture looks beyond machinery, culture hates hatred; culture has one great passion, the passion for sweetness and light" (Arnold, *Culture,* p. 112). Arnold's perhaps exessive rhetorical play here lends point to Nietzsche's comment, "The *'soul'* was an attractive and mysterious conception from which philosophers rightly have separated themselves only with reluctance" (*Nietzsche,* III, 453).

of science and commentator on the scientific mechanist, Jacques Loeb, writes,

> Flushed with a sense of triumph over his enemies, Loeb went to claim his victory at the First International Congress of Monists in September 1911—a veritable concourse of the omniscients convened by Ernst Haeckel at Hamburg. To this, the most radical, libertarian, and anti-Prussian of German cities, delegations of freethinkers, freemasons, ethical culturalists, socialists, pacifists, and internationalists swarmed from many countries for a feast of reason on the edge of an abyss which they were the last people in the world to suspect. For Loeb, these few days in Hamburg were a foretaste of the golden age, the Enlightenment come again but this time forever. In a state of fierce intoxication with his vision, he poured out "The Mechanistic Conception of Life" to an audience of several thousand. He portrayed the physiochemical explanation of life as making explosive progress in the opening decade of the twentieth century. . . . Best of all, the mysterious realm of the will had been brought within the scope of physiochemical explanations by Loeb's work on animal tropisms. The "wishes and hopes, disappointments and sufferings" of men were grounded in instincts "comparable to the light instinct of the heliotropic animals," and for some of these the "chemical basis" was already sufficiently understood to make it "only a question of time" before they were fully accounted for on mechanistic lines. . . .
>
> Monists had a raw sensitivity to the charge that they were undermining ethics and morality. Loeb could not have been one of them or commanded their respect if he had failed to explore the ethical implications of the mechanistic conception of life. He ended by asking the question they dreaded to hear but were ashamed to dodge: "if we ourselves are only chemical mechanisms—how can there be an ethics for us?" His answer was that we approve what instinct compels us "machine-like" to do.[100]

Loeb's lecture was published in 1912 under the title, *The Mechanistic Conception of Life*. The rubric echoed a famous nineteenth-century statement by the great biologist Rudolf Virchow, "Über die mechanische Auffassung des Lebens," an essay published in 1858 and exactly translated by Loeb's English title. Virchow, though himself much more equivocal on the subject of possible ontological entities such as soul, nonetheless represented a rising tide of mechanistic commitment. Fleming notes that "a quadrumvirate of rising physiologists—Helmholtz, Ludwig, Du Bois-Reymond, and

[100]Fleming, pp. xxviii–xxix. For a proleptic opposition to this kind of view, see the paper of William James entitled "Are We Automata?" where he argues against the idea that "we are pure material machines" (*Mind* 4 [Jan. 1879], 1–22).

Brücke—swore a famous mutual oath in 1845 to account for all bodily processes in physicochemical terms";[101] and there existed a still more extreme situation among a group of

> medical materialists, led by Jacob Moleschott of *Das Kreislauf des Lebens* (The Circulation of Life, 1852), Ludwig Büchner of *Kraft und Stoff* (Force and Matter, 1855), and Carl Vogt of *Köhlerglaube und Wissenschaft* (Superstition and Science, 1855). These men are best remembered for their outrageous dicta that man is what he eats, genius is a question of phosphorus, and the brain secretes thought as the kidney secretes urine. The core of their doctrine was that force and matter are always conjoined, with no necessity for materialists to account for the conjunction. . . . The medical materialists were philosophical monists, vindicating for mechanistic materialism an infallible omnicompetence to the entire occasion of the universe. (pp. viii–ix)

Such accumulations point us to the answer to an important question: Why did not organism and imagination, which are the two conceptions most frequently identified as occupying the very center of the Romantic view of the world—and were in the Romantic era virtually identical in mystery and aura— historically maintain an equal metaphorical and emotional prestige? That they did not is clear from even a brief consultation with our own experience. Organism has virtually lost its status as soul-fact in the present day, while imagination has not.

What happened is that the nineteenth-century mechanistic chemists, biologists, and physiologists just noted, and others like them, managed to turn the awareness of organism from the realm of soul to the realm of cognitive science. As Loeb said, "a mechanistic conception of life is not complete unless it includes a physicochemical explanation of psychic phenomena";[102] and organism today is the province of those who investigate the structure of DNA.

Those scientists who attempted to save the soul-aura of organism have been shunted aside by history. Fleming notes of one of the advocates of soul-fact in organic theory, Hans Driesch:

> In another remarkable experiment of the 1890's, Hans Driesch proffered a sensational challenge to his own master, Roux of the *Entwicklungsmechanik.* . . . This justly famous discovery by Driesch [about the developmental capacities of sea urchins] began as a piece of empirical research, but the more he reflected upon it, the more it seemed a colossal refutation of all mechanistic philosophies in biology. If a machine was taken apart, the individual pieces never turned

---

[101]Ibid., p. viii. For the rise of mechanism in the seventeenth and eighteenth centuries, see, e.g., Schofield. See further Koyré.
[102]Loeb, p. 35.

into complete functioning machines of the original type. Driesch
eventually set up as a twentieth century vitalist, propounding a neo-
Aristotelian doctrine of "entelechy."[103]

Shortly afterward, however, Fleming sums up the fate of Driesch's
standpoint as follows: "The definitive overthrow of Drieschian
neovitalism was not accomplished so much by other people's
emendation of his empirical findings as by his own increasingly
mystical formulations. Most biologists took one look at these and
fled in dismay" (p. xxvi).

No later excursions of soul-fact into the realm of organism have
held out better hopes.[104] When Crick and Watson discovered the
structure of DNA, there was no upsurge of hope in soul. On the
contrary, the mechanists seemed ever closer to claiming the secret
of life for materialistic philosophy.

Indeed, some lectures by Crick himself, called *Of Molecules and
Men*, carry the mechanistic predispositions of Loeb into the absolute mainstream of molecular biology in our own day. "The ultimate aim of the modern movement in biology," writes Crick in
1966, in words that could have been Loeb's in 1912, "is in fact to
explain *all* biology in terms of physics and chemistry."[105] Crick is
unequivocal in his rejection of soul. "I myself, like many scientists,
believe that the soul is imaginary and that what we call our minds
is simply a way of talking about the functions of our brains" (p. 87).
He is concerned to evict all vestiges of vitalism and substitute
mechanical materialism in the description of life. "I can hardly
delay any longer considering what I mean by the word 'vitalism.' . . . It implies that there is some special force directing the
growth or the behavior of living systems which cannot be understood by our ordinary notions of physics and chemistry. . . . It will
be my general thesis that the reason the need is felt for a doctrine
like vitalism is because we see a complicated pattern of behavior
which we cannot easily explain in terms of the concepts that are
immediately available to us" (p. 16). Speaking of "the borderline
between the living and the nonliving," he observes:

> It is difficult, then, having analyzed the cell into its various
> operations, to see which of the operations is in fact as mysterious as

---

[103]Fleming, pp. xxiv–xxv.
[104]Three of them argued against by Crick are Walter Elsasser's *The Physical Foundations of Biology* (1958), Peter Mora's "Urge and Molecular Biology," *Nature* (1963),
and Eugene Wigner's "The Probability of the Existence of a Self-reproducing Unit,"
The Logic of Personal Knowledge: Essays Presented in Honor of Michael Polanyi (London:
Routledge & Kegan Paul, 1961).
[105]Crick, p. 10.

it appeared before we had all this detailed knowledge. What emerges quite clearly is that the cell is a very complicated object, and that it will indeed be extremely difficult for us to synthesize it from scratch. It will not be easy for us, therefore, to create life in the strict sense. On the other hand when we examine any bit of the mechanism, and see how it is made and how it works, there seems to be no difficulty in principle in synthesizing it ourselves, starting from rather simple chemical materials. (pp. 56–57)

Looking to the future, and to the possibilities opened up by computers, Crick directly attacks the interests of soul; he says that

machines are going to take on many of the functions of human beings, and that it is going to be quite disturbing for us to associate with them. There are people, Fred Hoyle for example, who believe that machines will eventually take control of our civilization. . . . I doubt myself whether we shall reach quite such a stage, but nevertheless I am convinced that it is going to be quite upsetting having to associate with very complicated and sophisticated machines, and that this development is likely to happen during our own lifetime.

I think the people who are most disturbed by this sort of thing are those who believe in some sense in the soul. What is never very clear is what is meant by "the soul," but one of its attributes appears to be that it can associate with the body but is separate from it, and, in particular, that it can in some circumstances exist separately from the body and especially, so many people think, after death. (pp. 83–84)

Crick's view that the machine will invade our most profound sense of self is not only one shared by the vague fears of the man in the street, but is also identical with the conceptions of those who actually design such machines. Of one of the chief theorists of computer possibilities, Alan Turing, a commentator speaks in this way: "A mechanical approach to the mysteries of consciousness was Alan Turing's dream and by the late 1930's he was a thorough believer in the possibility of a properly organized machine that could be intelligent and conscious and could have free will—at least to the extent that we or any physical object can do so."[106]

So the machine makes ever greater inroads into the ultimate human concerns: the freedom of the will, the immortality of the soul, and the existence of God. Organism, at one time virtually the synonym for Romantic hopes, has faded as a theoretical guarantee of the possibility of soul. One icon of a priori human domain, however, has still not been overthrown; it remains intact, mysterious, and uneroded. The others have faded or shrunken along

[106]Hofstadter, p. 25.

with organism. Symbol, though once the very heart of Christian theology, is today a conception largely limited to literary theory, and somewhat passé even there; genius functions mostly as a word in an adolescent's vocabulary; the sublime is merely a topic in the history of ideas. But imagination is still vital, incommensurable, and current. Imagination still stands against the mechanism of Loeb, and of later formulators such as B. F. Skinner and Jacques Monod. It is still inexplicable, and still irreducible to physical conceptions. Even Crick, though he does not use the word *imagination*, and though he is reluctant to leave any area as incapable of mechanical formulation, admits at least temporary bafflement before those higher functions of the brain of which imagination is the apex.

> In our brains the nervous system seems to be organized into rather thickish sheets. It is as if it were a structure based on two and a half dimensions rather than on either two or three, but apart from one or two hints from recent work the way in which nerves are grouped together is not really understood. Nor is it understood how nerves know how to find their way to the right place and make the right contacts. . . . This information must largely be carried in the genetic material, and we do not have the remotest idea, at the moment, of how this genetic information is expressed. . . . Presumably it is done on some repetitive principle, with general instructions and the more special instructions, but the details of this are at the moment completely unknown.
>
> When we come to consider how the brain learns—how it remembers—we are even more in the dark. . . .[107]

Thus imagination still is as mysterious as it is powerful. That has been its status since the earliest formulations of the mechanistic threat. Indeed, an eighteenth-century representative of mechanism as extreme as Loeb's twentieth-century *Mechanistic Conception of Life* was La Mettrie's notorious *L'Homme machine* of 1747. The title tells all. Men, said La Mettrie, "ne sont au fond que des Animaux, & des Machines perpendiculairement rampantes";[108] he argued that "l'Homme est une machine; & qu'il n'y a dans tout l'Univers qu'une seule substance diversement modifiée" (p. 197). But into this relentless Spinozism, with its mechanistic denial of the freedom of the will, the immortality of the soul, and the existence of God, there intrudes a single unaccountable element: imagination. "By the imagination," La Mettrie concedes, or rather rhapsodizes, "the cold skeleton of reason takes on living and ruddy flesh, by the

---

[107]Crick, pp. 72–74.
[108]La Mettrie, pp. 191–92.

imagination the sciences flourish, the arts are adorned, the wood speaks, the echoes sigh, the rock weeps, marble breathes, and all inanimate objects gain life. . . . Foolishly decried by some, vainly praised by others, and misunderstood by all . . . it not only describes, but also can measure nature" (pp. 165–66).

In such a statement imagination, then as now, is surrounded by the undissipated aura of soul. And then as now, imagination subsists as something mysterious and incommensurable. In fact La Mettrie, the ultimate mechanist, salutes those characteristics of imagination essential to its aura: he hails "l'imagination, ou cette partie fantastique du cerveau, dont la nature nous est aussi inconnue, que sa manière d'agir"—"the imagination, that fantastical part of the brain, whose nature is as unknown to us as is its manner of acting" (p. 165).

So there it is. Imagination and its cognate, originality, still retain their aura and still exist as soul-facts. The idea of originality is most vitally conceived not as firstness, which for the most part can be revealed under scrutiny to be factitious, but as an intensity that honors personality. Originality denotes dynamic individuality rather than inert temporality. It is inextricably linked to imagination. Standing in for soul, imagination gains in power and mystery in Romanticism. "Man is All Imagination," wrote Blake, "God is Man & exists in us & we in him." "Imagination is the Divine Vision not of The World nor of Man nor from Man as he is a Natural Man but only as he is a Spiritual Man."[109] And imagination still stands in for soul. It holds aloft the banner of a priori human domain even for those who think in directions that run counter to soul. As the radical atheist Jean-Paul Sartre insists, "imagination is not an empirical and superadded power of consciousness, it is the whole of consciousness as it realizes its freedom."[110]

Such bastions, dwindled in number though they are, are defenses for the hopes and dignity of the human. In the implications of modern knowledge, as opposed to the conventions of morality—which dissipate more slowly than scientific likelihood expands, and to the uninformed still seem rooted in the nature of things—the hopes and dignity of the human seem ever more tenuous. The bleaker picture at the ultimate frontiers of science is the one limned by the eminent physicist Steven Weinberg, at the close

[109]*Blake*, pp. 654, 655.
[110]Sartre, *Imagination*, p. 270. He goes on to say that "there could be no developing consciousness without an imaginative consciousness, and vice versa. So imagination, far from appearing as an *actual* characteristic of consciousness turns out to be an essential and transcendental condition of consciousness (p. 273).

of a discussion of whether the universe has a beginning and end, or whether it oscillates forever between expansion and contraction.[111]

> However all these problems may be resolved, and whichever cosmological model proves correct, there is not much of comfort in any of this. It is almost irresistible for humans to believe that we have some special relation to the universe, that human life is not just a more-or-less farcical outcome of a chain of accidents reaching back to the first three minutes, but that we were somehow built in from the beginning. As I write this I happen to be in an airplane at 30,000 feet, flying over Wyoming en route home from San Francisco to Boston. Below, the earth looks very soft and comfortable—fluffy clouds here and there, snow turning pink as the sun sets, roads stretching straight across the country from one town to another. It is very hard to realize that this all is just a tiny part of an overwhelmingly hostile universe. It is even harder to realize that this present universe has evolved from an unspeakably unfamiliar early condition, and faces a future extinction of endless cold or intolerable heat. The more the universe seems comprehensible, the more it also seems pointless.[112]

It is against this encompassing darkness that originality and imagination hold aloft their flickering torches.

---

[111]Cf. Schelling in 1813: "The whole spatially extended universe is nothing but the swelling heart of the Godhead. Held by invisible powers, it persists in a continuous pulsation, or alternation of expansion and contraction" (*Schelling*, VIII, 326).
[112]Weinberg, p. 154.

Index

Thomas McFarland is Murray Professor of English
at Princeton University. His most recent book
is *Romanticism and the Forms of Ruin*.

The Johns Hopkins University Press

ORIGINALITY AND IMAGINATION

This book was set in Palatino text and display type
by The Composing Room of Michigan
from a design by Susan P. Fillion.
It was printed on S.D. Warren's 50-lb. Sebago Eggshell paper
and bound by The Maple Press Company.